AN WELFARE STATES

EUROPEAN **WELFARE STATES**
COMPARATIVE PERSPECTIVES

MEL COUSINS

⑤SAGE Publications

London ● Thousand Oaks ● New Delhi

First published 2005

 SAGE Publications Ltd
1 Oliver's Yard
55 City Road
London EC1Y 1SP

SAGE Publications Inc.
2455 Teller Road
Thousand Oaks, California 91320

SAGE Publications India Pvt Ltd
B-42, Panchsheel Enclave
Post Box 4109
New Delhi 110 017

British Library Cataloguing in Publication data

A catalogue record for this book is available
from the British Library

ISBN 1-4129-0172-3
ISBN 1-4129-0173-1 (pbk)

Library of Congress Control Number: 2005926161

Typeset by C&M Digitals (P) Ltd., Chennai, India
Printed on paper from sustainable resources
Printed in Great Britain by TJ International Ltd, Padstow, Cornwall

CONTENTS

LIST OF BOXES, FIGURES AND TABLES

BOXES

FIGURES

TABLES

ACKNOWLEDGEMENTS

I would like, in particular, to thank Zoë Elliot for her support in the development and writing of this book. A number of anonymous referees commented on both the original proposal and the text and contributed greatly to the structure of the book. I would also like to thank a number of colleagues who have commented on different sections of the book: Mary Daly, Frans Pennings, and Simon Roberts. The usual disclaimers apply.

ONE INTRODUCTION

The objective of this book is to provide an up-to-date and comparative analysis of European welfare states. It covers three main issues:

1 Key theories about welfare states (for example, political theory, globalisation and gender).
2 A description and analysis of the development of European welfare states and a comparative outline of a small number of states drawn from different welfare 'families'.
3 A discussion of current key challenges and possible options for future policy development.

The theoretical perspective is directly linked to empirical country examples providing a coherent and detailed picture of European welfare states.

This chapter defines the scope of the book. If we are to look at European welfare states, it is first necessary to ask what we mean by these terms, that is, 'Europe' and 'welfare state'. The chapter also provides an introduction to comparative welfare state analysis. Why should we study welfare states in a comparative context? What are the advantages and disadvantages of doing so? It outlines the reasons for comparative studies and the potential disadvantages of this approach. It also discusses methods of comparative welfare state analysis. Finally, the chapter outlines the contents of this book.

EUROPE

Sykes has correctly stated that 'most studies of social policy in Europe focus either explicitly or implicitly on the Member States of the EU' (1998: 15). But it is clear that Europe and the European Union (EU) are not co-terminus. Even in the case of Western Europe, nations such as Norway and Switzerland have chosen to remain outside the EU. More fundamentally, the ongoing accession of a large number of Central and Eastern European countries has emphasised the shifting nature of the EU's boundaries. On the one hand, the accession of 10 countries (including eight Central and Eastern European countries) in 2004 has brought a significant section of

Europe within the EU. On the other hand, however, it has emphasised the fact that a large number of European countries remain outside the European Union.

Yet, as Therborn has argued, 'the territoriality of Europe is itself a historical construct' (1995: 34). Current Europe, he argues, is less than two hundred years old. There are fairly clear physical boundaries both to the North and West of Europe. However, culturally and in terms of policy influences it is often argued that the United Kingdom and Ireland are influenced in social policy terms at least as much by the United States as they are by mainland Europe. To the South, the Mediterranean now also forms a clear geographic and economic boundary between the wealthy countries of Europe and the under-developed countries of Northern Africa. As Therborn points out, there is a degree of irony in this in that 'the same sea once held a common civilization together' (1995: 35).

It is to the East that the fuzzy nature of Europe's boundaries is now most evident. The fall of Communism (and the Iron Curtain), the creation of a whole host of new nation states, and the enormous size of Russia and Turkey (both spanning two continents) all mean that it is very difficult to define exactly where Europe's eastern border lies. As Therborn argues, 'the Urals are a cartographer's demarcation, hardly a natural physical border' (1995: 35).

This study will look at Europe in broad terms rather than focussing narrowly on the European Union. Nonetheless, its main focus will be on those nations which are now members of the European Union. One reason for this is that 'the logic of the comparative research design ideally requires that the countries be maximally different on the dimensions of their study and maximally similar on all other dimensions' (Goodin et al., 1999: 14). Thus it is more difficult to engage in any real way in a comparative study of countries like Sweden with an average per capita income of US$26,000 per annum and a country such as Albania with an average income equivalent to US$400. There are, of course, also practical constraints in covering both an excessively large number of countries and countries for which very limited data is yet available. The study looks in detail at about twenty European countries. It is obviously impossible to make any detailed reference to such a large number of countries in one study. In Chapter 7, five specific countries from different welfare state approaches are discussed in more detail. These are not intended to be 'representative', but they are intended to be indicative of the different 'families' of welfare state which exist within Europe. The rationale for the selection of these particular countries is set out in Chapter 7.

EUROPEANISATION

Europe is not simply a geographic area but also a political, economic and cultural construct. Accordingly, in our study of European welfare states it is important to consider the impact that 'Europeanisation' is having in this area. Europeanisation 'can be taken as designating processes of economic, socio-cultural and political integration in Europe' (Kelstrup, 2001) and is mainly related to the recent process of integration specifically through the development of the European Union. Of course, this process is not confined to the current members of the EU but, due to the accession and related processes, extends far beyond the borders of the EU itself.

The term 'Europeanisation' is used in two different ways:

- First, the term has been used to describe the emergence and development at the European level of distinct structures of governance, that is, of political, legal and social institutions associated with political problem-solving which formalise interactions among the actors and policy networks specialising in the creation of authoritative rules. (Börzel and Risse, 2000)
- Second, that term has been used to describe '[a] set of processes through which the EU political, social and economic dynamics become part of a logic of domestic discourse, identities, political structures and public policies' (quoting Radaelli, 2000: 3).

Both these processes, the development of distinct structures of governance and the processes through which EU dynamics become part of the domestic discourse, are important in the development of European welfare states.

One of the difficulties in this area is to separate out the analysis of Europeanisation from the broader process of globalisation. The two processes are clearly related, but Europeanisation can be seen both as part of the broader globalisation process and as a reaction against it, 'which makes it possible to exercise political influence on the ways in which globalisation transforms societies' (Kelstrup, 2001). These issues are discussed in more detail in Chapters 7 and 10.

WELFARE STATE

The rationale for studying *European* welfare states is strengthened by the fact that, as Peter Flora has argued, 'the modern welfare state is a European invention' (1986: xii). But there is a perhaps surprising absence of any clear definition of the meaning of the term 'welfare state'. As Flora and Heidenheimer have stated, 'welfare and state are among the most ambiguously employed terms in contemporary English political vocabulary' (1981: 5). They might have added that the combination of the two words in the term 'welfare state' has not diminished in any way the ambiguity involved.

ORIGINS OF THE TERM

The term 'welfare state' appears to have originated in its German form *Wohlfahrsstaat* in the later nineteenth or early twentieth century. As early as 1922 it could be stated that 'today the state regards itself in principle as the bearer of primary responsibility for social welfare ... it does not aspire simply to be a state of order, police and law, but also wants to be a culture and welfare state as well' (quoted in Hong, 1998: 36). However, by the 1930s in Germany the term had become one of political abuse. In 1932 the German Chancellor, von Papen, accused the Weimar government of having 'attempted to make the state into a sort of welfare state and, in this way, weakened the moral forces of the nation' (quoted in Hong, 1998: 208).

In the United Kingdom, the term, in its English form, appears to have come into common use in the late 1930s and 1940s (Bruce, 1961). Ironically, the Beveridge Report, sometimes referred to as the blueprint for the welfare state, did not use the term. Indeed Beveridge himself, sometimes referred to as the father of the welfare state, disliked the term because of what he saw as its 'Santa Claus' and 'Brave New World' connotations and never used it (Harris, 1977: 448). As Harris points out he preferred the term 'social service state' which, he felt, implied that citizens had duties as well as rights (1977: 459).

Despite Beveridge's reservations, the term became widely used in English (see, for example, Asa Briggs' (1961) definition of the term 'welfare state' in Box 1.1).

WHAT IS A WELFARE STATE?

Today a typical example of the definition of a welfare state is:

> A system in which the government undertakes the chief responsibility for providing for the social and economic security of its population, usually through unemployment insurance, old age pensions, and other social-security measures; A social system characterized by such policies. (Collins English Dictionary, 2000)

As can be seen, this definition brings together three different issues. First, there is the policy intention of the welfare state, in this case suggested to be government undertaking the responsibility for providing for the social and economic security of its population. Second, there is the method by which this is achieved, in this case suggested to be unemployment insurance and other social security measures. Third, the definition recognises the fact that the term 'welfare state' has come to be used in respect of the overall social system characterised by such an approach.

A COMMITMENT TO 'WELFARE'?

Some approaches adopt a normative approach to the definition of the welfare state. In other words, they argue that, in order to be a welfare state, the cluster of state policies must have a specific objective whether this be emancipatory, de-commodification or the pursuit of equality. Marshall (1950), for example, argues that social citizenship constitutes the core idea of a welfare state. A recent German history of the welfare state argues that one should distinguish between two aspects of the welfare state: first, the welfare state as a range of social services or institutions, and second, as 'patterns of political action based on welfare-related normative orientations' (Leisering, 2003: 179). This approach identifies a welfare state only where social services are linked to normative orientations. Thus some countries, such as the United States of America and the former Soviet Union (and other former communist countries), cannot be identified as welfare states.

For the purposes of this study, however, it does not seem useful to delimit the scope of the term 'welfare state' by a preconception of what that state *should* aim to achieve. To do so would raise very difficult definitional issues about the precise degree of normative commitment required to qualify as a welfare state and the timing of transitions in and out of welfare statehood. (For example, would the United States of America qualify as a welfare state at the time of the New Deal in the 1930s, and if so when did it cease to be defined as such?) In addition, such an approach to the definition of welfare states does not perhaps correspond with the common use of the term. If, for example, we found that the social policies of a particular European country were neither de-commodifying nor emancipatory and, in fact, increased inequalities, one might criticise these policies but few would suggest that the term 'welfare state' could not still be applied to the country.

THE SCOPE OF THIS BOOK

A second issue arises in distinguishing between the bundle of policies normally referred to as the welfare state and the 'social system' characterised by such policies. This can be seen in Esping-Andersen's definition of the welfare state (see Box 1.1). Esping-Andersen refers to a narrow and broad approach to the welfare state. The first sees it in terms of the traditional social policies of income transfers and social services. The broader view focuses on the state's larger role in managing and organising the economy. This broader view, which considers issues such as the state's role in the overall macro-economic steering of the economy, has produced many interesting studies. However, for present purposes, it would bring in a very wide range of policies including, for example, the role of the Central Banks and the role of corporatism in developing macro-economic policy.

Box 1.1: Definitions of 'welfare state'

[A] welfare state ... will be seen to have three immutable characteristics. The first is that the term refers not simply to a discrete range of social services but to a society in which government actively accepts responsibility for the welfare (broadly defined) of all its citizens. The second and third characteristics concern its chronology and core functions, both of which require further elaboration. Chronologically, welfare states were the unique creation of the 1940s. ... [In terms of its core functions] ... a welfare state is a society in which government is expected to ensure the provision for all its citizens of not only social security but also a range of other services – including health, education and housing – at a standard well above the barest minimum. In so doing it consumes resources (through expenditure on goods and the employment of manpower) on such a scale that it cannot but affect the working of the economy. For this reason, and in order both to finance its own expenditure and to minimise political dissatisfaction or unrest, it is concerned with the underlying health of the economy. (Lowe, 2004)

A 'Welfare State' is a state in which organized power is deliberately used (through politics and administration) in an effort to modify the play of market forces in at least three directions – first, by guaranteeing individuals and families a minimum income irrespective of the market value of their work or property; second, by narrowing the extent of insecurity by enabling individuals and families to meet certain social contingencies (for example, sickness, old age and unemployment) which lead otherwise to individual and family crises; and third, by ensuring that all citizens without distinction of status or class are offered the best standards available in relation to a certain agreed range of social services. (Briggs, 1961)

The welfare state has been approached both narrowly and broadly. Those who take the narrower view see it in terms of the traditional terrain of social amelioration: income transfers and social services, with perhaps some token mention of the housing question. The broader view often frames its questions in terms of political economy, its interests focused on the state's larger role in managing and organizing the economy. In the broader view, therefore, issues of employment, wages, and overall macro-economic steering are considered integral components in the welfare-state complex. (Esping-Andersen, 1990)

Box 1.1: (Continued)

In a narrow sense, the welfare state may refer to state measures for the
provision of key welfare services (often confined to health, housing, income
maintenance and personal social services). Increasingly broadly, the welfare state is
also taken to define (1) a particular form of state, (2) a distinctive form of polity
or (3) a specific type of society [For the purposes of this study the author defines
the welfare state under capitalism] as defining a society in which the state
intervenes within the processes of economic reproduction and distribution to
reallocate life chances between individual and/or classes. (Pierson, 1998)

I define the welfare state, or state social provision, as interventions by the
state in civil society to alter social forces, including male dominance, but I do not
judge a priori that all interventions are aimed at, or actually produce, greater
equality among citizens. (Orloff, 1996: 53)

The welfare state is the institutional outcome of the assumption by a society
of legal and therefore formal and explicit responsibility for the basic well-being of
all its members. Such a state emerges when a society or its decision-making
groups become convinced that the welfare of the individual ... is too important
to be left to custom or to informal arrangements and private understandings
and is therefore a concern of government. (Girvetz, 1968)

As Pierson has argued, the broad approach to the understanding
of the welfare state has had 'salutary effects' and has illustrated 'the
extent to which welfare states are nested in a set of broader institutional arrangements' (2001: 420–1). But as Pierson has pointed out,
such a broad approach also has disadvantages. It inevitably brings
together the discussion of quite different policies and issues under
the umbrella of the term 'welfare state'. First, it leads to a situation
where studies of the welfare state are 'talking past each other'
because they are examining quite distinct aspects of the welfare
state. Second, a study of a wide range of different policies and institutions makes comparative study more difficult both because of the
difficulties involved in analysing a wide range of different policy
measures and due to data limitations. A related reason for a focus
on one particular area of the welfare state is that, as Castles has
argued 'the causes and consequences of the policy actions of the
state differ widely from one policy area to another and within particular areas over time' (1998: 300). An effort to analyse all the different
sectors of welfare state policies can lead to so many answers that
one has forgotten the question.

For the purposes of this study, we will take a somewhat pragmatic
approach to understanding of the term 'welfare state'. We will look
in particular at the policies which are included in the term 'social
protection' by the European Union (that is, social security and, to a

lesser extent, health) and at closely related labour market policies (in particular active labour market policies).

Daly suggests that a focus on cash benefits can be justified on the basis of 'their power to reveal the nature and quality of social rights' (1997: 132). She argues that cash benefits are 'the most tangible expression of social rights' and thus 'are wonderfully revealing of the terms on which individuals can make claims on public resources and the types of solidarity which are fostered by systems of public support' (1997: 132). Tempting as this line of argument may be, it is not necessarily clear that cash benefits are any more revealing than labour market, health care or social services policies. I would prefer to defend a focus on cash and (to a lesser extent) health benefits on more pragmatic grounds. These benefits are undeniably important, constituting on average over half of total government spending in European countries. They impact on the lives and opportunities of the majority of the populations of European countries and are indeed revealing of key trends in public policy.

WELFARE STATE – AN ENGLISH LANGUAGE TERM

A final point in relation to the term 'welfare state' is that despite its frequent use in international social policy discourse it is very much an English language term. Despite its German origins, the term 'welfare state' in German has negative connotations and such terms as 'social policy', 'social market economy' or 'social state' are more common (Alber, 1986). While the Latin languages have developed their own versions of the term such as the French *État Providence* or the Italian *Stato del Benessere*, these terms are not very commonly used.

COMPARATIVE WELFARE STATE ANALYSIS

WHY STUDY COMPARATIVELY?

In this section we look at why one might study welfare states in a comparative context and at the advantages and disadvantages of doing so. Then we look briefly at the approaches to comparative welfare state study.

Why should we study welfare states comparatively? In this, and most, studies of welfare states, the unit of analysis is the nation. The focus is on what is happening at the level of the individual country. Thus this book examines European welfare *states* rather than 'the European welfare state'. However, there are a number of international influences which are perhaps shaping the development of national welfare states, and it is arguable that these influences may be increasing over time. First, as we shall examine in Chapter 3, economic integration and globalisation are argued to have an increasing impact on the national welfare states. Second, and this is particularly relevant in Europe, international agencies are increasingly having a role in the development of welfare state policies. In the European context, the work of the European Union is particularly relevant in this area. While social policy remains a national competence, the European Union has an increasing role to play in shaping the development of social policies, even if this is through 'soft' methods such as the open method of co-ordination rather than through the 'harder' methods of legislation. The Organisation for Economic Cooperation and Development (OECD) also plays an important role in influencing policy and, in Central and Eastern Europe, organisations such as the World Bank and the International Monetary Fund (IMF) have had an influential role. Finally, and this is a factor which can be seen over the lifetime of the welfare state, there is a high degree of policy diffusion, particularly in a European context. If, for example, we look at the introduction of old age pensions in any particular country, it may seem that national factors have been most influential in the. timing and form of that introduction. However, when we look at this in a comparative context we see that old age pensions were introduced across Europe in a surprisingly narrow timeframe. The same applies to the introduction of sickness benefits, unemployment insurance and family allowances. This is discussed in more detail in Chapter 5.

The advantages of a successful comparative approach are obvious. We can hope to understand much more about the development of the national welfare state if we see how welfare states have developed in other, broadly similar, countries and if we can identify common trends or divergences across countries. A comparative approach can help us to question aspects of our own national welfare states which we may have taken for granted. Similarly, a comparative approach may help to explain particular developments which may otherwise appear anomalous. A comparative approach can also help us to generate general theories about the operation of welfare states and societies. While a study of one country (or even a group of countries) may suggest that, for example, government by left-wing parties is the factor most likely to lead to an extensive welfare state, broader comparative analysis can help us to ask whether, in fact, other types of government (such as Christian democratic parties) can lead to a similar destination by a different route. Similarly, comparative analysis can help us to examine whether globalisation has a different impact on a large and largely closed economy than it does on a small and more open economy. Finally, comparative analysis can help us to take into account the different stages of economic development between core and peripheral countries in Europe and the impact this has on the development of welfare states.

THE DIFFICULTIES OF COMPARATIVE STUDY

Comparative study of welfare states is, however, difficult. First, there are the practical difficulties of language and data. In order to study comparatively, we have to be sure that we are studying the same thing. However, at least in a European context, this difficulty has been increasingly overcome by the development of more comparative data banks by organisations such as the EU and the OECD and by the (fortunate or unfortunate) increasing availability of English language studies of European welfare states.

There is also the perhaps more important danger of attempting to impose grand explanatory theories on diverse countries. Many welfare state studies can be criticised for their tendency to focus on a small number of rich, core countries and for assuming that more peripheral countries were simply 'backward' and that they would inevitably develop towards the same type of welfare state (Cousins, 1997). It has been argued that 'social scientists compare to escape cultural hegemony' (Janoski and Hicks, 1994: 6). However, rather than escaping from cultural hegemony, many social scientists can be accused of attempting – consciously or unconsciously – to impose cultural hegemony in their study of welfare states. While the study of other welfare states can help to inform both general theories of welfare and our knowledge of our own welfare state, it is important to ensure that our approach does not seek to turn the other into the same (Docherty, 1993).

HOW DO WE STUDY COMPARATIVELY?

The approach to the comparative study of welfare states varies on a continuum from the very detailed, *qualitative* study of a small number (perhaps two, three or four) of welfare states in great detail to the large-scale *quantitative* study of a large number of welfare states. In many cases, such studies involve about eighteen OECD countries, although some involve as many as sixty or more countries.

There are advantages and disadvantages to both approaches. The small-scale qualitative approach involves very detailed study of the development of welfare states over time. Inevitably, however, there is a limit to the number of countries which a researcher (or even a small team of researchers) can hope to study in detail. In contrast, the larger-scale quantitative studies can allow a wide range of factors to be taken into account over a considerable period of time in a much larger number of countries. Such quantitative studies frequently use sophisticated econometric methods to analyse the relationship between factors such as the level of economic development or the strength of particular political parties and the development of welfare states. Unfortunately, however, the availability of data and the linking of the data to the theory rarely matches the reliability or sophistication of the econometric methods used and there have been a number of recent important criticisms of aspects of quantitative approaches (see Shalev, 2002; Hall, 2003; Ebbinghaus, 2003).

Korpi argues that while quantitative comparative studies 'cannot compete with the rigor of deductive theorizing nor with the richness of life in detailed case studies, they have a greater capacity for theoretical disillusionment via confrontation with specific aspects of reality' (1989: 324). This would, however, suggest that greater emphasis in quantitative comparative studies should be placed on rejecting theories due to lack of causal relationship rather than on attempting to 'prove' a causal relationship from a statistical one.

Hall argues that a substantial gap has opened up between ontology (in the sense of 'the fundamental assumptions that scholars make about the nature of the social and political world and especially about the nature of the causal relationships within that world') and methodology ('the means scholars use for ensuring that their inferences about the social and political world are valid') (Hall, 2003: 373–4). Most ontologies now assume that policy outcomes are the result of complex interaction effects and various forms of multiple causality, whereas many statistical methods are based on much more restrictive assumptions about causal relationships (for example, independence of variables, steady impact over time and space, absence of multiple causality). Increasingly there is a move towards more qualitative comparative approaches (QCA), which seek to combine the detailed study of the qualitative approach with the mathematical rigour of the more quantitative studies (Ragin, 1994 and see Box 1.2). However, as Hall points out, such approaches retain an essentially correlational approach to causal inference and, all too often, conflate causality with co-occurrence (2003).

Box 1.2: What is qualitative comparative analysis?

Qualitative Comparative Analysis (QCA) is a method of comparative analysis that uses Boolean algebra – an algebra based on binary numbers and a collection of binary logic operations – in the study of social phenomena. Qualitative studies generally examine only a relatively small number of cases, but these analyses are both detailed and look at how different factors interact together to produce specific

(Continued)

Box 1.2: (Continued)

outcomes. QCA formalises the logic of qualitative analysis in a mathematical model which allows researchers to apply the logic and empirical detail of qualitative approaches to studies that embrace a larger number of cases (which would normally require the use of statistically complex quantitative methods).

QCA involves the categorisation of each potential variable (identified on the basis of previous theoretical study) into either/or. A truth table is then prepared, setting out the categorisation of dependent variables and that of the independent variables. These combinations are compared with each other and logically simplified. The objective of the simplification is to represent the information in the truth table, regarding the different combinations of conditions that produce a specific outcome, in the most concise manner possible.

One of the disadvantages of QCA is the requirement that all variables be dichotomised. While this can be acceptable for some variables (for example, whether a person is or is not a Catholic), it may represent an unrealistic reduction of 'reality' in others (for example, strength of unionisation) where it may be more realistic to provide a continuum of values from very low levels of unionisation, through medium levels to very high levels.

A development of QCA, which takes account of this limitation, is 'fuzzy sets'. A fuzzy set allows measurement in the interval between 0 and 1. Thus the fuzzy set of trade union strength could include nations who are 'fully in' the set (membership = 1.0), some who are 'almost fully in' the set (membership = .90), some who are neither 'more in' nor 'more out' of the set (membership = .5), and so on down to those who are 'fully out' of the set (membership = 0). This gives considerably more flexibility. However, it may also lead to researchers attaching a spurious scienticity to apparent relationships between degrees of a particular 'cause' and an outcome such that this development of QCA can, in incautious hands, begin to resemble traditional quantitative methods.

This is not to deny the value of statistical methods. However, it is to insist on the importance of inspecting not only the correspondence between the data representing 'causes' and those representing 'outcomes', but also the process whereby those causal factors operate so as to lead to those outcomes (Hall, 2003). All too often, comparative researchers posit a possible relationship between cause and effect, then proceed to 'show' such a relationship (both through quantitative and qualitative methods) and then conclude that *quad erat demonstrandum*. As Hall (2003) argues, the essence of explanation does not simply lie in specifying a set of 'explanatory variables', particular levels of which can be said to correlate with an outcome, but in explaining the mechanisms whereby one factor leads to another.

OVERVIEW OF THE BOOK

This book is divided into three sections. Part I looks at theoretical perspectives on the welfare state. Chapter 2 reviews the range of approaches developed to explain the development of welfare states. It is not confined to 'political' theory in the narrow sense, examining also factors such as economics, sociology, and religion. It outlines the recent theories about welfare state retrenchment and the 'new politics of welfare'.

Chapter 3 focuses on the wealth of recent writings on globalisation and outlines the (sometimes conflicting) approaches. In particular, it looks at what is meant by globalisation both generally and specifically in relation to welfare state theory. It outlines the different theses which have been put forward in relation to the impact of globalisation on welfare states and looks at the extent to which research indicates support for these theses in a European context.

Chapter 4 looks at criticisms of existing approaches from a gender perspective and at recent studies which apply a more gendered analysis of the welfare state. In particular it outlines the theoretical criticisms which have been made of existing theories and it draws on more recent work which has attempted to develop gendered criteria for analysing the impact of welfare states.

Part II looks at issues in comparing European welfare states. Chapter 5 gives a history of the development of welfare states in Europe, including the factors that have influenced those changes. It also gives some key data on the variations in welfare states that exist in Europe.

Chapter 6, which looks at typologies of welfare, examines the literature on these typologies and at how this applies in a European context. It looks at the general debates about 'typologising', at the criticisms that have been advanced of Esping-Andersen's approach and at the defences of that approach. It also looks at alternative approaches such as the 'families of nations' developed by Castles and his colleagues. It examines the extent to which typologies can inform our understanding of European welfare states and the extent to which 'actually existing' welfare states match the typologies.

Chapter 7 provides a concise overview of current welfare regimes in five contrasting European countries. Each country's system is outlined using a common analytical framework.

Chapter 8 looks at public opinion and the welfare state. It examines recent data on public opinion in Europe from surveys such as Eurobarometer, the International Social Survey Programme and the European Value Study. There is now a considerable body of international opinion poll evidence on support for the welfare state. This evidence has, to some extent, called into question the 'legitimacy crisis' thesis, as opinion poll evidence does not generally show a decline in support for the welfare state. But if, internationally, there has not been a decline in the level of support for welfare spending, why has there been a tendency for governments – to varying degrees – to introduce policies of retrenchment or restructuring? This chapter looks at the theoretical issues relating to public opinion in the broad sense and at opinion polls and the extent to which public opinion can help to explain welfare state developments.

Part III looks at the future of European welfare. Chapter 9 looks at the challenges facing European welfare states including demographic issues (such as ageing and falling birth rates), international economic integration and globalisation, changes in the labour market, the expansion of the European Union, and their impact on the need for support in key policy areas such as caring and pensions. It refers, in particular, to issues arising in the countries featured in Chapter 7 and also links back to the theoretical discussion of the new politics of welfare in Chapter 2 to provide a comparative study of welfare reforms.

To conclude, Chapter 10 on policy options looks at current philosophies of welfare, and at possible policy directions for the future including privatisation and basic income and EU developments such as 'open co-ordination'. In particular, this chapter examines developments at an EU level and, in the light of EU expansion, assesses the extent to which a European welfare state may be developing.

Summary

This chapter has discussed:

- how Europe is a social, political and cultural as well as a geographical entity;
- the definition of the term 'welfare state' and whether a normative commitment to welfare is an essential part of that definition;
- the advantages and disadvantages of comparative study; and has
- provided an outline of the contents of this book.

Discussion points

1   Where does Europe's eastern (or southern) border lie? What implications does this have for the study of European welfare states/the development of European welfare policies?
2   We can only speak of a *welfare* state where there is a normative commitment by that state to the welfare of its people. Discuss.
3   '[S]ocial scientists compare to escape cultural hegemony (or ethnocentrism)' (Janoski and Hicks, 1994: 6). Is this true?

Supplementary reading

Despite its ubiquity, there is a surprising absence of discussion about the meaning of the term 'welfare state'. For an overview of the issues see Flora and Heidenheimer (1981). Therborn (1995) provides one of the most imaginative and comprehensive discussions of 'Europe' from a social policy perspective. There is a wide range of texts on comparative social policy analysis. Janoski and Hicks (1994) provide a detailed overview of more qualitative, comparative research methods. Said (1993) provides a useful caution to an excessively 'Eurocentric' approach to any area of study.

PART ONE
THEORETICAL PERSPECTIVES

TWO WELFARE STATE THEORIES

This chapter looks at the range of theories which have been advanced to explain the development of the welfare state. In the first part of this chapter we look back over the development of welfare state theories and outline a number of theses which are representative of some of the main themes in welfare state theorising. In the second part we look at a range of theoretical approaches which are currently being used to analyse the development (or retrenchment) of European welfare states.

THESES ON THE WELFARE STATE

In this section we look at a number of key theses on the welfare state that are representative of the main approaches to welfare state theorising which have developed over the last decades. These are:

1 The welfare state emerges as part of the 'logic of industrialisation'.
2 The welfare state develops in response to the needs of advanced capitalism.
3 The welfare state is a product of modernisation of societies.
4 The welfare state is shaped by struggles over politics and social class.
5 Welfare states are shaped by the social organisation of production.
6 The welfare state is determined by the structure and interests of the state or polity.

A broadly chronological approach is adopted. This emphasises both the extent to which welfare state theories are inevitably creatures of their time (for example, at the height of the popularity of functionalism we see a functionalist understanding of welfare states) and the manner in which theory develops by reacting (either developing or rejecting) earlier approaches. For ease of exposition, we focus on one or two key texts in each area. In most cases there is, of course, extensive literature in each area with considerable variations between different authors.

THE WELFARE STATE EMERGES AS PART OF THE 'LOGIC OF INDUSTRIALISATION'

The earliest theories tended to adopt a structural or functionalist approach to the development of welfare states. In other words, they saw the welfare state as emerging to meet the needs of society at a certain stage of industrialisation, modernisation or advanced capitalism (as the case may be). The functionalist understanding of the development of the welfare state is, perhaps, best exemplified in Kerr et al.'s (1960) study *Industrialism and Industrial Man*. 'The world', Kerr and his colleagues announced, 'is entering a new age – the age of total industrialization' (1960: 3). By industrialisation the authors meant 'the actual course of transition from the preceding agricultural or commercial society towards the industrial society' (1960: 14). In this context, Kerr and his colleagues saw the development of social security and the welfare state as a key step in the building of the industrial labour force.

They argued that:

> ... in the very early stages of industrialization, the state and the managers typically make little or no provision for the maintenance of the working forces. The worker is thrown back upon his family if he becomes injured, ill, unemployed, or too old to work. In effect, therefore, the family is his only available system of social security. (1960: 152)

However, as industrialisation progresses, wider family ties tended to be broken. Workers, therefore, demanded that the state and business 'share some responsibility for their maintenance' (Kerr et al., 1960: 153). Arising from these pressures:

> ... advanced industrialising societies characteristically have formal programmes of accident compensation, sickness benefits, unemployment insurance, and old age pensions for industrial workers. There is general agreement that neither the individual nor his family should assume the major responsibility for the hazards involved in being a permanent member of the industrial working force. The society is called upon to maintain persons who cannot work for reasons beyond their control as well as those who were engaged in productive activity. The responsibility for guaranteeing the minimum welfare and security of industrial man rests in large measure upon his managers and his government. This completes the severance of his dependence, both materially and emotionally, on kinship and family ties. (Kerr et al., 1960: 153)

Kerr et al. did recognise that different countries might adopt 'different tactics in effecting labor force development' (1960: 160) and that this would have implications for the state's approach to the development of social security. They also recognised the role of worker protest and elite response in leading to the development of greater social security (1960: Ch. 6). Nonetheless, the main emphasis in this highly functionalist approach was that welfare states emerged at a certain stage of industrialisation in response to the different needs of industrial societies as compared to 'traditional' pre-industrial societies.

A number of specific studies of welfare states at around this time drew on this theoretical approach (for example, Wilensky, 1975). Rimlinger's study of welfare policy and industrialisation in Europe, America and Russia concluded that 'the need for a highly organized form of income protection increases as a society becomes industrialized and urbanized and that this need is independent of the nature of the socio-economic order' (1971: 334). While emphasising that social security was 'as essential under socialism as it is under capitalism', Rimlinger's study also recognised the quite different approaches that had been taken in different regimes and emphasised the importance of a range of other factors in the development of welfare states. These included 'an emphasis on class relations as a determinant factor in the development of social protection', 'the nature of the political system' and the role of ideas (1971: 8–10).

Myles and Quadagno have distinguished between the weaker and stronger versions of industrialisation theory. They argue that the weak version of the theory, that is 'that industrialism and its correlates (economic growth, population ageing) are necessary to account for the common trend line in welfare state expansion' is rarely questioned (2002: 36). However, the stronger version of the theory which 'rests on the assumption that public policy is the product of large, impersonal, economic forces' and that politics 'if it matters at all, does not matter very much' is much more contentious (2002: 37).

THE WELFARE STATE DEVELOPS IN RESPONSE TO THE NEEDS OF ADVANCED CAPITALISM

If functionalism emphasised the positive role that welfare spending had to play in ensuring the smooth functioning of industrial society, a Marxist approach, while also adopting a highly functionalist understanding of the welfare state, emphasised instead that welfare spending was a contradictory process which created tendencies towards economic, social and political crisis.

This understanding of the welfare state can be seen in O'Connor's study of the *Fiscal Crisis of the State* (1973). O'Connor argued that 'the capitalistic state must try to fulfil two basic and often mutually contradictory functions – *accumulation and legitimisation*' (1973: 6). In other words, the welfare state in advanced capitalist society assists both in ensuring the continuation, stability and efficient working of the economic system and in ensuring the integration of social classes and groups and the maintenance of social order. O'Connor argued that because of the 'dual and contradictory character of the capitalist state' nearly all welfare state spending was involved in both the accumulation and legitimisation functions and served both purposes simultaneously (1973: 7). He argued that, for example, some education spending – such as that needed to reproduce and expand workforce technical and skill levels – served the accumulation function, whereas other expenditure served the legitimation function. Similarly, he argued that the main purpose of some transfer payments, such as social insurance, was to reproduce the workforce whereas the purpose of others, such as income payments to the poor, was to 'pacify and control the surplus population' (1973: 7).

Like the functionalist approach, but in quite a different way, O'Connor also saw the development of the welfare state as being linked to the current stage of capitalism. Modern monopoly capitalism differed, he argued, in two fundamental respects from earlier competitive capitalism. First, an economy dominated by large corporations operating in monopolistic industries generated more inequality. Second, there was an important difference in the manner in which economic and social imbalances were perceived and acted upon under monopoly capitalism. O'Connor argued that under competitive capitalism, issues such as unemployment and wage levels appeared to be 'the consequence of impersonal forces beyond human control' (1973). In contrast, under monopoly capitalism, the inequalities generated by capitalist development 'begin to be attributed to the conscious policies of large corporations, big unions, and government agencies rather than impersonal market forces' (1973). Thus O'Connor argued that 'the growth of the state sector and state spending is functioning increasingly as the basis for the growth of the monopoly sector and of total production' and conversely 'the growth of state spending and state programmes is the result of the growth of the monopoly industries' (1973: 7–8). In other words, he argued that the growth of the state was both the cause and effect of the expansion of monopoly capital (1973: 8). However, O'Connor also argued that the 'accumulation of social capital and social expenses is a contradictory process which creates tendencies towards economic, social, and political crisis' (1973: 9).

THE WELFARE STATE IS A PRODUCT OF MODERNISATION OF SOCIETIES

Both the 'logic of industrialisation' and the functionalist Marxist approach outlined above obviously operated at a high level of generalisation. They did not, at least in their pure forms, explain much about the different manners in which welfare states developed. A more nuanced, if still functionalist, approach was developed drawing on the concept of modernisation. This saw the welfare state as a general phenomenon of modernisation, as a product of the increasing differentiation and the growing size of societies, on the one hand, and of processes of social and political mobilisation, on the other (Flora and Heidenheimer, 1981). Flora and Alber argued that the concept of modernisation had largely replaced the traditional concept of development as well as more specific concepts such as industrialisation and democratisation. While accepting that its meaning was somewhat 'vague and ambiguous', they argued that the concept of modernisation was useful in the analysis of welfare states because of its 'emphasis on the multidimensionality of societal development', that is, the assumption of causal interrelationships among economic and population growth, social and psychic mobilisation, political development, cultural change and the transformation of the international economic and political order (1981: 38).

Flora and Alber (1981: 41) argued that the development of the welfare state could be analysed according to at least three different aspects:

- the processes of differentiation of individual and household income, of working and living place which created specific labour market problems that must be solved by the state;
- the evolution of social rights as a consequence of (or compensation for) the institutionalisation of political rights; and
- the increasing control, substitution and supplementing of markets (and to some degree of associations) by state bureaucracies.

In their examination of the introduction of social insurance legislation in Europe (which we consider in more detail in Chapter 5), Flora and Alber utilised the following key variables drawing on the modernisation approach:

- socio-economic development (that is, the level of industrialisation and urbanisation);
- the political mobilisation of the working class (the percentage of votes in national elections for working class parties); and
- constitutional structures (that is, the extension of suffrage and the contrast between constitutional–dualistic monarchies and parliamentary democracies).

Contrary to what might have been expected, their study found that in contrast to the pioneering countries which first established social insurance legislation in different areas, the follower countries established their systems 'usually at a slightly higher level of socio-economic development and generally at a much higher level of political mobilisation' (Flora and Alber, 1981: 61). However, consistent with the modernisation approach, they found that countries which introduced social insurance schemes at relatively low levels of socio-economic development were characterised by relatively high levels of political mobilisation of the working class and, conversely, that countries which introduced social insurance schemes at relatively low levels of political mobilisation were characterised by relatively high levels of socio-economic development, leading to social problems which 'necessitated' the introduction of such institutions.[1] Flora (1986: xx) argues that in Western Europe 'the modern welfare state originated as an answer to specific problems of the new industrial working class' and that 'the fact that the modern welfare state originated in the late-nineteenth century in Europe may thus be simply explained by the comparatively high levels of industrialization and democratisation achieved in this region of the world' (1986: xiii).

However, while Flora saw the evolution of the welfare state as a universal aspect of modernisation, he did also recognise the diversity of welfare states which exist in Europe. In looking at the diversity of welfare states, Flora (1986) argued that at least two basic dimensions of institutional infrastructure were relevant:

- the degree to which the state had 'penetrated' the welfare institutions, that is, the *stateness* of the welfare state; and
- the degree to which the welfare institutions reflect social differentiations. Amongst other things, Flora argued that different class structures tended to lead to different types of welfare state and that, for example, the more homogenous the industrial working class, the greater were the chances for the development of a uniform system of income maintenance.

This latter point leads us to our next range of theses, which focus in much more detail on the role of politics and social class in the development of welfare states.

THE WELFARE STATE IS SHAPED BY STRUGGLES OVER POLITICS AND SOCIAL CLASS

A subsequent range of studies criticised the emphasis in the structural approach on the functional necessities in terms of the requirements

---

1 There were, however, a number of outlying countries which introduced social insurance legislation 'too early' to fit into this analysis; this is discussed in more detail in Chapter 5.

of industrialism and the composition of the population and instead focused on the role of politics and social class in determining the structure of welfare states (Korpi, 1980). In particular, studies emphasised the importance of the mobilisation of workers (or wage earners) and of social democratic or left-wing parties. One of the best theoretically grounded approaches in this tradition is that outlined by Walter Korpi in a series of studies.

POWER RESOURCES

The main principles of the 'power resources' approach can be outlined as follows (Korpi, 1980; 1989):

- Control over power resources is a major factor affecting the functioning of the distributive processes within society, what the outcomes of these processes are and how distribution conflict is patterned. Therefore, control over power resources played a major role in determining the structure of the welfare state.
- Distribution of power resources in capitalist democracies can vary between nations and also change over time.
- Major power resources in capitalist democracies are assumed to be related to class structures. The types of power resources that can be mobilised and used differ in class-related ways. In the market, capital and economic resources form the basis of power. In contrast, in the field of politics the principal power resources are the right to vote and the right to organise for collective action.
- Political democracy plays an important role in the processing of conflicts of interest.

SOCIAL DEMOCRACY

The power resources approach is not necessarily confined to an analysis which argues that social democracy is the key to the development of the welfare state. It could also be utilised to analyse the impact of other key social classes and political actors. Indeed Korpi argued against any interpretation of the power resources approach as a 'one-factor theory claiming to explain welfare state development more or less exclusively in terms of working class or left strength' (1989: 312). Thus he argued that 'the power resources approach does not ... imply that social policy development is based on the organisational and political power of the working class and left parties alone' (1989: 313). Nonetheless, Korpi and his colleagues, many from a Scandinavian background, did, in fact, focus mainly on the role of social democracy and the mobilisation of wage earners in the development of welfare states. Further, their findings tend to support the social democratic thesis. For example, in a study of the development of sickness benefits in 18 OECD countries since 1930, Korpi (1989) found that left party government participation had been an important factor during both the pre-War and the post-War periods in the development of sickness insurance (1989).

Some of those operating within the broad social democratic approach have recognised the limitations of relying exclusively on an emphasis on the role of the working class in the development of the welfare state. Esping-Andersen (1985), in his study of the development of the welfare state in Scandinavia, emphasised the importance of class coalitions. Nonetheless, in this approach, the social democratic party remained the key player in building the cross-class coalitions. However, the social democratic approach has, subsequently, been subjected to more sweeping criticisms. In particular, it has been criticised for its failure to take into account the key role of the middle classes (Baldwin, 1990) and the role of employers (Swenson, 2002; Mares, 2003). It is important to note that these criticisms are not necessarily of the power resources approach per se, but rather of its narrow application to social democracy and the working class.

THE ROLE OF THE MIDDLE CLASSES

Baldwin, in his study of the development of social insurance in Britain, France, Germany, Denmark and Sweden in the period from 1875, has emphasised the important role of the middle classes and argued that the social democratic approach should be seen as 'but one instance of a broader logic of social interest behind the welfare state and its development' (1990: 8–9). He has made the case for the importance of including other classes, in particular the middle classes, in the analysis of welfare state developments. Baldwin has argued that 'the concerns of particular social groups did determine social policy in an immediate sense' (1990: 289) and that the middle classes were one of the key social groups in this regard. His detailed historical study questions the social democratic interpretation even in its heartland of Scandinavia where 'the unique features of the Nordic welfare states were determined by the interests of the politically emergent agrarian middle classes neither to be excluded from the benefits of social policy, nor to bear more of the costs than could be displaced to their urban opponents' (1990: 289). Similarly, he argues that welfare state development in Britain and Scandinavia after the War 'reflected not only the interests of the poor, but equally so the middle-classes' desire to be favoured by statutory generosity'

(1990: 289–90). Similarly, van Kersbergen (1995) has highlighted the role that Christian democracy has played in developing the welfare state in many European countries.

BRINGING EMPLOYERS BACK IN

A number of recent studies, also critical of the social democratic approach, have emphasised the role of employers in the development of welfare states (Swenson, 2002; Mares, 2003). Swenson, for example, points out that the power resources approach (at least in its social democratic variant) cannot explain the development of the New Deal in the United States of America. Swenson states that much theorising to date has simply assumed (rather than demonstrated) that employers were opposed to the development of welfare states and that the level of opposition was broadly the same across time and across nations. He argues that this assumption is unsustainable and that without examining in detail employers' positions across times and across nations, an emphasis solely on social democracy can be misleading. It cannot, for example, determine whether the strength of social democracy is correlated (either negatively or positively) with the strength of capital. In practice, Swenson (2002), in his historical study of the development of welfare states in Sweden and the United States of America, outlines how employers have frequently favoured the development of social policy measures. He argues that there is usually a 'regulatory logic' to the interests of employers who often 'like government regulation when they see a net benefit and little risk' (2002). Welfare policies can provide such regulation. There are, however, many obstacles and handicaps in the way of employers attempting to implement such interests and in practice 'reformers with considerable organizational distance from the capitalist world (mostly liberal democrats in the US and social democrats in Sweden), were usually responsible for taking the policy initiative' (2002).

Mares (2003), drawing on evidence from the development of welfare states in France and Germany, makes broadly similar criticisms of existing approaches. Mares argues that 'social policies play an important economic role for the labour market strategies of firms' (2003: 9). She suggests that the presence of skilled workers, firm size and the relative incidence of risk facing a firm can affect employer preferences for social policy developments. Swank and Martin (2001) also provide evidence in support of this approach, arguing that the organisation of employers shapes social policy support amongst firms and affects social policy outcomes. In particular, the authors argue that the centralisation and cohesion of employer groups and economic co-operation across enterprises positively affects welfare state outcomes.

RECENT STUDIES

A number of recent studies have re-emphasised the role of the working class or of social democracy in the development of welfare systems – albeit with some modification of earlier theories (Hicks, 1999; Huber and Stephens, 2001). Hicks' interesting qualitative and quantitative study of the development of welfare states over the period from about 1880 argues that 'the political organizations and organizational politics of employees ... are the most persistently powerful forces operating to advance income security policy' (1999: x). Huber and Stephens, again combining quantitative and historical approaches (focusing on the period from 1945), utilise a 'power constellations' approach involving (a) class power, (b) the structure of the state and of state–society relations, and (c) the complex of relations in the international economy and the system of states. Their basic conclusions are that 'social democratic incumbency led to the construction of large welfare states, with generous entitlements, a heavy emphasis on public provision of social services, on labor mobilization and on redistribution through the tax and transfer system' (2001).

WELFARE STATES ARE SHAPED BY THE SOCIAL ORGANISATION OF PRODUCTION

A nuanced theory of the development of the welfare state, drawing on a structural neo-Marxist approach but having regard to the role of social classes and the state, has been developed by Quadagno (1988). Quadagno argues that welfare programmes are not a unique feature of advanced capitalist countries and that, since at least the sixteenth century, public welfare benefits have performed the functions of providing support to the vulnerable and in allocating labour (1988: 6). Thus welfare programmes have developed in response to the progression of industrial capitalism, and the nature and form of welfare states is determined by the social organisation of production. Recognising that the timing and structure of welfare programmes vary considerably between countries, she argues that 'the link between welfare state development and forms of social production may be modified in an advanced capitalist state if labor obtains the political resources to free welfare programs from market criteria'. She argues that 'the welfare state may be, but certainly is not invariably or even usually, in opposition to property and market forces' and that 'workers' ability to wrest social benefits from the market depends on their position in the state hierarchy' (1988: 7).

In this social organisation of production thesis, Quadagno draws on two key insights from neo-Marxist writing. First, that the state is (only) relatively autonomous in mediating between different social classes, and second, that the political process operates at a number of different levels. Poulantzas argues that the capitalist state has 'a precise role as political organizer and unifier and as a factor for the establishment of the "unstable equilibrium of compromises", which role is constituitively connected with its relative autonomy' (1973: Ch. 4, 1976: 71). The concrete form taken by this relative autonomy depends upon 'the precise conjuncture of the class struggle at any one time'. The term 'relative' in the expression 'relative autonomy of the state' refers to the relationship between state and dominant classes, that is, it refers to the class struggle within each social formation and to its corresponding state form. The principles of the Marxist theory of the state lay down the general, negative limits of this autonomy, that is, that the state (in the long run) can only correspond to the political interests of the dominant class or classes. But within these limits, the degree, extent and form of autonomy can only be examined with reference to a given state and to the precise conjuncture of the corresponding class struggle (the specific configuration of the power bloc, the degree of hegemony within that block, the relations between the differing classes and fractions) (1976: 72). Poulantzas does not take account of factors such as race and gender, which must now also be incorporated into such an analysis.

Offe (1984: 159–60) provides an analysis of the nature of the political process in which political outcomes are decided. This, he argues, can best be conceived of as consisting of three tiers (or three cumulative arenas of conflict). The first and most visible is the arena of political decision making within the state apparatus. Here the actors are the political elites competing with each other for electoral victories and scarce resources who decide on social policy programmes, legislation and budgets. This, he points out, is the most superficial and most visible level of politics and is the level at which analysis tends to focus. But, Offe argues, 'the space of possible decisions of political elites is determined by societal forces that, on a far less visible level, shape and change the politicians' view and perception of reality, i.e. of the alternatives open to decision makers and the consequences to be expected from each of the alternatives. This is the level at which the agenda of politics and the relative priority of issues and solutions is determined ...' (1984: 159). At this level it is more difficult to identify specific actors and 'the forces operating here are most often the aggregate outcome of a multitude of anonymous actors and actions' (1984: 159). The important point, he argues, is that although the power to structure the politicians' reality, agenda and attention cannot be as easily traced back to personal actors, as is the case on the first level of political conflict, there is a 'matrix of social power according to which social classes, collective actors and other social categories have a greater chance of shaping and re-shaping political reality, opening or closing the political agenda, than others' (1984: 160). Underlying this is a third level at which changes within the matrix itself occur, that is, changes in the relative weight that collective actors enjoy in shaping the agenda of politics.

Combining these two approaches, Quadagno (1988) locates the development of old age pensions in the United States of America in a complex set of economic, political and social forces. In particular she argues that in the United States the late unionisation of mass production workers, a powerful private sector and the dualism of the US economy (that is, primary production in the South as against industrialisation in the North), all help to explain the particular form which pension policy took in that country.

THE WELFARE STATE IS DETERMINED BY THE STRUCTURE AND INTERESTS OF THE STATE OR POLITY

STATE-CENTRED

This approach emphasises the role of the state (or polity) in the development of the welfare state (Skocpol, 1985). There are two distinguishable aspects to the state-centred approach that Skocpol puts forward. First, in contrast to the neo-Marxist theory, and drawing on the basic understanding of the state of scholars such as Max Weber, Skocpol argues that states 'are not simply reflective of the demands or interests of social groups, classes or societies' (1985: 9). This is, in itself, not inconsistent with the neo-Marxist argument that states are in the last instance reflective of these interests. However, Skocpol goes further by referring to the possibility of 'fully autonomous state actions' (1985: 15).

Second, Skocpol advances 'an alternative frame of reference ... perhaps even more important than the view of state as actor' (1985: 21). This 'Tocquevillian' view sees states as 'configurations of organization and action that influence the meanings and methods of politics for all groups and classes in society' (1985: 28). Skocpol sees this approach as 'entirely complimentary' to the state as actor interpretation.

Weir and Skocpol (1985) apply this approach to explaining the different responses to the Great Depression in Sweden, Great Britain and the United States of America. The authors outline how Sweden aimed to become a full-employment society with high levels of public spending on social welfare, the United States of America also adopted a broadly Keynesian approach but Great Britain, despite being a pioneer in establishing public social welfare programmes, did not adopt a Keynesian approach nor extend public social benefits until after the Second World War (1985: 108–9). Having rejected a number of possible explanatory theories for these differences (such as functionalism and working-class strength), the authors outline a state-centred theory to explain the different responses. They suggest that two key factors explain the policy differences: the established policy approaches for addressing problems of unemployment; and the institutional mechanisms they provide for allowing economic experts to participate in public policy making. In Great Britain, policy discussions focused, in the absence of any tradition of extensive public works, on unemployment benefits. In contrast, the Swedish government was able to build on existing work on public works carried out by a national Unemployment Commission. Also, in Great Britain in the 1930s the authors argue that the Treasury was in effective control of policy development and 'a profound bias against policy innovations contravening economic orthodoxy spread throughout the entire British apparatus' (1985: 127). In contrast, Swedish economists were more readily involved in the policy-making process.

A BROADER INSTITUTIONAL APPROACH

The main protagonists of the state-centred approach have now all developed their theories further (see Orloff, 1993b; Amenta, 1998). Skocpol (1992), in her detailed study of the early development of the US welfare state, has outlined a 'polity centred' approach which sees the polity as 'the primary locus of action, yet understands political activities, whether carried out by politicians or by social groups, as conditioned by the institutional configurations of governments and political party systems' (1992: 41). This framework, which includes not only the state but also 'party organizations' and 'politically active groups' as part of the polity, draws attention to four types of processes: (a) state and party formation and transformation; (b) the effects of political institutions on the identities, goals and capacities of social groups; (c) the fit between the goals and capacities of groups and the points of access and leverage allowed by political institutions; and (d) the effects of policy feedback. Skocpol argues that the reasons why the United States of America developed distinctive types of social policies can only be understood by situating policy making within a broader, organisationally grounded, analysis of American political development (1992: 526).

A variation on this approach, from the Tocquevillian perspective, has emphasised the manner in which formal and informal constitutional structures impact on welfare state outcomes (Immergut, 1992). Much recent work in an 'institutional' vein has tended to focus on the nature of political institutions rather than the 'state as actor'. Institutional theorists have argued that the diffusion of political authority has been a key impediment to the development of the welfare state in the United States (for example, Steinmo and Watts, 1995), while Huber and Stephens (2001), in their comparative study of the development of post-War welfare states, also argued that political structures have played a key role both in the development of welfare and in facilitating or blocking its retrenchment.

DISCUSSION

The theories outlined above are not necessarily mutually exclusive and comparative studies have argued that factors emphasised by a number of different approaches have an impact on welfare state development (Huber and Stephens, 2001). It should also be emphasised that the approaches outlined above are certainly not exhaustive and are simply indicative of some of the main trends in welfare state theorising in recent decades. In a number of cases, there is considerable variation in the approach taken by different authors within different approaches.

There are a number of important aspects of welfare state theory which it is not possible to incorporate into the approaches outlined above. These include the impact of religion and of the family. Castles suggests that 'differences in religious adherence and/or in degrees of secularisation between advanced nations may be as relevant to understanding cross-national variants in a wide range of public policy outcomes as the impact of socio-economic and political factors' (1994: 19). Using Catholicism as an example, he argues that religion can have an impact on policy areas as diverse as welfare expenditure, family policy and labour market policy outcomes, particularly where gender related outcomes are at issue. Fahey (2002) argues that there is a need for greater emphasis on the role of the family and on agrarian social classes as influences in the formation of welfare states. He seeks to bring together and extend these perspectives by exploring the role of state support for family based economic production, especially family farming, in the evolution of welfare regimes. He argues that family employment is a decommodified alternative to wage labour and that such family employment received extensive support in many welfare states at various points during the past century.

CURRENT STRANDS IN WELFARE STATE THEORY

In the previous section, we looked at some of the main strands in welfare state theory. In this section, we conclude this chapter by looking at some of the key issues in current welfare state theories. Many of these issues are discussed in more detail in coming chapters (Globalisation in Chapter 3, Gender in Chapter 4, and Typologies of Welfare in Chapter 6). The key strands in current welfare state thinking can be summarised under the following headings:

1   Further development of existing theories
2   Gender and the welfare state
3   Typologies of welfare
4   The return of structural theories
5   Politics *with* markets

FURTHER DEVELOPMENT OF EXISTING THEORIES

The further development of existing theories includes both approaches which seek to add new elements to existing theories and those which seek to bring together and make sense of a number of the different approaches outlined in the first section of this chapter. The former group includes studies which have added to the politics and social class approach by investigating the role of employers in the development of welfare states (Swenson, 2002; Mares, 2003) and those which have applied the power resources approach in the context of welfare state retrenchment (Korpi and Palme, 2003; Allan and Scruggs, 2004). The latter approach, seeking to draw on a range of alternative theories to the development of the welfare state, includes studies such as Huber and Stevens (2001) and Castles (1998). Many of these studies have already been discussed in the previous section.

GENDER AND THE WELFARE STATE

There has been little reference to gender in this chapter. This issue is addressed in Chapter 4, but its absence here is not due to the organisational structure of this book but rather to the fact that most of the approaches outlined here made little attempt to integrate gender into their analysis of welfare state developments. Unfortunately, despite its importance, gender remains a minority topic in the study of welfare states. Despite the undoubted increase in the number of studies of gender and welfare, research in this area is starting from a very low base. There are still only a minority of 'mainstream' welfare state theorists who seriously attempt to incorporate gender into their analysis of the welfare state (see, for example, Huber and Stephens, 2001) and serious study of issues of gender and welfare has tended to be confined to a small number of (almost all female) researchers.

TYPOLOGIES OF WELFARE

Although a number of earlier authors did examine the issue of welfare state typologies, it is really only since the publication in 1990 of Esping-Andersen's classic study *The Three Worlds of Welfare Capitalism* that the study of welfare state typologies has really taken off. Since then the 'welfare modelling business' (Abrahamson, 1999) has been booming and this despite Peter Baldwin's description of typologising as 'the lowest form of intellectual endeavour' (1996: 29). Given the importance of welfare state typologising in the social policy debate, Chapter 6 of this book is dedicated to an examination of these studies.

THE RETURN OF STRUCTURAL THEORIES

As Myles and Quadagno aptly put it, 'at the very moment when political theories of the welfare state seemed to have relegated the 'logic of industrialism' thesis with its emphasis on the over-determining role of large impersonal economic forces to the critical list, the theory was revived in new form' (2002: 41). The new spectres haunting welfare state theorising include globalisation, deindustrialisation and the 'new politics of welfare'.

GLOBALISATION

Just like typologising, studies of globalisation and the welfare state are a growth industry. Whatever impact globalisation may have had on the welfare state itself, it has certainly led to a massive increase in articles and books examining the impact of economic integration. As outlined in Chapter 3, these studies have yet to arrive at a consensus as to whether globalisation leads to increased welfare state spending, significant reductions or restructuring in the welfare state or to some element of convergence.

DEINDUSTRIALISATION

An alternative structural explanation for recent changes in the welfare state is the role of deindustrialisation (Iversen, 2001; Iversen and Cusack, 2000). Iversen and Cusack (2000) have challenged the importance of globalisation in a radical manner, arguing that the relationship between trade openness and welfare state expansion is spurious and that such expansion has, in fact, been driven by deindustrialisation, that is, by the major changes in occupational structures which have occurred in all advanced industrial societies in recent decades. They reject the globalisation thesis on the basis that a causative link between indices of globalisation (such as trade) and welfare state pressures cannot be found. Drawing on data from 16 core countries they found no evidence of greater variation in output, employment and wages in more open economies (in terms either of trade or capital market openness) than in more closed economies.

Having rejected the globalisation thesis, Iversen and Cusack (2000) argue that, in fact, the main sources of labour market risk are to be found in domestic economic processes and, in particular, in the labour market dislocations associated with major shifts in occupational structures. Their argument is both that labour market risks 'are generated across the interfaces between economic sectors requiring very different types of skills' and that employers that provided social benefits are also constrained by the transferability of skills (2000: 325). Where a worker has to cross the interface to a different occupational sector, he or she may be left unemployed or only able to find work at a substantially reduced wage (including social benefits). Accordingly, there will be a demand on the state to provide protection against these risks.

Testing their theory econometrically, Iverson and Cusack found that none of the globalisation measures gave a statistically significant impact on spending. In contrast, deindustrialisation was found to be correlated with an increase in welfare state spending as predicted by their theory. They argue that 'exposure to risk in the labour market is a powerful determinant of peoples' preferences for state protection and public risk sharing' (2000: 324). The main source of this risk, they believe, is to be found in the domestic economic process. In particular, they argue that the 'labour market dislocations associated with major changes in the occupational structure have been a driving force behind the expansion of the welfare state'(2000: 324–5). In the period from 1960, they highlight the 'massive sectoral shift' from agriculture and industry to services (2000: 325). Such changes in the occupational structure, they argue, are mediated by 'the transferability of skills and social benefits' (2000: 325). Skills allow people to cross over into different economic sectors (to 'transgress the interfaces defined by skills discontinuities') and benefits provide compensation to people during a transition or on a failed transition. As Iverson and Cusack point out, where large numbers of people face the risk of having to make such 'travels', demand for state-sponsored compensation and risk-sharing will be high (2000: 326).

NEW POLITICS OF WELFARE

A further, largely structural, approach to the analysis of the welfare state is the 'new politics of welfare' developed primarily by Paul Pierson (1996, 2001). Pierson argues that, in contrast to previous decades when the growth of the welfare state was under examination, a different approach is needed in a context of retrenchment and austerity.[2] Pierson argues that welfare state expansion involved the enactment of popular policies but, by contrast, welfare state retrenchment requires governments to pursue unpopular policies that must stand the scrutiny of both voters and entrenched interest groups (1996: 143–4). He adopts a largely structural account of the pressures on welfare states and argues that the power resources approach does not greatly help to explain retrenchment.

Pierson identifies four main 'post industrial' pressures on the welfare state:

- *The slowdown in productivity growth and consequently economic growth associated with the shift from manufacturing to service employment* Pierson (2001: 83) argues that, over time, productivity improvements are the key to sustained economic growth. However, the massive occupational shift which has been and is taking place in most advanced nations from manufacturing to service employment threatens to undermine that productivity growth. While the precise levels of productivity growth in the different sectors may be open to question, Pierson argues that it is highly unlikely that services will be able to match the productivity growth typical of manufacturing. Inevitably, Pierson argues, this will lead to slower economic growth over time. This in turn will generate 'acute problems for welfare states' (2001: 86). First, slower economic growth will impact on the level of funding available (through taxation) for the welfare state. In addition, if slower economic growth leads to higher unemployment, this creates extra pressures on the welfare state. Further, the growth of service employment creates pressures

---

2 Despite Pierson's nuanced approach to the issues of retrenchment, his choice of the terms 'retrenchment' and 'austerity' is perhaps somewhat problematic. It is difficult to reconcile a situation where most European countries are, in economic terms, richer than they have ever been and spending on average 20 per cent of this wealth on social protection with a situation which could be classified as 'permanent austerity'.

between the goals of employment growth, wage equality and budgetary constraint. Service sector employment can only occur through the private sector at the price of increased inequalities in wages or through the public sector at the cost of increased budgetary pressures. Countries which do not allow an increase in wage inequalities and at the same time impose budgetary restraint are likely to constrain service employment and hence see rising levels of unemployment (Iverson, 1998).

- *The gradual expansion, maturation and 'growth to limits' of government commitments* Pierson (2001: 88) identifies a second source of pressure as being the maturation of welfare states. Policy measures introduced in previous decades have now grown to their mature levels with consequent increases in the level of funding required. Pierson cites healthcare and pensions as the most important components of this process.

- *The demographic shift to an older population* Pierson (2001) argues that the well identified tendency to an ageing of the population in all developed countries will create significant pressures on the welfare state, for example, through increased healthcare and pension costs. The ageing of the population arises from increased longevity and from the fall in the birth rate, which means both that older people are living longer (and therefore that there are more of them) and also that there are fewer people in the younger age brackets.

- *The transformation of household structures* The final key pressure identified by Pierson (2001) has been the change in household structures and the relationship between households and work. This includes a number of interrelated issues such as the massive increase in female participation in the paid labour force, falling fertility rates and a change in household structures arising both from an increase in lone parenthood and the increasing tendency for single people and older people to live on their own. These changes have created pressures on welfare states which were originally designed on the basis of a traditional male breadwinner household structure. Increased female participation, Pierson (2001) argues, not only generates additional revenue for the welfare state but also creates demands for new types of public social services such as childcare. Pierson also sees the increase in lone parent households as creating pressures on welfare states, given that such households are more likely to have low incomes in the absence of state supports.

While this account is broadly structural, applying across the board to all advanced welfare states, Pierson does recognise that the pressure on welfare states 'retains a distinctly national character' (2001: 99). There are, for example, significant variations in the degree to which countries are facing pressures from population ageing. Facing these pressures, Pierson identifies the sources of the welfare state's political strength as of two basic types: the electoral incentives associated with the programmes which retain broad and deep popular support and the 'institutional stickiness which further constrains the possibilities for policy reform' (2001). The issue of popular support for the welfare state is discussed in more detail in Chapter 8. In relation to institutional stickiness, Pierson argues that there are both formal and informal institutional veto points which can make more difficult measures to retrench welfare state spending and also that there are 'path dependent' processes which 'tend to lock existing policy arrangements into place' (2001). These issues, and Pierson's more detailed analysis of measures of retrenchment, are discussed in more detail in subsequent chapters.

It should, however, be noted here that some studies focusing on replacement rates, rather than overall welfare state spending, have argued both that there has been a greater degree of retrenchment than accepted in Pierson's account and that class related politics remain relevant to welfare outcomes (Korpi and Palme, 2003; Allan and Scruggs, 2004). Clayton and Pontussen (1998), looking at public services, inequality and poverty, also argue that there has been a greater degree of retrenchment than identified by Pierson. These debates will be discussed in more detail in Chapter 7.

POLITICS *WITH* MARKETS

An important debate in recent welfare state studies has been the emphasis on the extent to which welfare states are complimentary to markets. This is, of course, in contrast to some earlier approaches (in particular the social democratic approach), which assumed that welfare states were the outcome of politics *against* markets (Esping-Andersen, 1985). One strand of this research, referred to above, is that which emphasises the role of employers in shaping the welfare state. A second strand, drawing on regulation theory, emphasises the complementarities between the welfare state and modes of production. Boyer (2002), for example, in a detailed study of the French welfare state in a comparative context, argues that in the past the welfare state has been the logical compliment of the Fordist growth regime (2002: 13). Boyer identifies a number of challenges facing this paradigm including technological change, globalisation, a shift in political alliances and what he describes as 'alarmist discourses on the inefficiency of social security' (2002). From a broadly similar perspective, a number of researchers, whose work is brought together in Ebbinghaus and Manow's (2001) edited volume *Comparing Welfare Capitalism*, have highlighted that there are certain 'institutional complementarities' between different production regimes, industrial relation practices and social protection systems. In particular, this approach emphasises that 'the productive function of social protection has often been overlooked due to the focus on redistribution as the main goal of welfare state policies' and argues that for a 'better understanding of modern capitalism we ought to take into account the important impact of the welfare state on employment, skill acquisition, wage setting and investment' (2001: 2). Ebbinghaus and Manow's study looks in particular at possible linkages between social protection and three areas of political economy. First, the system of industrial relations, second, the production system and employment regime and third, the financial and corporate finance system. The detailed studies identify a number of important linkages in these areas; for example, they suggest 'intricate interdependencies between labour relations and labour market outcomes' (2001: 13). Similarly, they argue that 'welfare states may also serve an important function in stabilising, maintaining and enhancing production regimes by providing an educated and healthy labour force which is shielded from social risks' (2001: 14). These issues are discussed in more detail as they arise in concrete national situations in subsequent chapters.

Summary

This chapter has:

- outlined the different theses on the development of the welfare state which argue that the welfare state is shaped by factors including: the logic of industrialisation; the needs of advanced capitalism; the modernisation of societies; the influence of politics and social class; the social organisation of production; and the structure and interests of the state or polity; and
- looked at a number of current strands of welfare state theory including: the impact of globalisation (see Chapter 3); gender (see Chapter 4); typologies of welfare state (see Chapter 6); deindustrialisation; the 'new politics of welfare'; and a new focus on the importance of employers and business on the development of the welfare state.

Discussion points

1   Economic development has been more important in the development of European welfare states than the impact of political parties. Discuss.
2   The state and institutional structures have been one of the key influences in the development of welfare states in Europe. Do you agree?

3 Using the example of a recent important policy development in your chosen European country, discuss the extent to which the factors influencing policy match the different theses outlined in this chapter.

Supplementary reading

There is an extensive literature on welfare state theories. A helpful summary is Myles and Quadagno (2002). The key texts in the development of welfare state theorising are set out in the relevant sections of this chapter. Important contributions include Baldwin's (1990) excellent account of the development of welfare policies in a number of European countries, which adopts a class coalition approach; a modified application of the social-democratic approach by Hicks (1999); and Huber and Stephens (2001), which usefully bring together a number of theoretical approaches.

THREE GLOBALISATION AND EUROPEAN WELFARE STATES

This chapter focuses on the wealth of recent writing on globalisation and outlines the (often conflicting) approaches. In particular, it looks at what is meant by 'globalisation' both generally and, specifically, in relation to welfare state theory. It outlines the different theses which have been put forward in relation to the impact of globalisation and looks at the extent to which research indicates support for these theses in a European context.

WHAT IS GLOBALISATION?

Globalisation is one of the discussed and debated issues in current political and social policy discourse. Yet the concept of globalisation itself and its precise meaning is highly contested. The term 'globalisation' is used by a wide range of people, from neo-classical economists to the radical left. It is hardly necessary to add that the understanding of the term and the uses to which it is put vary greatly along this spectrum. Indeed, linked to these differences in understanding, there are a wide range of views as to when precisely globalisation began.

Box 3.1: Definitions of 'globalisation'

The description is the widening and deepening of international flows of trade, finance and information in a single, integrated global market. The prescription is to liberalize national and global markets in the belief that free flows of trade, finance and information will produce the best outcome for growth and human welfare. (UNDP, 1997: 82)

As experienced from below, the dominant form of globalisation means a historical transformation: in the economy, of livelihoods and modes of existence; in politics, a loss in the degree of control exercised locally – for some, however, little to being with – such that the locus of power gradually shifts in varying proportions above and below the territorial state; and in culture, a devaluation of a collectivity's achievements or perceptions of them. This structure, in turn, may engender either accommodation or resistance. (Mittelman, 2000: 6)

Some authors, for example, argue that a global economic system is a centuries-old process. Frank, writing from a world-systems perspective, argues that 'there was a single global world economy with a worldwide division of labour and multilateral trade from 1500 onward' or indeed even earlier (1998: 52). O'Rourke and Williamson (2002) argue for a more modest backdating, arguing that globalisation in the sense of the integration of the world economy began in the early eighteenth century. In contrast, Hirst and Thomson (1997), while accepting that the world economy was highly integrated at least as far back as the nineteenth century and that in the period 1870 to 1914 flows of merchandise trade, capital investment and labour migration were all comparable to or greater than those of today, distinguish between a 'worldwide international economy' and a 'globalised international economy'. They argue that, in contrast to an *international* economy, in a *globalised* economy 'distinct national economies are subsumed and rearticulated into the system by international processes and transactions' (1997: 339). These authors argue that the current economy is not globalised in this strong sense but remains an international economy.

As can be seen, like the term 'welfare state', a wide variety of meanings have been attached to the term 'globalisation' (see Box 3.1). It is not necessary for the purposes of this book to decide which is the correct approach. It is, however, necessary to define a particular understanding for the purposes of this study. In relation to its current impact on the welfare state, it does not seem useful to apply the term retrospectively to past centuries. Even if one were to do so, it would be necessary to ask what is different about globalisation today. Bearing in mind the points made by Hirst and Thomson in relation to the level of international integration in earlier centuries and accepting that a world-economic system has existed for many centuries, it does seem useful to employ the term 'globalisation' in a weak sense to reflect the current level of internationalisation of the world economy and the growing interconnectedness (both in terms of trade, investment and communication) which is a feature of recent decades. Characterising globalisation as a process rather than as an end state does allow us to capture some essential new features of the world economy.

CONCEPTS OF GLOBALISATION

Using globalisation in this weak sense to reflect current key processes of the world economy, it is still necessary to examine precisely what we mean by this increasing interconnectedness and how we can measure its features. Carroll (2003), in a review of concepts of globalisation in welfare research since the mid-1990s, identifies no less than nine broad categories of understanding:

1 *Trade*: the impact of international trade on the welfare state. It is usually measured in terms of the level of imports and exports as a percentage of gross domestic product.
2 *Competition*: the impact on the welfare state of increased competition including competition from low-wage countries, labour market competition, tax competition and cost-cutting pressures.
3 *International organisations*: the influence of a wide range of international organisations in the social policy area. Clearly, in a European context, the European Union is a key player.[1] However, particularly in Central and Eastern Europe, organisations such as the IMF and World Bank also play an important role.
4 *Global markets*: international trends such as increased privatisation of public services and increased marketisation.
5 *Spatial reorganisation of social life*: the extent to which spatial distances are being reduced by travel and, perhaps more importantly, by communications technology.
6 *Trans/multi-national corporation activity*: the impact of trans- and/or multi-national corporations on the welfare state.
7 *Capital market de-regulation and/or openness*: related to the previous category, the extent to which trends in capital mobility can influence the development of the welfare state.
8 *International capital flows*: the level of foreign direct investment (FDI).
9 *Information centred*: the extent to which we are living in a global information society.

Obviously, a number of these aspects of globalisation are interrelated. The extent to which these aspects of globalisation have been examined and the impact (or lack thereof) which they have been

---

1 As discussed in Chapter 1, Europeanisation can be seen as both a part of and a reaction against globalisation. Insofar as Europeanisation is leading to the development at the European level of distinct structures of governance and processes through which the EU political, social and economic dynamics become part of a logic of national policies, it goes beyond globalisation. Accordingly, we do not discuss here the detailed impact of EU development and Europeanisation on welfare state policies will be discussed in Chapters 7 and 10.

found to have on the welfare state will be discussed in more detail below. However, it is important not simply to focus on the empirical indices of globalisation, as to do so would be to treat globalisation as 'an unproblematic dependent variable' (Hay et al., 1999). Hay and his colleagues emphasise the importance of 'the independent causal and constitutive role of *ideas about globalisation* in the generation of the effects attributed to globalisation itself' (1999: 2).

GLOBALISATION IN EUROPE

Before proceeding to look at the theses which have been put forward about the impact of globalisation on the welfare state, it is perhaps important to look at the data on commonly used indices of globalisation in Europe. Rather than looking at Europe as a block, we look at the data for individual countries to emphasise the variation in the degree to which different aspects of globalisation affect different countries.

It is first worth recalling the fact that international economic integration is not a new concept. In terms of trade, in Western Europe, exports (as a percentage of GDP) reached a peak just before the First World War. Trade declined dramatically in the period up to the Second World War, increasing thereafter. However, the level of exports from Western Europe, although at an historic high, is not dramatically different today than it was a century ago. Looking at other aspects of economic integration, labour migration in the nineteenth and early twentieth centuries was significantly higher than it is today as millions of emigrants made their way from Europe to the United States. In terms of capital mobility, the share of capital outflows was much higher in the United Kingdom during the period of the Gold Standard than it has been since (Rodrik, 1997).

However, economic integration today is qualitatively (and in some respects quantatively) different to that experienced in previous decades. As we have seen, trade is now somewhat higher than it was in previous centuries. Europe, or at least Western Europe, is now a country of immigration rather than emigration. Restrictions on capital flows have been largely abolished and the level of capital flowing from one country to another has reached unprecedented levels. These indicators have significantly different impacts in different European countries. Two of the main indicators of globalisation that are commonly used are the level of trade (imports and exports as a percentage of GDP) and the level of foreign direct investment. Table 3.1 sets out these indicators for 21 European countries for which comparable data are available.

In terms of trade, the level of exports and imports as a percentage of GDP varies from about 40 per cent in the United Kingdom to a

Table 3.1   Trade openness and foreign investment in selected countries, 2003

	Trade/GDP	Inward FDI/GDP	Outward FDI/GDP
Austria	71	21	19
Belgium	169		
Czech Republic	113	55	2
Denmark	61		
Finland	59	27	53
France	43	28	46
Germany	55		
Greece (2001)	33		
Hungary	110	44	4
Ireland	118	135	33
Italy	41	11	16
Netherlands	99		
Norway	49		
Poland	53		
Portugal	52	36	26
Slovenia	131	32	2
Spain	44	33	33
Sweden	62		60
Switzerland	64		
Turkey	43		
United Kingdom	40	41	66
EUR average	**72**	**42**	**30**
USA	18		
JAPAN	19		

Source: OECD (2003)

high of 100 per cent and over in countries such as Belgium, Czech Republic, Hungary, Ireland, the Netherlands and Slovenia.[2] In terms of foreign direct investment there is also a significant variation with the level of inward foreign direct investment varying from a low of about 11 per cent in Italy to a high of 135 per cent in Ireland (Table 3.1). Similarly, in terms of outward foreign direct investment there is also a significant variation with the countries of Central and Eastern Europe and many Southern European countries having almost no outward FDI, while countries such as Sweden and the United Kingdom have reached levels of 60 per cent of GDP.

It is more difficult to develop meaningful indicators for some of the other aspects of globalisation discussed above. In particular, it is difficult to gauge the impact of international organisations and to

---

2 Despite these variations, in comparative terms all European countries are relatively open. In contrast, other major trading blocks are much more closed, with the United States and Japan having a trade ratio of about 20 per cent. The level of trade is, of course, inversely related to the size of a country's population, with countries with smaller internal markets being more heavily dependent on external trade.

separate out the policy impact that an international organisation such as the OECD or IMF has in a specific country from the general influence which the diffusion of particular policy paradigms have and always have had on policy-makers. However, studies indicate that the impact of organisations such as the World Bank and the IMF has been quite significant in some or all of the countries of Central and Eastern Europe (Box 3.2). It is important to bear these variations in the impact of globalisation on different European countries in mind when we look at the different theses which have been advanced in relation to the impact of globalisation on the welfare state.

Box 3.2: Globalisation and Central and Eastern Europe

Many of the general studies discussed in this chapter have not included (or have not specifically considered) the impact of globalisation in Central and Eastern Europe (CEE). However, the dramatic economic and social transition that has and is occurring in these countries may mean that globalisation has a particular impact on their welfare states. A number of recent studies have examined aspects of globalisation and CEE.

Looking at globalisation in post-communist countries in both Europe and Asia, Frye (2003) found that trade openness and volume were related to lower total government spending and lower spending on health and education. In contrast, FDI – which in most countries was quite small and directed at exports – was modestly related to higher total spending. Frye found that integration into the EU (that is, the stage in the accession process) was also associated with higher total spending and spending on health and education. He suggested that the trade relationship might be due to the weakness of trade unions in post-communist countries.

Orenstein and Haas (2002) argued that the impact of globalisation differed greatly depending upon a country's position in the international economy and geopolitical relations. They found that leading CEE accession countries had experienced a radically different welfare trajectory than had their neighbours in the former USSR and, in line with Frye's argument, attributed this to a 'Europe effect'. In particular, Orenstein and Haas argued that the impact of globalisation on a particular country was mediated by politics in three ways; first, by a country's geopolitical position (that is, proximity to the EU), second, by the domestic politics of decision making, and third, by the role of international actors (including the WTO, World Bank and IMF in addition, of course, to the EU) influencing the paths countries take.

Ferge (2001) takes a somewhat more negative view, arguing that there appears to be a higher degree of compliance to the new (neo-liberal) ideology of globalisation in CEE countries than in Western Europe. This she attributes to: the poverty of the transition countries; the 'economic necessity' of cutbacks in state spending during the transition; the cultural impact of the structural shift from state socialism to capitalism; the delegitimisation of social policy values because of their association with state socialism (although see Chapter 8); and the weakness of civil society.

Box 3.2: (Continued)

She suggests that transition countries, particularly those with significant debt, require the 'goodwill' of foreign capital and international organisation. However, Ferge emphasises that the story to date is very much an interim one.

Looking specifically at the political aspects of globalisation, Anderson (2003) argues that international organisations do impact on policy developments in two ways: first, by creating political and material incentives for domestic policy actors to adopt legislation, and second, by lending political and technical support to domestic actors proposing unpopular legislation. However, she concluded that nation states still guide welfare state development.

In summary, the evidence would seem to suggest that indicators of globalisation per se (such as levels of trade and foreign direct investment) have had a limited impact on CEE welfare states. Nonetheless, there can be no doubt that their sudden integration into the world economic system has had a dramatic effect on social wellbeing in individual countries and led, at least in the short term, to significant changes in poverty and income inequality. In this context of sudden change, the limited evidence to date would suggest that international organisations have played a significant role in influencing policy. In particular, it has been argued that EU accession has been important. One might question, however, the extent to which the 'Europe effect' is an independent cause of these welfare changes. In order to examine this, one would need to compare the path of moderately developed CEE countries which chose not to enter the EU – but there is none. Albania, for example, illustrates that geographical proximity to the EU is in itself insufficient. As Orenstein and Haas point out, the CEE accession countries' 'better prospects of EU membership were determined not only by external, but also by internal factors, particularly their greater similarity and proximity to core EU member states in politics, economics, and culture' (2002: 33).

SEVEN THESES ON GLOBALISATION

No consensus has emerged as to the impact of globalisation on the welfare state from the studies which have been carried out to date. Rather, a number of different theses have emerged from this first wave of globalisation research. These are:

1   Globalisation leads to a 'race to the bottom'
2   Globalisation leads to compensatory social spending
3   Globalisation has no significant impact on the welfare state
4   Globalisation imposes a constraint on government action
5   The impact of globalisation is outweighed by other factors
6   The impact of globalisation varies across nations and is shaped by national institutions
7   Globalisation leads to convergence of policies.

The first three theses follow a straightforward continuum. Perhaps the most common thesis about globalisation is that it will lead to a serious reduction in welfare state expenditure. However, a contrary theory is that globalisation will, in fact, lead to an increase in social spending to compensate for the impact of globalisation. Finally, some studies have found no impact for globalisation.

GLOBALISATION LEADS TO A 'RACE TO THE BOTTOM'

Perhaps the most common thesis on globalisation and the welfare state, albeit one that is advanced in a strong sense by relatively few social policy academics, is that increased global competition (in particular capital mobility) will necessitate a 'race to the bottom', with both taxation and welfare measures being cut to attract highly mobile capital (or what is in effect the same thing, to avoid the flight of capital). In a European (and indeed OECD) context, it is difficult to find clear data to support this thesis. Macro-level data on welfare state spending do not show any overall reduction in effort in recent decades (Castles, 2004) and studies have found it difficult to find a causal link between increased globalisation and any significant reduction in welfare state effort (Garrett and Mitchell, 1999).

On the other hand, there has arguably been welfare state retrenchment in a number of European countries, for example, Central and Eastern Europe, and this can perhaps be attributed to aspects of globalisation (Ferge, 2001). One possible explanation for this is that globalisation creates conditions to which policy makers can react in different ways. As Hay et al. point out, 'governments acting in accordance with restrictive views of the constraints imposed by globalisation are likely to contribute further, by the consequence of their actions, to the evidence enlisted in support of such a view' (1999: 2). In other words, governments 'acting in a manner consistent with ... the globalisation thesis may well serve to summon the consequences the thesis would predict, irrespective of the accuracy of the thesis itself' (1999: 2).

GLOBALISATION LEADS TO COMPENSATORY SOCIAL SPENDING

An alternative thesis is that trade openness (and possibly capital mobility) leads to compensatory social spending. The argument is that globalisation increases economic insecurity for workers in the exposed sectors of the economy and that greater welfare state spending is required to compensate for this increased insecurity (Cameron, 1978). Several econometric studies have found evidence in support of some variant of this thesis. Rodrik (1997) finds that trade openness is positively associated with high levels of welfare spending in both developed and developing countries. He highlights the important distinction between trade openness per se and exposure to external risk, which is a function of both the level of trade and volatility in the terms of trade. Rodrik argues that increased spending arises from the risk factor associated with trade rather than from trade itself. His study found that exposure to external risk is positively associated with higher spending, both for OECD countries and for a wider sample of countries, including those with lower incomes. Looking at trends over time, he found that countries with high terms of trade volatility combined with high levels of trade were likely to have increased social spending, while in countries with low terms of trade volatility, such as many OECD countries, increased trade was likely to be related to lower levels of social spending. Garrett (1998) also found that open capital markets leads to higher spending in situations where the political left is strong and unions are encompassing.

GLOBALISATION HAS NO SIGNIFICANT IMPACT ON THE WELFARE STATE

Studies such as those by Rodrik and Garrett have, however, been questioned by an alternative thesis which suggests that recent changes in the welfare state are due to domestic rather than international factors (Iversen and Cusack, 2000). Iversen and Cusack have argued that the relationship between trade openness and welfare state expansion is spurious and that such expansion has in fact been driven by deindustrialisation. They argued that it is necessary to find a causative link between indices of globalisation and welfare state pressures. However, using data from 16 countries, they found no evidence of greater volatility in output, employment and wages in more open economies (in terms either of trade or capital market openness) than was to be found in more closed economies. Re-analysing Garrett's (1998) findings of a positive relationship between capital openness and welfare spending (given left labour power), they found them to be highly sensitive to the precise specification of control variables and that the relationship disappeared using alternative measures (see Chapter 2). This is, however, one of the few studies to find *no* impact for globalisation.

More recent studies have generally returned more nuanced findings, accepting that globalisation can have an impact on welfare states but arguing that its impact varies depending on the political and economic context, or that it is out-weighed by other factors.

GLOBALISATION IMPOSES A CONSTRAINT ON GOVERNMENT ACTION

While the 'race to the bottom' thesis (in a strong sense) has garnered relatively little social policy support, there is considerable support for a weaker thesis that globalisation imposes significant constraints on the autonomy of national governments (Scharpf, 2000). Scharpf argues that international competition is driving up productivity and skills requirements and limiting or reducing employment opportunities in the exposed sectors of the economy. He points out that employment in the exposed sectors of the economy (internationally traded manufacturing and services) is generally shrinking, while employment gains have been made in sheltered sectors of the economy. On the one hand this puts greater pressure on the welfare state to achieve egalitarian welfare goals but, on the other, he argues that globalisation severely constrains opportunities for increasing welfare state revenue.

Garrett and Mitchell (1999), in a study of welfare state spending in 18 OECD countries over the period 1961 to 1994, found some empirical support for the thesis that globalisation does impose constraints on the welfare state. In particular, they found that 'total trade had a negative and significant effect' on welfare state expenditures. On the other hand, they found that imports from low-wage economies had scant impact on welfare effort, that foreign direct investment was not associated with less welfare effort, and that international financial openness did not have an effect on welfare state spending (although it was weakly associated with lower total government spending). However, Garrett and Mitchell suggested that there might be a benign reason for the seeming constraint imposed on spending by increased trade in that trade may, in fact, lead to macro-economic benefits and that the political dislocations associated with trade are relatively small.

Genschel (2002), who examines the funding side of the equation, argues that while aggregate data on OECD countries do not show a drop in tax levels, it would be a mistake to conclude from that that tax competition is not a serious challenge to the welfare state. He argues that spending would have been higher had it not been for tax competition and that globalisation constrains national tax autonomy in a serious way in that it both prevents governments from raising taxes in response to growing demands for greater welfare state spending and from reducing taxes on labour in response to rising unemployment. However, rather than supporting the argument that globalisation involves a 'race to the bottom', Genschel argues that it 'traps the (welfare state) between external pressures to reduce the tax burden on capital and internal pressures to maintain revenue levels and relieve the tax burden on labor' (2002: 246). This leads to 'more austerity, more deficit finance, and a less employment friendly tax mix' than would otherwise have been the case (2002: 246).

THE IMPACT OF GLOBALISATION IS OUTWEIGHED BY OTHER FACTORS

In contrast to the approach outlined above, which sees globalisation as a key constraint on the welfare state, this approach, while accepting that globalisation does constrain national autonomy, sees it as being outweighed by other pressures on the welfare state. Pierson (2001) has pointed to a range of factors which constitute potential sources of the strains generally attributed to globalisation (see Chapter 2). These include slower productivity growth, particularly in the services sector, the maturation of welfare states, demographic changes (in particular ageing of the population) and the transformation of household structures (such as an increase in divorce and one-parent families). Globalisation, he argues, is essentially unrelated to the final three of these factors and only modestly linked to the first. His argument is that while globalisation 'accompanied these transitions' and 'undoubtedly accentuated and modified the pressures on welfare states in important respects', it was these four factors which imposed real constraints on welfare state growth (2001: 83).

THE IMPACT OF GLOBALISATION VARIES ACROSS NATIONS AND IS SHAPED BY NATIONAL INSTITUTIONS

Developing Garrett's (1998) argument that globalisation is consistent with higher welfare state spending when the political left is strong, a number of studies have suggested that the impact of globalisation varies depending on national political and production regimes. Swank, in a study of the impact of global capital in 15 countries, argues that 'the actual domestic policy impacts of international capital mobility are complex and variable, and are fundamentally and systematically shaped by national political institutions' (2002a: 5). Swank carried out a detailed quantitative analysis of the impact of global capital flows on welfare state developments in those 15 countries. His principal conclusion was that 'international capital mobility is not systematically and directly linked to social welfare policy change' (2002a: 275). If anything, he found some support for the compensation thesis, that is that globalisation may lead to some increase in welfare spending. Only in cases of 'high fiscal stress' (that is, high budget deficit) did he find a relationship between capital flows and reductions in welfare spending. However, Swank did find that liberal welfare states showed links with retrenchment which, he argued, arose from the different political structures inherent to such states compared to corporatist or social democratic regimes.

Swank (2002b) also examined the direct effects of capital mobility, global and European trade, and European monetary integration on welfare expenditures in 16 West European welfare states in the period from 1979 to 1995. He found that trade integration may have contributed to modest retrenchment in European welfare states. In contrast, however, he found no relationship between capital mobility and welfare state effort but that, consistent with the compensation thesis, financial liberalisation was positively associated with welfare spending. His analysis indicated that neither membership of the Exchange Rate Mechanism (ERM) nor the advent of the European Monetary Union (EMU) convergence criteria were significantly associated with welfare state effort (having regard to other key factors). Taking account of the interaction between financial liberalisation, European trade and monetary integration, Swank found that:

> ... in European nations that had achieved high international liberalisation and experienced high levels of trade with other European nations, social welfare expenditure generally, and the social wage specifically, were reduced. Similarly, nations with high levels of liberalisation and full membership in the narrow bands of the ERM were also likely to experience reductions in aggregate welfare effort and the social wage. (2000b: 177)

In contrast in countries with low to medium levels of trade integration and which did not participate in the ERM narrow bands, he found no reduction in the social wage.

In related work looking at the impact of production regimes, Swank (2003) found that globalisation had not led to welfare state retrenchment in co-ordinated market institutions which tended to shape the interests, choices and capacities of labour, capital and the state in ways favourable to welfare state maintenance or expansion (generally corporatist and social democratic countries). However, it had contributed to retrenchment in unco-ordinated market economies. It is worth recalling Hay et al.'s (1999) point here as to whether it is globalisation in itself which leads to retrenchment or policy makers' chosen response to the issues raised by globalisation.

GLOBALISATION LEADS TO CONVERGENCE OF POLICIES

A final thesis is that while policies may not necessarily be retrenched or expanded due to globalisation, there will be a trend towards policy convergence in view of the increased openness of the global economy and greater competition between countries. In an EU context,

Table 3.2   Variation in social protection expenditure in 16 European countries, 1960–2001 (co-efficient of variation of spending amongst countries as percentage of GDP)

	1960	1980	2001
All	0.37	0.27	0.14
EU 5	0.12	0.14	0.11
EU 8	0.21	0.18	0.18
'Northern'	0.25	0.21	0.14

Source: Calculations based on data in Castles [1998] for 1960; OECD [2004] for 1980 and 2001. The 'Northern' group includes all countries except Greece, Portugal and Spain.

in particular, it can be argued that the removal of trade barriers between countries, the move to economic and monetary union and limited harmonisation and convergence of social policy measures should all lead to greater policy convergence.

It is possible to examine trends in relation to welfare state expenditure over a reasonably long period in 16 European welfare states for which comparable OECD data is available. An analysis of the coefficient of variation (that is, an indicator of the degree of variation) of social spending in European countries over the period from 1960 to 2001 shows a significant fall in the variation amongst spending levels for the full group. However, this is strongly influenced by the inclusion of the three Southern countries (Greece, Portugal and Spain) which initially had low levels of spending. The original members of the EU (which had quite similar spending levels in 1960) and those which joined in the first expansion in 1972 show much more limited convergence. However, the group of richer countries which joined in 1995 (Austria, Finland and Sweden) and the two rich non-EU countries (Norway and Switzerland) also show significant convergence – albeit that the reasons behind national trends are often quite different. Overall spending increased significantly from an average of 10.3 per cent of GDP in 1960 to 24.5 per cent in 2001. This evidence unambiguously rejects a simple race to the bottom thesis and does provide limited support for a more general convergence trend towards a common level of social expenditure.

Castles (2004) found a relationship between the degree of trade openness in 1981 and subsequent changes in social expenditure in OECD countries. However, this relationship disappeared when controlled for domestic factors such as deindustrialisation and initial levels of expenditure. Castles suggests that what we are seeing is 'a process of programme maturation and convergence'(2004: 113). His view is that '[t]rade openness leads not so much to permanently higher levels of public and social expenditure as to the early adoption of public sector programmes designed to minimise the impact of exposure to the world market' (2004: 113). Thus, early studies which appear to link trade openness and higher levels of social expenditure were simply picking up early examples of countries with high levels of trade expanding their programmes. But as programmes in these countries mature, rates of expenditure increase decline while rates in late adopters start to catch up.

GENDER AND GLOBALISATION

Most of the studies already discussed have paid little attention to the relationship between globalisation and gender. Indeed, there have been relatively few studies looking specifically at this issue in the area of the welfare state. Nonetheless it is clear that (at least) some aspects of globalisation may have gendered impacts (both positive and negative). For example, a relationship has, in general, been established between policies of export-led industrialisation and increasing female participation in the paid labour force.

A number of recent studies have looked at the gender aspects of changes in the labour market arising from a range of factors, including globalisation. Standing (1999) has argued that the changing character of labour markets has led to a rise in female labour force participation and a relative fall in male participation, as well as to a 'feminization' of jobs traditionally held by men (in the dual sense of increased female participation in such jobs and in that 'male' jobs had become more insecure).[3]

Beneria (2001) argues that increasing flexibilisation of work processes and trade liberalisation have resulted in profound changes in employment structures and conditions which have had different impacts on men and women. These changes include a shift of employment to smaller firms and individual contractors, a reduction in hierarchal levels within firms, a tendency towards unstable employment and a rise in labour market insecurity (for example, unemployment), polarisation in job opportunities (which are better for skilled labour and worse for the low skilled), and a reduction in workers' commitment to firms. In terms of the specific gender impact of these developments, Beneria argues that, first, the feminisation of the labour force has 'intensified the reliance of many women on informal employment' (2001: 9). Second, women's employment has been affected by economic restructuring, for example, through increased subcontracting and homeworking. Third, women's

---

3 Whether it is advisable to use the term 'feminisation' as a synonym for a reduction in job security may be debateable.

continued primary involvement in unpaid domestic and childcare responsibilities 'diminishes women's mobility and autonomy to design their labour market strategies' (2001: 11). Beneria recognises that there have also been positive aspects in recent labour market developments including the rise in women's education levels (though this has contributed to an increase in income inequality *amongst* women) and the rise in women's wages relative to men in most countries (albeit that no country has achieved equality of wage levels).

Unfortunately, there has, to date, been much less research on the specific impact of globalisation on welfare state policies from a gendered perspective. Developments related to globalisation such as trade liberalisation and the transfer of manufacturing industry to less developed countries have had gendered labour market impacts. These, in turn, are likely to give rise to specific issues for the welfare state. However, the overall changes in labour market structures are related to factors broader than globalisation and these impacts are mediated in different ways by different national regimes (and by the EU as a whole). Globalisation can be a different experience for women and men depending on a range of factors including their labour market and family circumstances. However, as in the case of globalisation and welfare spending overall, it is difficult to identify general policy trends in the area of gender and welfare policies which are *caused* by globalisation.

CONCLUSION

We will return to the issue of the impact of globalisation on welfare states in future chapters in looking at the ways in which particular welfare states have developed and at the future challenges to welfare state development. While, as we have seen, quantitative studies have attempted to identify causal links between various aspects of globalisation and welfare state change, from a qualitative perspective, as Daly has argued, globalisation is 'above all, a process that is difficult to pin down in a concrete relationship to welfare states' (2001: 100). As she argues, it is 'difficult if not impossible' to separate 'the changes which it invokes as against those from other sources' (2001: 100). Nonetheless, a number of general points can be made:

1   There is little support for the thesis that globalisation will lead to significant reductions in welfare state expenditures across nations (the 'race to the bottom' thesis).

2   While there is limited support for the thesis that globalisation will lead to compensatory social spending in particular countries at particular times, there is again an absence of evidence that

globalisation would have any general tendency to increase social spending.

3   There is significant support for the thesis that globalisation is a factor in welfare state policy – indeed, it is important to emphasise that it may be a positive factor leading to a reduction in welfare state spending – not simply because of the negative pressures arising from capital flight but also for the more benign reasons that globalisation can lead to additional economic growth and a fall in unemployment.

4   The impact of globalisation is mediated in different ways by different national policy regimes and by the EU.

5   While globalisation does give rise to labour market pressures which can impact on men and women in different ways, it is difficult to identify general policy trends in the area of gender and welfare policies which are *caused* by globalization.

In so far as conclusions can be drawn from the findings of studies reported above, it is that the research to date does not show that globalisation has anything other than a relatively moderate direct impact on welfare state efforts in developed countries, and one which varies depending on the extent to which a country is integrated into the world economic system and depending on the national political and production structures and policy responses to that integration (for the CEE countries see Box 3.2). Swank has carried out some of the most nuanced studies on the impact of globalisation and of the EU on European welfare effort. His conclusions are that the direct effect of increases in global and European trade and capital mobility on welfare states appear to be limited. On the other hand, European monetary integration, particularly for countries with high debt, has created moderate pressures for welfare retrenchment. One of his most important arguments is that 'the relationship between the international economy and welfare state is cross-nationally varied' and that 'policy reform is fundamentally shaped by the institutions in which the system of social protection is embedded' (Swank, 2002b). Sykes et al. come to a broadly similar conclusion, arguing that globalisation should not be treated as 'a homogenous exogenous force impacting on nation-states and causing them to adapt their welfare states, but as a differentiated phenomenon, the character of which is constructed and interpreted differently in different types of welfare system' (2001: 198).

Authors such as Pierson and Iverson and Cusack have highlighted the importance of factors other than globalisation in the development of welfare states, and it is arguably the case that there has been insufficient study of the interrelationship between these factors to date.

Indeed, one might suggest that globalisation principally influences welfare systems through its overall effect on the economy, rather than directly. In this way, it is a little different to similar macro-economic trends such as industrialisation, deindustrialisation or the development of a knowledge-based economy. It arguably would be better for the development of welfare state theory if the 'logic of globalisation' was integrated into broader welfare state theory.

Summary

This chapter has:

- discussed the meaning of globalisation and how it might be measured in terms of trade, foreign investment, capital market flows and deregulation, and the influence of international organisations;
- provided data on indicators of globalisation in Europe;
- outlined different theses about the impact of globalisation on the welfare state, ranging from globalisation leading to a reduction in welfare effort through to the opposite thesis that the pressures of globalisation give rise to increased welfare spending;
- examined the relationship between globalisation and gender; and
- summarised the current state of knowledge.

Discussion points

1 '[T]he truth effects of discourses of economic globalisation are somewhat independent of the veracity of the analysis' (Rose, 1996). Read a recent speech by a senior political figure on the effects of globalisation. Is Rose correct?
2 The world was just as integrated in terms of capital and labour flows in the late nineteenth century as it is today. Discuss.
3 Chose one particular area of recent national welfare policy reform in Europe and discuss the impact which globalisation has had (or has not had).
4 Which definition of globalisation (of those listed in this chapter or elsewhere) do you find most useful. Why?

Supplementary reading

Rodrik (1997, in particular Ch. 4), provides a useful and clear introduction to the issue of globalisation and the welfare state. Swank (2002a) provides one of the most detailed studies of the impact of globalisation on welfare states, drawing on both qualitative and quantitative evidence. Iverson and Cusack (2000) provide an interesting challenge to the received wisdom and argue for domestic factors rather than international factors as the key issue in recent developments in the welfare state. Mittelman (2000) provides a useful broader account of globalisation, while So (1990) outlines a clear introduction to world-systems theory.

FOUR GENDER AND THE WELFARE STATE

This chapter looks at theories concerning the relationship between gender and the welfare state. It outlines the criticisms that have been made of existing theories and draws on more recent work which has attempted to develop gendered criteria for analysing the impact of welfare states. Issues specifically related to gender and typologies of welfare states will be addressed in Chapter 6.

In the first part of this chapter we look at some of the main theses advanced in the literature on the role of gender in the development of welfare states. In the second part we look at a number of key current debates. As in Chapter 2, we draw on a number of important key texts which illustrate the main lines of argument. Obviously, within each approach there is a wide range of variation. This is particularly the case in relation to the literature on gender and the welfare state. Literature in this area is much less extensive than that on the welfare state in general and, almost by definition, much less comprehensive. It is also the case that the literature does not fit as readily into clear schools of thought, as does much general welfare state literature.[1]

Box 4.1: What is gender?

Originally a grammatical term only (Scott, 1986), gender has now become an important concept in the analysis of power relations between the sexes. The meaning, in this context, of the term gender has usefully been summarised by the Council of Europe:

> Gender is a socially constructed definition of women and men. It is the social design of a biological sex, determined by a conception of tasks, functions and roles attributed to women and men in society and in public and in private life. It is a cultural-specific definition of femininity and masculinity and therefore varies in time and space. (1998: 10)

---

1 Much of the work on gender and welfare states draws on broader debates about gender issues more generally. Unfortunately space does not allow reference to this broader context.

Box 4.1: (Continued)

As the Council of Europe points out:

> The construction and reproduction of gender takes place at the individual level as well as at the societal level. Both are equally important. Individual human beings shape gender roles and norms through their activities and reproduce them by conforming to expectations. There is a growing awareness that gender has to be considered also at a political and institutional level. (1998: 10)

But, for these purposes, gender is often not only taken to refer to a socially constructed definition of women and men, but it is also:

> ... a socially constructed definition of the relationship between the sexes. This construction contains an unequal power relationship with male domination and female subordination in most spheres of life. Men and the tasks, roles, functions and values attributed to them are valued – in many aspects – higher than women and what is associated with them. It is increasingly recognised that society is characterised by this male bias: the male norm is taken as the norm for society as a whole, which is reflected in policies and structures. (1998: 10)

WHY IS GENDER RELEVANT TO THE WELFARE STATE?

Much of the welfare state studies, discussed in previous chapters, made no particular reference to gender and appeared to assume that gender issues were not relevant to the way in which the welfare state developed. It is probably more likely that the gendered division of welfare was simply taken for granted by these authors. Many of the key schemes covered by these studies, such as sickness or unemployment insurance, were applicable mainly to male workers. But, in practice, women have made up a significant proportion of those in receipt of welfare benefits, particularly means-tested benefits, over the centuries (see Table 4.1).

Thus it is clear that over a very long period women have made up a majority of those in receipt of certain welfare benefits. Not only that, but women's recipience of welfare benefits varied significantly depending on the type of scheme. For example, women were more likely to receive means-tested benefits than social insurance benefits because of their generally lower participation in the insured labour force. Thus schemes like sickness and unemployment insurance tended to be of major relevance to men. On the other hand, schemes such as maternity benefits were only relevant to women. On this ground alone, there is a need to take into account issues of gender in the development of welfare states.

Table 4.1   Women on welfare, 1500–2000

In Strasbourg in 1523, 69% of adults in receipt of poor relief were women
In Toledo in 1573, 63% of those in receipt of poor relief were women
In 1760 women made up about 70% of all welfare recipients in England
At about the same time 60% of the adult inmates of the Hôpital General of Grenoble were female
In Ireland in 1960, 72% of adults on the means-tested home assistance scheme were women
At the start of the twentieth century in the United Kingdom, 61% of adults on all forms of poor relief
    were women and in the 1980s 60% of adults for whom supplementary benefit was paid were women

As we discuss in more detail below, agency is a further reason to have regard to gender issues. A number of authors have argued that women's agency has played an important role in the development of aspects of the welfare state through the input of women's organisations or women administrators and policy makers.

Finally, it is important to take into account the role of gender because of the influence it has had on the structure of welfare systems. To take just one important example, many welfare systems, reflecting the assumed structure of families, were built around a model of the male breadwinner (See Box 4.2 for a discussion of this type of assumption in the Beveridge Report). In designing welfare systems, it was assumed that the main breadwinner in the family was male and that the wife did not work outside the home or only worked to a limited extent. Benefit systems were, therefore, designed to reinforce this structure with payments being made to the male breadwinner with 'dependency' additions for his wife and children. It is only quite recently that discrimination against one gender in terms of access to welfare benefits has been made unlawful and this still does not apply to all areas of welfare policy (see Box 4.3).

Box 4.2: Gender and the Beveridge Report

One interesting example of an engagement between a more structural and more historical account has been in relation to gendered criticisms of the Beveridge Report. Given the importance of the Beveridge Report in UK policy making, many sociologists or social policy writers, primarily from a socialist/feminist background, developed a number of criticisms of the report's assumptions. These criticisms were, in turn, critiqued in Blackburn (1999).

The feminist authors, according to Blackburn, argued that Beveridge reduced married women to second-class citizens when it came to social security. This was done in three ways. First, Beveridge proposed that married women in insured employment would pay reduced national insurance contributions and qualify for lower benefits. Beveridge argued for this approach on the basis that a man, unlike a married woman, was making contributions on behalf of himself and his wife.

Box 4.2: (Continued)

This, it was argued, obviously perpetuated gender inequality. Second, Beveridge proposed that married women should be entitled to opt-out from paying national insurance contributions if they so chose. This resulted in only a minority of married women becoming fully insured and, it was argued, helped to reinforce their financial dependence within marriage. Third, feminist authors criticised Beveridge for his assumption that the majority of married women would leave paid work to be supported by a male breadwinner. Beveridge proposed that on leaving insurable employment, such women were to be entitled to a marriage grant in return for which they would lose their rights to benefits based on their previous insurance record. Beveridge had assumed, relying on pre-War data, that 88 per cent of married women would be economically dependent on their husband and that the wartime increase in female employment would not continue after the War.

Blackburn points out that this line of critique has been undoubtedly of great value but argues that it is itself open to some criticism. First, she points out that the criticism fails to take seriously the 'real gains that the welfare state bestowed on women' (1999: 374) citing, for example, improved healthcare, milk and food supplements, family allowances paid to the mother and a guaranteed minimum of subsistence. The expanded social services also provided for increased work opportunities for women.

Second, Blackburn points out that the Beveridge Report was widely accepted because it was popular with both men and women. She points out that the report was broadly acceptable to the Trade Unions and was strongly endorsed by leading left-wing intellectuals and the Liberal and Labour party constituency groups. Support for the male breadwinner family was not particular to Britain at the time but was also the predominant ideology in a number of other countries including Norway, Germany and the Netherlands. Indeed, as Harris argues, 'Beveridge's views were largely in accord with those of the majority of the organised women's movement in Britain in the 1930s and 40s' (1977). In fact, the majority of women voters in 1945 voted for Labour. Harris argues that it is futile and somewhat patronising to berate Beveridge for failing to adopt the views of half a century later.

Third, Blackburn argues that some of the criticisms of Beveridge should be more justly ascribed to the Treasury whose opposition meant, for example, that the proposed level of family allowances was significantly reduced. Blackburn argues that Beveridge's insurance principle was 'replete with problems' for *both* men and women and that therefore a gender sensitive analysis cannot focus exclusively on women. She points out that not only dependent women but a wide range of other groups, including the long-term unemployed, the chronically sick and the young, were forced to rely on means-tested benefits.

Fourth, Blackburn argues that socialist/feminist criticisms fail to appreciate the complexities of the social policy process. She points out that the development of welfare policy is frequently the outcome of competing interest groups, leading inevitably to uneasy compromises. Thus she argues that 'it is not possible to interpret the welfare state as simply a product of Beveridge's desire to control women' (1999: 379).

In conclusion, Blackburn argues that the socialist/feminists are correct to argue that women were unjustly treated by the welfare state. However, she argues that it is also essential to take account of the fact that there were some real gains for women and that 'women were also active in moulding the welfare state, and they supported governments pledged to implement the Beveridge Report' (1999: 382).

> ### Box 4.3: EU law and equality in social security
>
> EU law has played an important role in ensuring greater equality in social security for women. The EU Treaty requires equal pay for men and women. However, this does not extend to public pension schemes (although it does apply to occupational pensions, which are considered to be deferred pay). The EU agreed a directive in 1979 which required equal treatment for men and women in relation to most areas of social security (for example, unemployment, old age, sickness and disability). At that time, many EU member states still discriminated against women by, for example, paying lower levels of benefits or paying benefits for shorter periods of time. The EU directive came into force in 1986 but a number of EU countries (in particular Ireland, the Netherlands and the United Kingdom) had not fully implemented the directive in their national legislation. This led to a number of court cases both before the national courts and, ultimately, the European Court of Justice. The ECJ held that the directive was directly effective in national law and could be relied on by women to claim equal benefits to men.
>
> The EU directive, combined with broader trends towards equality and the rising number of women in European labour forces, all led to important changes in the gender structure of welfare schemes and the introduction of (at least) formal gender equality in most areas of welfare. A number of areas, however, including family and survivors' benefits, fall outside the scope of the directive and the personal scope of the directive is confined to workers or persons seeking work. Thus women who give up work to care for children fall outside the scope of the directive and cannot claim equality of treatment. In 1985 the EU commission proposed a directive to 'complete' the implementation of the principle of equal treatment, but this was never agreed by member states. Detailed directives have, however, been agreed in relation to equal treatment in occupational pensions.

THESES ON GENDER AND THE WELFARE STATE

THE WELFARE STATE MAINTAINS THE SOCIAL CONDITIONS OF REPRODUCTION

This approach adopts a structuralist or functionalist perspective similar to some of those which we have seen in Chapter 2. However, coming generally from a socialist, feminist background, authors adopting this perspective see the welfare state as being shaped by both capitalism and patriarchy. McIntosh, for example, argues that 'the state plays a part in the oppression of women ... through its support for a specific form of household: the family household dependent largely upon a male wage and upon female domestic servicing' (1978: 255). McIntosh sees this household system as being related to capitalist production in that it, albeit inadequately, serves for the reproduction of the working class and for the maintenance of women as a reserve army of labour. McIntosh makes the important point that in evaluating the link between the welfare state and gender issues 'we must look at the whole structure of benefits, the part they play in the economy as a whole and the patterns of social relations that they establish and sustain' (1978: 257).

McIntosh seeks to analyse the role which the state plays in establishing and sustaining systems in which women are suppressed and subordinated to men. She identifies the two key systems as being the family household and wage labour. Drawing in particular on the British experience, McIntosh outlines a number of ways in which the state played an important role in sustaining the family. These include the manner in which the income maintenance system assumed that married women would be financially dependent on their husbands and the (then) ineligibility of wives for many social security benefits. Conversely, the provision of support such as the widow's pension made it less necessary for wives to engage in the paid labour force. Thus McIntosh argues that the family household is not 'merely the social expression of an instinct' but is structured and constrained by welfare state policies.

In a more nuanced form of this thesis, Siim argues that there have been two contradictory aspects of welfare state development, the oppressive and the supportive:

> On the one hand the welfare state is being supportive towards women and has helped to decrease women's personal dependence on individual men as mothers and workers. On the other hand the welfare state has also been oppressive towards women, has subsumed women under a new kind of centralized power hierarchy and has disregarded the collective interests of women or subsumed women's interests and values under the dominant state rationality. (1987: 265)

There is much of value in this type of analysis. In particular, it emphasises the extent to which welfare systems are structured differently based on gender divisions. It should be remembered that until the 1970s and 1980s many European welfare systems contained provisions which were directly discriminatory against women (in particular married women) and that in some cases these were only removed due to EU legislation and as a result of a number of legal challenges (see Box 4.3). However, as in the case of the structural approaches in Chapter 2, this type of analysis operates at a high level of generality and does not attempt to account for differences between countries. It also abstracts from the question of whether it is possible for women's organisations or trade unions significantly to improve provisions in favour of women.

WOMEN'S AGENCY HAS PLAYED AN IMPORTANT ROLE IN SHAPING WELFARE STATES

The second major type of analysis of the development of welfare states has emphasised the historical role of women's agency in shaping aspects of European welfare states. Bock and Thane (1991) have analysed the influence of women's movements on the emergence of Europe's welfare states from the 1880s to the 1950s. They looked in particular at three major groups of women 'whose history was shaped by the emergence of state welfare actions' (1991: 1): women, and in particular mothers, living in poverty; women's movements; and women who administered welfare provisions and policies. They criticise mainstream approaches for having underestimated or obscured the degree to which welfare schemes were related, directly or indirectly, to women. They argue that the indirect impact was 'to reinforce women's dependency on husbands who benefited from the welfare measures, and hence also to reinforce the gender gap in terms of income and (relative) poverty' (1991: 4). However, Bock and Thane point out that some welfare provisions, which are rarely addressed in mainstream work, were 'aimed directly at women and contributed to relieving some aspects of female misery and poverty, particularly those related to maternity' (1991: 4). They emphasise the fact that women's movements, which were active throughout Europe from the early or mid nineteenth century, 'helped to bring about or influence the introduction of maternity benefits, family allowances and other maternity and family-centred policies' (1991: 6).

Similarly, Koven and Michel (1990, 1993) highlight the fact that 'the emergence of large-scale state welfare programs and policies coincided with the rise of women's social action movements in France, Germany, Great Britain, and the United States in the late nineteenth and early twentieth centuries' (1990: 1076). In their study of maternalist policies and the origins of welfare states in France, Germany, Great Britain and the United States in the period 1880 to 1920, Koven and Michel argue that 'women's reform efforts and welfare states not only coincided in time, place and sometimes personnel but also reinforced and transformed one another in significant and enduring ways' (1990: 1076). They argue that women in each of the four countries succeeded, in varying degrees, in shaping at least one area of state policy, that is, that concerning maternal and child welfare. They emphasise three important factors that helped to shape policy in these areas: first, the growth of welfare bureaucracies with the consequent expansion of women's employment in areas such as social work, health visiting and district nursing; second, maternalist discourses which, they argue, 'extolled the private virtues of domesticity while simultaneously legitimating women's public relationship to politics and the state, to community, workplace and marketplace'; and third, the development of policies to meet the needs of mothers and children through a wide range of charitable organisations (1990: 1078-9). Ironically, however, they argue that 'the power of women's social action movements was inversely related to the range and generosity of social welfare benefits for women and children' (1990: 1079). They attribute this fact to the argument that strong states, that is, those with a well-developed bureaucracy and a long tradition of government intervention 'allowed women less political space in which to develop social welfare programmes than did "weak states" where women's voluntary associations flourished' (1990: 1079-80). They argue that Germany, which had the strongest state, had politically ineffective women's movements but developed the most comprehensive programmes for women and children. In contrast, the United States, with the strongest female reform movement and the weakest state, yielded the least extensive and least generous benefits for women.

While both these studies provide a valuable corrective to the absence in mainstream theories of an analysis of the role of women, it is important, as each study points out, to emphasise the limited achievements of women's organisations. Bock and Thane highlight the fact that the maternity and gender policies which they study emerged in all the countries examined 'largely out of discourses in which concern about the quantity and quality of the population and the responsibilities of mothers in relation to this were prominent' (1991: 10). They point to the fact that the decline in the birth rate was a matter of great concern throughout Europe in this period and that this led to pro-natalist policies. In relation to the introduction of family allowances, they point out that 'women had played an important part in placing and keeping family allowances on the political agenda, but lacked the power to bring about their implementation' although, they argue that in liberal democracies women were able to wield some influence over the final shape of legislation on family allowances, in particular in ensuring that allowances were paid directly to women (1991: 13).

Koven and Michel similarly emphasise that women's organisations 'were more likely to be effective when their causes were taken up by male political actors pursuing other goals, such as pro-natalism or control of the labor force' (1990: 1080). They emphasise that issues concerning population and efficiency were highly important in the decades before the First World War and that these, and then the War itself, 'prompted legislators to establish many programmes that might not have received State support under other conditions' (1990: 1080). However, they find that the programmes owed their existence to the models, organisation and momentum created by female activists. On balance, Koven and Michel argue that 'women in all four countries contributed substantially to the development of private, voluntary, maternal and child welfare programmes, some of which served as models for State programmes and others of which were themselves taken over by the State'. However, they find that 'in all four countries, women often lost control over maternalist discourses when they were debated in male-dominated legislatures or became linked with other causes' (1990: 1106).

SOCIAL DEMOCRACY HAS DEVELOPED MORE GENDER-FRIENDLY WELFARE POLICIES

As part of the general application of the 'social democratic' argument on the development of the welfare state (discussed in Chapter 2), authors have argued that social democratic welfare states have tended to develop more gender-friendly policies. The commitment, in particular in the Nordic countries, to high levels of employment and of public services has tended to lead both to high levels of female employment (particularly in public social services) and to policies to support female employment such as childcare. Both factors – high public service employment and gender-friendly employment policies – have tended to reinforce each other (Huber and Stephens, 2001).

In contrast, Christian-democratic (or Christian-centrist) welfare states have tended to adopt labour and welfare policies that are focussed on a male-breadwinner model and which discourage (or at least do not encourage) female (or maternal) employment. Christian-centrist welfare states, such as Germany, tend to provide much lower levels of public support for policies such as childcare and eldercare. In general, the emphasis in such welfare states is much more on cash benefits, with expenditure on social services being much lower than in most Nordic countries (see Chapters 5 and 7). Most Christian-centrist states also have lower levels of female and maternal employment. Southern welfare states also tend to have low levels of service employment and low levels of public care services. In general, as we will see in Chapters 5 and 7, a detailed study of welfare states does support this thesis, although there are some anomalies such as France, which – while social democracy has historically played a very limited role in the development of the welfare state – has developed high levels of early education support and achieved relatively high levels of female employment.

THE SECULARISATION OF POLITICAL LIFE
LEADS TO GENDER FRIENDLY POLICIES

Focussing in particular on the case of France, Morgan (2003) has argued that it is the secularisation of political life in France, the weakness of Christian democracy as a political force and the subordination of the voluntary sector to the state which has led to a French policy trajectory markedly different to other centrist welfare states. However, rather than contributing directly to gender-friendly policies, Morgan argues that 'the creation of an early childhood care and education system that aids women's employment has been an indirect consequence of the achievement of other governmental objectives' (2003: 261). This has led to a situation where 'policies to support mothers' employment have been vulnerable to the shifting machinations of political elites who prioritise economic and fiscal outcomes over feminist policy goals' (2003: 289).

Morgan's argument is a convincing explanation for the apparent anomaly of French policy. The greater degree of secularisation and the long-term absence of any specific Christian democratic party in government can go far to explain the difference between the structure of the French system and that of, for example, Germany. However, Morgan suggests that the secularisation thesis has broader implications, with a weakness of Christian democracy and the relatively minor role of the voluntary sector linking the otherwise disparate Scandinavian and French cases. Thus she argues that secularisation has also been important in Scandinavia and that the development of gender-friendly policies cannot be attributed to social democracy alone. Here she points to the example of Norway, which is less secularised that its neighbours, having the largest and most successful Christian democratic party in the region. Norway has a more developed voluntary sector and is also seen as having somewhat less gender-friendly policies than, for example, the more secularized Sweden (Sörensen and Bergqvist, 2002).

DISCUSSION

The studies that emphasise the role which women's organisations had on the development of the welfare state are important and require to be integrated into theories of the overall development of the welfare state. However, while there have been a number of important studies of the development of the welfare state which have incorporated the role of women (see, for example, Skocpol and Ritter, 1991; Pedersen, 1993), there is still an absence of any comprehensive account of the role which gender played in the development of the welfare state. To take the theses we have outlined, there is no necessary contradiction between a structuralist account (in a weak sense) which emphasises the gendered division of welfare and its links to broader economic and gender inequalities, a more detailed account which emphasises the role that women's organisations *did* play in shaping the welfare state, and an approach which emphasises the importance of secularisation or social democracy. Yet such an account has yet to be written. And, despite the plethora of cross-national studies of factors influencing the development of welfare states, there remains an absence of such studies either from a gender perspective or properly incorporating gender issues into a more general analysis.

CURRENT THEMES IN RESEARCH ON GENDER AND THE WELFARE STATE

There are perhaps three main strands of current welfare state theorising in which the impact of gender is being considered. The first, and smallest, is that which seeks to incorporate gender issues into mainstream theorising. The second seeks to develop gendered typologies of welfare regimes. The third, and arguably the most important, seeks to develop criteria by which we can analyse welfare states from a gender perspective.

GENDER AND MAINSTREAM THEORIES

Despite the fact that mainstream welfare state theories have been heavily criticised for disregarding gender, and despite the fact that those criticisms are valid, there has been a very limited attempt to incorporate gender issues into mainstream theories. Walter Korpi (2000) provides an important exception to this and seeks to combine gender and class in an analysis of patterns of inequality in different types of welfare states in 18 countries. As his study concerns typologies of welfare, we will examine it further in Chapter 6. Huber and Stephens have also sought to integrate aspects of gender into their analysis of welfare states. They analyse the impact which women's employment has had, arguing that it has been 'an important determinant of the expansion of public, social welfare services net of other social, political and historical factors' (2000). They argue that rising women's labour force participation creates a dynamic in which it feeds demands for social services, which both enable women to enter the labour force and provide employment for them.

This can, in turn, lead to increased support amongst women for the maintenance and expansion of welfare state services. These examples are, unfortunately, the exception rather than the rule.

GENDER AND TYPOLOGIES OF WELFARE

A second important strand (in at least quantitative terms) in welfare state theorising is that which seeks to develop gendered typologies of welfare state regime. As outlined in Chapter 2 and discussed in more detail in Chapter 6, the area of welfare state typologies has been a growth industry. However, a very considerable proportion of the quite limited number of studies on gender and the welfare state have, for reasons which are somewhat unclear, focused on this area.

Much important work, which is discussed below, has emerged from these studies. However, it is not necessarily clear that, at this stage in the development of gendered welfare state theories, a focus on typologies is most productive. Many of these studies, which are discussed in more detail in Chapter 6, draw on or criticise Esping-Anderson's *The Three Worlds of Welfare Capitalism*. But it must be remembered that Esping-Anderson's study was not primarily about developing measures to analyse welfare state policies. Rather, Esping Anderson's account was based on a theoretically informed, politically driven understanding of the factors that had led to three quite different welfare regimes. Esping Anderson's development of instruments such as decommodification and stratification were intended to assist in empirically identifying the differences between different welfare state regimes. However, many of the studies from a gender perspective have focused on criticism of, for example, decommodification as being inappropriate from a gender perspective, ignoring the fact that there is no theoretically driven, politically based, gender account of why there are, might be or should be different welfare regimes in the first place. In addition, as Duncan has pointed out, 'gender remains essentially an optional add on' in these typologies (1995: 267). As Duncan argues, it is the pre-existing theoretical core of the welfare regime model, which is firmly rooted in capital–labour divisions in a capitalist society, which 'continues to provide the explanatory dynamic' to the existence of different welfare regimes. These issues are discussed further in Chapter 6.

ANALYSING WELFARE FROM A GENDER PERSPECTIVE

One of the positive aspects which has emerged from much of the work around welfare state regimes (and indeed from other work on gender and the welfare state) has been attempts to develop an understanding of how we might analyse welfare states from a gender perspective. As we have seen, the structuralist account simply assumed that the welfare state 'steps in to maintain the social conditions of reproduction' (McIntosh, 1978: 254). It assumed that the welfare state acted to the disadvantage of women and did not seek to analyse how a welfare state might be more gender friendly (although, in practice, many socialist feminists were involved in welfare campaigns). Much recent scholarship concerning gender and the welfare state has focused instead on issues as to how one might measure the gender impact of the welfare state, in particular the search for what might be described as a 'gender-friendly' model. It must be noted that there is an explicitly normative aspect to much of this research. The purpose is not simply to analyse the welfare state but rather to develop a type of analysis which will enable the development of a more gender-friendly welfare state. While such a normative approach is implicit in much mainstream theorising, it is considerably more to the forefront of much feminist accounts.

A number of key foci can be detected in recent work. First, there is an emphasis on the *central role which care plays in welfare states*. Second, and combined with this, is a focus on *access to paid work for women*. Third, there are those authors who emphasise *the importance of personal autonomy and 'defamilization'*. Finally, drawing on a number of these strands of thought, Daly (2000) has proposed a comprehensive framework for analysing *the gendered division of welfare*.

THE ROLE OF CARE WORK

A number of authors have focused on the importance of care work in the analysis of welfare states, both from the point of view that welfare states are, at least in part, structured around a particular understanding of who will carry out care work and also from the perspective that increased support for care work is vital to the development of a more gender-friendly welfare state. In early work, Lewis argued that one of the central issues in the structuring of welfare regimes was the valuing and sharing of the unpaid work that is done primarily by women in providing welfare, mainly within the family (1992: 160, 170). Lewis developed an analysis of welfare regimes (which we will discuss in more detail in Chapter 6) based around different 'breadwinner' models. She argued that countries such as the United Kingdom and Ireland adopted a *strong breadwinner* model where the assumption was that the man went out to work and the woman was primarily responsible for care work. In contrast, Sweden adopted a *dual earner* model where both spouses had access to the paid labour force (weak breadwinner model). Lewis noted that while in moving to a dual earner model Sweden may have gone a long way towards solving the issue of valuing unpaid work, it had not addressed the question of sharing unpaid work. Finally, she identified France as an example of a *modified breadwinner* model where women's labour market participation had been encouraged and where the French welfare system had recognised women's claims as wives, mothers and paid workers.

Jenson criticised Lewis's original focus on unpaid work on the basis that unpaid work cannot serve as a synonym for care and that it is care work that is a central issue in the structuring of welfare states (Jenson, 1997). Indeed, in subsequent work, Lewis has placed considerably more emphasis on care (1997). In recent work Lewis (2002) has argued that a gender-centred model of welfare state must emphasise the need to develop policies that value and redistribute care work.

Daly, however, while recognising the importance of care policies, argues that 'it may be misleading, especially in a comparative context, to ascribe comprehensive care policies to welfare states, for in many there is relatively little congruence between policies on caring for children and those of the elderly and other adults who may be in need of care' (2000: 58). She argues that while care is 'an essential component of any gender framework, it is on its own insufficient as an indicator of the gender dimension of the content of welfare states' (2000: 58).

ACCESS TO PAID WORK

A second line of argument, which also acknowledges the importance of care work, draws attention to the importance of welfare state measures to encourage equal access for both genders to the paid labour force. Sörensen and Bergqvist argue that 'gender-equality friendly policies *do not* support the traditional division of labour between women and men. On the contrary, they support women as well as men to abandon their traditional roles and identities by, for example, encouraging women's labour market participation and men's care work' (2002: 1). Orloff (1993a), in her analysis of gender and the social rights of citizenship, has argued for the inclusion of access to paid work as one of the dimensions to capture the effect of welfare states on gender relations (in addition to the treatment of paid and unpaid labour). Orloff (1993a: 318) argued that for many women access to the paid labour force is, in fact, potentially emancipatory. She refers to research which has found that many women want paid work because it provides independence within marriage and the patriarchal family.

PERSONAL AUTONOMY

A further strand of research has emphasised the importance of personal autonomy and defamilisation. Orloff (1993a), in addition to the criteria of access to paid work, has also proposed that the capacity to form and maintain an autonomous household should be one of the dimensions utilised to analyse the effect of the welfare state on gender relations. Drawing a parallel with the concept of de-commodification, that is, when a person can maintain a livelihood without reliance on the market (Esping-Anderson, 1990: 22), Orloff argues that a measure is needed of the extent to which persons who carry out domestic and caring work (almost all women) can form and maintain autonomous households without having to marry to gain access to a breadwinner's income. Orloff argues that 'the capacity to form and maintain an autonomous household relieves women of the compulsion to enter or stay in a marriage because of economic vulnerability' and thus that 'the state is woman-friendly to the extent that it enhances women's leverage within marriage ... or increases the absolute and relative standards of living of women-maintained families' (1993a: 321). Similarly, O'Connor argues that 'the concept of de-commodification must be supplemented by the concept of personal autonomy or insulation from dependence, both personal dependence on family members and/or public dependence on state agencies' (1993).

A related concept is that of defamilisation, which can be seen as relating to autonomy from family relationships. Here, however, there is considerable disagreement between feminist authors as to whether this is a positive measure or to whether a development towards individualism without adequate social supports may, in fact, be hazardous for women and children. Rather, it has been argued that 'the key issue is whether women are able to choose freely between marital and other relationships or whether they are coerced by financial need into dependence on private patriarchy' (Ginn et al., 2001: 7).

THE GENDER DIVISION OF WELFARE

Daly (2000) has developed a very useful conceptualisation of welfare states from a gender-sensitive perspective. She argues that at the micro level the ordering principles linking the welfare state, the economy and the family include 'the nature of the individual's ties to state, family and market, and in particular the terms and conditions under which claims can be made on public resources' (2000). She states that a gender-friendly analysis of the welfare state must 'capture the material resources provided by the state to women and men, as individuals and as members of families, the conditions under which re-distribution is effected between them, and the outcomes in terms of gender-based processes of stratification' (2000). She focuses, in particular, on the *structures* of welfare state provision, the *processes* of the welfare state and the *outcomes* that follow:

- In terms of *structures*, Daly examines the distributive principles, that is, the type of risks covered by the benefit system, the basis of entitlement to benefits, the treatment of different family types, and the nature and extent of social services.
- As regards welfare state *processes*, Daly focuses on defamilisation in relation to the manner in which the maintenance responsibilities of family members are constructed as public or private obligations and in which care work is constituted as paid or unpaid.
- In terms of *outcomes*, Daly looks at stratification flowing from welfare state measures including income inequality, poverty and the capacity to participate in the labour market and/or the family.

Drawing on this framework, Daly provides an analysis of the gender impact of the British and German welfare states. Her findings illustrate the difficulties involved in making such a gender based analysis. In terms of reducing income inequalities, her analysis indicates that the British model has the edge but that when it comes to households, the German welfare system leads not only to greater income redistribution overall but also brings the income of men and women's households closer together. In terms of income poverty, her analysis shows that the German is the better model, with poverty levels less than half those of Britain and with German women having a poverty rate less than half that of women in the United Kingdom. In terms of incentive structures, she focuses on the impact that marriage has on labour market participation. Here she finds that for women in Germany marriage does, in theory, offer a reasonable standard of living. However, this is subject to the caveat that German women must more or less give up their own earning opportunities to avail themselves of the 'security' of marriage and that they remain dependent on their husbands or partners passing on the income that the German welfare state provides to men on behalf of their families. In contrast, in the United Kingdom women are less dependent on family incomes and more likely to be in the labour market or in receipt of welfare benefits. However, Daly suggests that it is 'debateable whether working for relatively low incomes without the benefit of the enabling services that are so important to mothers can be represented as a broadened choice for women' (2000: 216). In conclusion, Daly states that 'judged in terms of overall poverty levels and the income standard attainable by lone mothers, Germany is the better place to live, for women as well as men' but, highlighting the dilemmas of a gender-friendly approach, this is subject to the fact that the vast majority of women do not provide for themselves but are supported by male incomes (2000: 217). Thus the British model, which performs better on gender grounds, performs less well overall than the German model for both men and women.

CONCLUSION

In conclusion, it is clear that while gender is a very important issue in relation to the development, current structure and future of welfare states, it remains somewhat peripheral to welfare state theorising. Indeed, as we will see in subsequent chapters, gender issues are rarely central to debates about ongoing welfare reforms, although many such reforms have important gender implications. There is a clear need both for a further development of gendered tools for analysis and for the use of such gendered measures in discussions of welfare state policies.

Summary

In this chapter we have:

- outlined the relevance of gender to welfare states;
- outlined a number of theses on the role of gender in the development of welfare states including the arguments: that the welfare state maintains the social conditions of reproduction; that women's agency has played a role in shaping welfare states; that social democracy has developed more gender-friendly welfare states; or that the secularisation of political life leads to gender-friendly policies; and
- discussed current theorising, in particular the development of criteria to analyse welfare states from a gender perspective.

Discussion points

1 Gender has been central to the development of the European welfare state. Why has there been so little focus on gender in mainstream welfare state theorising?
2 Choose one recent welfare reform in Europe. What criteria and information might one use in analysing this reform from a gender perspective?
3 The structure of the welfare state has been shaped at least as much by the social organisation of care as by employment-related risks. Do you agree?

Supplementary reading

Scott (1986) provides a useful background to the development of the use of 'gender' as a concept. Daly (2000) provides one of the best discussions of the literature and an application of gender-based analysis to the British and German welfare states. Bock and Thane (1991) and Koven and Michel (1993) are edited publications discussing the role of gender in the development of specific national welfare policies.

PART **TWO**
COMPARISON OF EUROPEAN WELFARE STATES

FIVE WELFARE STATES IN EUROPE

This chapter provides an outline of the development of welfare states in Europe and the reasons behind that development. It also provides key data on the variations in welfare states which exist in Europe.

We first outline the development of European welfare states and look at some of the factors which have been influential in that development. There have, particularly for the period after 1945, been numerous studies of the factors influencing the development of welfare states. However, rather than attempting to summarise their (often conflicting) findings, we will examine some of the factors suggested in previous chapters to have been relevant to such development.

In this chapter we will focus on all those European countries for which long-term, comparable data are available. It is sometimes the case that Southern European countries are excluded from historical analysis on the basis of their non-democratic form of government for part of the post-War period. Some authors (for example, Hicks, 1999) also exclude Austria, Germany and Italy during their periods of non-democratic rule. This is on the basis of Lijphart's 'comparable-cases' or 'most similar systems' strategy (Korpi, 1989: 301). However, in the case of welfare state studies this begs the question as to whether democracy makes a difference and, indeed, some studies have found little relationship between democracy and welfare state development (Mulligan et al., 2002). As Dion has argued, '[e]ven authoritarian regimes ... must rely on some support base among the populance' (2005). Therefore, in so far as possible, such countries are included in the analysis here.[1]

In addition, a number of countries are sometimes excluded on the basis that they were part of a larger political entity at the time of introduction of welfare benefits (for example, Ireland, which was part of the United Kingdom up to 1922) or because of dependence on another country (for example, Finland, which was an autonomous grand duchy of Russia up to 1917 but subsequently highly dependent on the USSR). While the rationale for such exclusions is

---

1 Unfortunately, the non-inclusion of Spain, Greece and Portugal in the Social Citizenship Indicators Project and the absence of comparable data means that these countries must be left out of the analysis in so far as it relies on the SCIP.

clear, a total exclusion of such countries runs the risk of distorting analysis. For example, the finding from a number of studies that a certain threshold level of economic development was a necessary precondition for the introduction of new welfare benefits risks ignoring the possibility that some less developed countries may have had a system of social security imposed on them due to their then subaltern position as part of a more economically developed state. The importance of this aspect should be borne in mind when we consider that of the 25 countries currently members of the European Union, only about half were politically independent at the outbreak of the First World War. In looking at nation states as the unit of analysis it is worth recalling the extent to which the constitution of such states has changed over time. Around 1500, Europe consisted of some five hundred more or less independent political units, but by 1900 this had fallen to about twenty-five. Today this has risen again (even excluding micro-states) to around thirty-five.

POVERTY AND POOR RELIEF, 1450–1800

Measures to support disadvantaged persons can be found in most societies. In early modern Europe, religious bodies originally played a key role in providing such support (supplementing, of course, familial and informal communal support). Over time, however, secular public institutions began to play an important role in this area taking over, in many cases, the functions of religious bodies. Policies developed in different ways over time in different parts of Europe and it would be unwise to attempt to provide here an outline of the main lines of development. (see Lis and Soly, 1979, and Jütte, 1994, for details of the period to 1700–1750.) However, almost all systems of poor relief were based on the principle of actual need (in current terms they were based on a means test) and were closely linked to the needs of the labour market. In contrast to the later development of systems of social insurance and of universal benefits, poor relief was provided only where a person could prove an actual (and often acute) lack of resources. In addition, while the extent to which this was enforced varied over time and space, the poor were expected to work if at all possible and, just as today, much agonising took place about the nefarious effect of systems of poor relief on the labour supply and demography (for a classic example, see Malthus, 1798, but such views were widespread).

POOR RELIEF IN THE NINETEENTH CENTURY

The turn of the nineteenth century marked an important change in the direction of poor relief policies in many European countries. It is striking to note how the future directions of welfare policy in Europe were presaged in a debate arising from the ferment of ideas generated by the French Revolution. Condorcet (1795), a revolutionary on the run from his former colleagues, proposed the establishment of a system of insurance against social risks as part of his ideal future society. Tom Paine, actively involved in both the American and French revolutions, argued for the introduction of a universal lump sum payment at the age of 15 and to every person over 50 'to enable him or her to begin the World' and 'to enable them to live in Old Age without wretchedness and go decently out of the World' (1796/1992: 409). In violent response to similar revolutionary ideas, the Reverend Thomas Malthus (1798) advocated the abolition of the existing system of poor relief. In a number of European countries, the nineteenth century saw important changes in poor relief policy with the adoption of the New Poor Law in England in 1834 (and the establishment of a similar system in Ireland in 1838) and important reforms in Scotland, France and Prussia.

Perhaps surprisingly, there has been little comparative study of welfare policies in the nineteenth century. In one of the few quantitative studies, Lindert (1998) draws on an extensive range of data to describe public and private poor relief in Europe in the century from 1780 to 1880. Lindert finds that richer countries transferred a higher share of national income to the poor than did poorer countries, but that the share transferred did not increase in line with rising incomes over the nineteenth century. His study gives some explanation for the intensity of the UK debate on the Poor Law around the turn of the nineteenth century as his findings indicate that English poor relief stood out internationally as a share of national product in the period from 1795 to 1834 at about 2.7 per cent of gross domestic product (GDP). Before 1795 poor relief appears to have been at about the same level in England and the Dutch Republic. After 1834, reflecting the restrictions imposed by the 1834 legislation and, perhaps, the booming English economy, English relief dropped to levels matched by few other countries in Western Europe. Lindert suggests that the reason for the fall in the level of English relief may be that the newly franchised classes had stronger reasons to oppose tax-based relief than the elites who controlled parliament at the start of the century. He suggests that changes in political power partly explain the movements of English poor relief over time and space, as do changes in the ability of disenfranchised groups to exit from co-operating and supplying labour.

WELFARE BEFORE THE WELFARE STATE, 1880–1920

The critical period for the introduction of new forms of welfare benefits was in the period from the 1880s to the end of the First World

War, say about 1920. Beginning with the introduction of disability insurance in Wilhemine Germany by Bismarck in 1883, new forms of welfare benefits were introduced in a wide range of European countries over the following four decades.[2] The introduction of new welfare benefits has been studied in a comparative manner by a number of authors who have focussed in particular on the introduction of new benefits in the areas of old age, sickness (or disability), unemployment and workmen's insurance (that is, compensation for persons injured at work) (Collier and Messick, 1975; Flora and Alber, 1981; Usui, 1994; Carroll, 1999; Hicks, 1999). In this section we will re-examine their findings with particular reference to European countries.[3] There is no doubt that the introduction of such benefits marks an important change in policy direction with the introduction of large-scale national systems of welfare as opposed to locally based systems of poor relief. However, it is well to recall that, despite the introduction of these new forms of welfare, the old systems of poor relief remained very important in many countries and continued to do so throughout the twentieth century. Indeed, in most countries some aspects of means-tested payments today can still be traced back to the poor relief systems of the nineteenth century.

INTRODUCTION OF WELFARE SCHEMES

Table 5.1 sets out the date of introduction of benefits in the period 1880–1920 in 20 European countries for the four 'classic' welfare programmes: work accident, sickness, old age pensions and unemployment. As can be seen, work accident was the most common programme being in place in all countries by 1920 and, on average, was one of the earliest programmes introduced. Sickness benefits were also widespread and of course the first major programme to be introduced was sickness insurance in Germany. Next in time came old age pensions, again applying to the majority of countries. Last of all, and least common, was unemployment compensation. No country had introduced a major unemployment compensation scheme before France introduced a subsidised voluntary insurance scheme in 1905, and only four did so before the First World War (Alber,

---

2 It should be noted that these were not all social insurance benefits. Despite the frequent emphasis on social insurance (which is of undeniable importance) a number of key schemes – such as the old age pension in Denmark and the UK and workmen's compensation schemes – were not social insurance based at all.

3 Unfortunately this will not include benefits of relevance to women as there is little comparative date available to facilitate the inclusion of gender issues.

Table 5.1 Adoption of welfare programmes in European countries 1890–1920

	Work accident	Sickness	Old age	Unemployment	Total	Income	Income
United Kingdom	1897	1911	1908	1911	4	100	100
Austria	1887	1888	1906	1920	4	65	64
Belgium	1903	1894	1900	1920	4	76	78
Denmark	1898	1892	1891	1907	4	83	72
Ireland	1897	1911	1908	1911	4	61	55
Netherlands	1901	1913	1913	1916	4	69	78
France	1898	1898	1910	[1905]	3	63	65
Germany	1884	1883	1889		3	72	67
Romania	1911	1911	1911		3	35	36
Sweden	1901	1891	1913		3	66	59
Italy	1898	[1919]	1898	1919	3	43	56
Czechoslovakia	1887	1888	1906		3	47	63
Spain	1919		1919		2	37	49
Hungary	1907	1891			2	35	53
Norway	1894	1909		[1906]	2	57	52
Switzerland	1911	1911			2	84	91
Portugal	1913				1	31	26
Finland	1895			[1917]	1	49	46
Bulgaria	1907				1	23	29
Greece	1914				1	31	28
Average	1901	1899	1906	1915			
Median	1900	1896	1908	1916			

Dates for adoption are taken from Flora and Heidenheimer (1981), Hicks (1999) and a number of national studies. There are significant differences between the dating used in different studies. Authorial judgement has been exercised as to the appropriate dates based on a survey of the literature. Dates in brackets, e.g. [1905], indicate the introduction of schemes which cannot be considered sufficient in scope to warrant inclusion. Income is real product per capita relative to the United Kingdom, 1913 taken from Kennedy et al. [1988].

1981). The speed of diffusion of schemes and the manner of their adoption in waves (sickness and work accident, followed by old age, followed by unemployment) is striking.

WHY WERE SCHEMES INTRODUCED?

ECONOMIC DEVELOPMENT

In terms of causation, Hicks (1999: 35–7) argues that a certain level of economic development was (almost) a necessary condition for the consolidation of welfare benefits (by which he means introduction of programmes in at least three areas), with Romania being the only less developed country to do so by 1920. As set out in Table 5.1, it would appear that Hicks is broadly correct although Hungary and Spain, with a gross national product (GNP) per capita of under 40 per cent of that of the United Kingdom in 1913, introduced benefits in two areas. In both of these cases, however, alternative estimates of economic development put them at about 50 per cent of the UK level. Switzerland is the only country at a high level of economic development not to have adopted three or four schemes.

MODERNISATION

However, as Flora and Alber found, there is no clear relationship between the level of socio-economic development and the adoption of individual welfare schemes and, in fact, they found that 'follower' states established their benefit systems at a slightly *higher* level of socio-economic development than the initial adopters (1981: 61). In political terms, Flora and Alber also found that the follower states adopted legislation generally at a much higher level of political mobilisation. They did find support for the thesis that countries that introduce benefit schemes at relatively low levels of socio-economic development had relatively high levels of political mobilisation and conversely countries adopting at relatively low levels of political mobilisation were relatively highly developed in socio-economic terms (1981: 65) when adoptions were divided into three time periods (1880–1900; 1900–1920 and after 1920). The thesis that a combination of high socio-economic development and low political mobilisation (or vice versa) could predict adoption of benefit schemes was found to have validity for the periods after 1900. Flora and Alber found that countries adopting in this period (Belgium, Finland, Italy, the Netherlands, Sweden, Switzerland and the United Kingdom), while differing widely in levels of industrialisation and urbanisation and in levels of political mobilisation, enacted legislation at similar levels of socio-political development.

However, Flora and Alber also found small groups of countries which introduced legislation at either low or high levels of both socio-economic development and political mobilisation. The former introduced legislation 'too early' by reference to the central group, while the latter acted 'too late'. The early group included Germany, Denmark, Sweden, Austria and Italy. Of these only Italy was a parliamentary democracy in the relevant period and Flora and Alber hypothesised that constitutional-dualistic monarchies tended to introduce welfare legislation earlier (in chronological and developmental time) than the parliamentary democracies in order to solidify the loyalty of the working class in the face of a growing and hostile labour movement and because they already had stronger state bureaucracies capable of administering such schemes (1981: 70). In addition, these regimes were dominated by landed interests which were able to shift the costs of social measures to the urban upper, middle and working classes. In contrast, there was also a small group of countries which adopted benefits systems 'late' given their relatively high levels of socio-economic and political development. This group included

France and Belgium. Flora and Alber suggest that this may be due to political instability and political splits, particularly in the labour movement.

SOCIAL DEMOCRACY/POLITICAL MOBILISATION

Hicks (1999) adopts a different approach to analysis and comes to somewhat different conclusions. He utilises qualitative comparative analysis (QCA) (see Box 1.2) to analyse the factors relevant to what he describes as welfare state consolidation (that is, adopting at least three of the four main schemes). As discussed above, Hicks suggests that a certain 'threshold' level of economic development is necessary before extensive adoption of welfare schemes (consolidation) will occur. However, once that threshold is exceeded, his findings agree with Flora and Alber in finding that there is no link between a (higher) level of economic development and consolidation. Hicks also assesses the impact of political mobilisation, looking at the relationship between political mobilisation and welfare consolidation (measured as having reached a threshold of 20 per cent trade union density and/or 20 per cent social democratic votes). He finds that there is a correlation which is particularly strong for the combined worker mobilisation measure (that is, 20 per cent union density *or* 20 per cent left vote) and consolidation in 1920. This finding is not necessarily inconsistent with those of Flora and Alber and the differences can be explained by the different focus, with Hicks concentrating on 'consolidation' in 1920 while Flora and Alber focus on the conditions at the time of adoption.

Box 5.1: What is a correlation?

Correlation is a measure of association between two variables. It measures how strongly the variables are related, or change, with each other. When the events involve numbers, a positive correlation means that as one increases, the other increases as well. A negative correlation means that as one increases, the other decreases. A coefficient of linear correlation ranges from −1 for a perfect negative correlation, through zero for no relationship, to +1 for a perfect positive correlation. Correlation does not imply causation. In other words, just because two events are correlated does not mean that one causes the other. Strong correlation, however, does often warrant further investigation to determine causation.

ECONOMIC INTEGRATION

Given that the introduction of welfare measures coincided with the height of an earlier phase of economic integration, it is surprising that there has been so little study of the link between the two. Huberman and Lewchuck (2002) argue that increased trade openness was linked to the adoption of welfare benefits, a point we pursue below.

A REVIEW OF THE EVIDENCE

Table 5.2 sets out data on national welfare introduction and a range of potentially relevant factors such as levels of industrialisation, left vote and levels of trade unionisation. The analysis of individual adoptions is somewhat problematic given the difficulty in deciding whether a specific date should be chosen as countries often adopted somewhat limited measures before expanding their scope or making them compulsory. Accordingly we will adopt Hicks' concept of consolidation (although expanding it to countries adopting two or three programmes) and analyse the factors which appear to have been necessary for a country to achieve consolidation.

Table 5.2   Consolidation of welfare states in 1920

	Income 1	Income 2	Industrialisation	Left vote	Trade union density
Full consolidation					
United Kingdom	100	100	48	8	22
Austria	65	64	33	29	3
Belgium	76	78	48	19	7
Denmark	83	72	27	25	13
Ireland	61	55	14	–	–
Netherlands	69	78	36	15	11
	76	75	34	19	11
Partial consolidation					
France	63	65	29	34	5
Germany	72	67	34	35	11
Romania	35	36	8	–	–
Sweden	66	59	22	23	6
Italy	43	56	24	21	2
Czechoslovakia	47	63	37	–	–
Spain	37	49	21	–	–
Hungary	35	53	20	–	–
Norway	57	52	29	20	7
Switzerland	84	91	44	18	5
	54	59	27	25	6
No consolidation					
Portugal	31	26	22	2	–
Finland	49	46	13	41	2
Bulgaria	23	29	8	–	–
Greece	31	28	16	–	–
	34	32	15	–	–

Income is as in Table 5.1. Industrialisation is the proportion of the paid labour force employed in manufacturing and industry, taken from Cippola (1976). Voting data for left (including communist) votes in the period 1900–1919 from Mackie and Rose (2000). Trade union data are for 1913–1914 from Stephens (1979).

In fact, the answer is very simple. While, as Flora and Alber point out, the logic of industrialisation is not sufficient to explain the timing of welfare adoptions, it is (almost) a necessary and sufficient condition for welfare consolidation by 1920. No developed country, that is, with a level of GNP at least 40 per cent of the United Kingdom and with at least one-quarter of the population working in industry, has failed to adopt two welfare programmes and only Switzerland has failed to adopt three.[4] Only four European countries failed to meet these thresholds and yet consolidated. Of those countries failing to achieve these thresholds and yet adopting at least two programmes, Ireland (4) (which had a high level of GNP) was part of the United Kingdom and Hungary (2) was part of the Austro-Hungarian Empire. Only Spain (2) and Romania (3) have low levels of wealth and industrialisation and yet consolidated, and we do not have information on the scope of either countries' programme to assess how extensive they were in reality. No similar relationship can be seen between consolidation and left vote or union density. While the presence or absence of factors such as trade, left vote and trade union mobilisation may have affected the size or shape of welfare programmes (something we will examine in more detail for the period from 1930 when we have better information), the 'logic of industrialisation' (or membership of a more industrialised Empire) is largely sufficient to explain welfare consolidation in 1920 at a macro level.

WELFARE STATE DEVELOPMENT, 1920–1950

As we have seen in the previous section, by about 1920 almost all European countries had established at least one major social security programme and a good number had established two, three or four such programmes. In this section we describe the further expansion of such programmes and the post-War consolidation which took place in many countries in the period to about 1950. We focus in particular on the years 1930 and 1950.

WELFARE STATES IN 1930

Hicks (1999) studied welfare consolidation in the year 1930 and identified both the importance of worker mobilisation to the development of welfare states and three paths to welfare consolidation: an autocratic legacy (Germany, Austria), a Lib-Lab pact (UK, Denmark, Sweden) and Catholic paternalism (Belgium, the Netherlands). However, Hicks' analysis is problematic for two reasons. First, his

---

4 Norway did adopt three programmes, albeit that its unemployment scheme had very limited coverage.

focus on worker mobilisation means that he does not examine possible alternative factors such as the level of industrialisation or trade. Second, his definition of consolidation emphasises the coverage of different welfare schemes. However, this is very misleading in terms of the 'depth' of welfare commitment. Some countries, particularly Sweden, had schemes which, in 1930, satisfied Hicks' somewhat arbitrary cut-off point of minimum coverage of 15 per cent of the relevant population but paid extremely low benefits.

From 1930, we have the advantage[5] of being able to draw on more detailed measures of welfare effort through the Social Citizenship Indicators Project (SCIP). This provides details of both the level of benefits (as a percentage of average industrial earnings) and the coverage of the different schemes in relation to old age pensions, sickness and unemployment benefits.[6] This allows a more nuanced assessment on the scope of welfare schemes than the cruder measure of 'consolidation' which we used in the previous section. However, data are only available for 13 European countries, with all the southern countries (except Italy) and all CEE countries excluded. In the following sections we provide a new analysis of welfare development in 1930 drawing on SCIP data. We identify a number of different clusters of welfare state based on the scope and depth of their welfare schemes. Table 5.3 sets out a classification of welfare states in 1930 based on SCIP data.

WELFARE STATE GROUPINGS

Finland has a very minimal welfare system and can effectively be eliminated from the analysis. This leaves us with three main 'groups':

1 An 'autocratic legacy' group (Austria and Germany), which has the best-developed welfare system with schemes in all three areas covered (sickness, old age and unemployment), and scope and benefit levels at or above average in all cases.
2 The United Kingdom, with a high level of industrialisation and trade unionisation but where the welfare schemes have been established by Liberal and Conservative governments (Gilbert,

---

5 Albeit with some difficulty as the data is neither publicly available nor published in a readily usable form. For this chapter the data was drawn from a series of studies published by the Swedish Institute of Social Research (Palme, 1990; Kangas, 1991; Wennemo, 1994; Carroll, 1999).

6 For pensions we use data for recipience rather than for those insured for pensions. For short-term unemployment and sickness benefits we use the insurability data, as this gives a better idea of the scope of the scheme.

1966, 1970). The UK system generally had very wide scope but average to low benefits.[7]

3   A group of small, open, comparatively wealthy, countries (Belgium, Denmark and the Netherlands), with scope and benefit levels at about average. Schemes were introduced by either Liberal (DK) or Catholic (B, N) parties.

There are five countries with limited welfare schemes (France, Italy, Switzerland, Norway, Sweden). These were generally at a moderate level of industrialisation (only Switzerland exceeded 33 per cent) and were not particularly open. Trade union density was generally low, although most had a significant left vote. Finally, there are Finland and most other European countries not included in the SCIP analysis. These countries were generally at a lower level of economic development and of industrialisation.

Table 5.3   Welfare states in 1930

	Income I	Industrialisation	Left vote	Trade union density	Trade
Austria	2850	33	41	25	41
Germany	2870	40	38	18	30
	2860	36.5	40	22	36
United Kingdom	4340	46	33	23	36
Ireland	n/a	15	11	n/a	66
Belgium	3910	48	38	18	78
Denmark	3910	27	35	21	57
Netherlands	4470	36	24	20	69
	4097	37	32	20	68
France	3710	33	33	7	n/a
Switzerland	4580	45	27	17	46
Norway	2890	27	35	12	44
Sweden	3060	32	41	20	32
Italy	2490	31	–	–	24
Finland	2220	15	40	1	58

Income data are from Maddison (1991): GDP per capita in 1985 US$. Other data as per Table 5.2. Left vote is for the period 1920–1929. Trade data from Cippola (1976).

DETERMINANTS OF DEVELOPMENT

ECONOMIC DEVELOPMENT

There are a number of lessons from this analysis. First, economic development and industrialisation retain their importance. No country of

---

7 Ireland has a broadly similar welfare system to that of the UK but its status at this time relates almost entirely to its formerly being part of the United Kingdom as very limited initiatives were taken during the first decade of independence (Cousins, 2003).

the 12 with reasonably developed welfare states was at a low level of economic development (all having incomes at or over US$2,500 in 1985 terms) and all, except Ireland, had at least 25 per cent of the working population in industry. Conversely, there was no developed, industrialised European country which did not have a developed welfare system.

POLICY LEGACIES

Second is the importance of policy legacies. Germany and Austria were amongst the first nations to introduce welfare systems under autocratic rule. Almost fifty years after the introduction of the first welfare scheme in Germany by Bismarck, Germany and Austria retained their leadership position under dramatically different political conditions.

WORKER MOBILISATION?

Third, this analysis questions any simple link between worker mobilisation and welfare development. Undoubtedly social democracy in Germany had an important influence on the further development (and maintenance) of the German welfare state in the 1920s. However, in the United Kingdom, the main welfare reforms were introduced by the Liberals and Conservatives. Detailed historical studies do not indicate that the UK Labour party or trade unions had a major role in policy formation (Gilbert, 1970). As in Bismarck's Germany, no doubt UK governments were responding to the level of unionisation and growing Labour party voting, but to reduce this to a social democratic road to welfare is to replace the logic of industrialisation with an equally functionalist 'logic of mobilisation'.

CONSOLIDATION IN 1950

Moving on to 1950, we see significant changes in the structure of welfare systems. The Great Depression in the late 1920s led to significant cutbacks in welfare systems across Europe. Subsequently, many nations introduced family benefits in the 1930s and 1940s in a further wave of policy innovation (Wennemo, 1994). Finally, in the post-War period (and, no doubt influenced by the experiences of the Second World War) a number of European countries introduced consolidation and expansion of their existing welfare systems (Baldwin, 1990). Both the scope and generosity of benefits increased significantly over this period, with average coverage for pensions, sickness and unemployment benefits increasing from about one-third to half of the workforce and average pension rates increasing by about three-quarters. Increases in sickness benefits were more modest (about one-quarter), while there was little change in unemployment benefits.

WELFARE STATE GROUPINGS

In 1950 we begin to see a specific pattern of nations emerging, albeit that only two clear categories of welfare state are yet identifiable:

- First, building on the authoritarian group of the 1930s, we begin to see a recognisable 'Christian centrist'[8] group, consisting of Germany, Austria, the Netherlands and Belgium. These provide generous benefits but the scope of the schemes, while average or above, are far from universal.
- Second, we see a 'social democratic' group led by the United Kingdom and with Sweden and Norway beginning to develop with almost universal coverage in most areas but low to average benefits. Only the United Kingdom has a high level of public services at this time.

However, the remaining countries do not clearly adhere to any pattern. Ireland shows a considerable element of policy legacies with a structure quite similar to that of the United Kingdom, although it can hardly be described as social-democratic. Denmark displays a somewhat incoherent system (to an external eye) with broad sickness cover but low benefits and, conversely, very limited unemployment cover but high benefits. France and Switzerland retain their positions as countries with generally average benefits but France, a pioneer in the introduction of family allowances and with an above average level of public service employment, still lacks a compulsory unemployment scheme, while Switzerland has not introduced general family allowances and has only a very limited pension scheme. Italy now has a fairly comprehensive welfare scheme (only family allowances are lacking) but benefits are generally modest, and Finland still lacks a compulsory sickness scheme.[9] Comparative expenditure data would suggest that some other European countries (such as Czechoslovakia and Poland) had developed modest welfare states by this time.

EXPENDITURE DATA

Data is available from the International Labour Organisation (ILO) for the period from 1949 for 19 European countries (Table 5.4). This

---

8 The term 'Christian centrist' is preferred to the more usual 'Christian democratic' on the basis that some of these countries have not experienced rule by a specific Christian democratic party. The term 'Christian centrist' implies that parties of a Christian and centrist ethos (which of course includes Christian democracy) have played a significant role in the government of the relevant country.

9 Although see Kangas (1991) as to how employers' payment of sick pay provided a functional alternative to statutory sickness benefits.

Table 5.4 Welfare states in 1950

	Spending	Income	Industrialisation	Left vote	CD vote	Trade union density
Germany	14.8	3300	43	35	31	36
Austria	12.3	2800	35	49	47	62
Netherlands	6.7	4700	40	36	53	36
Belgium	10.6	4200	47	41	43	37
	11.1	*3750*	*41*	*40*	*44*	*43*
United Kingdom	10.1	5700	47	48	0	45
Sweden	8.3	5300	41	52	0	62
Norway	5.7	4500	33	66	8	54
	8.0	*5167*	*40*	*55*	*3*	*54*
Ireland	7.1	n/a	24	11	0	39
Denmark	8.4	5200	33	54	0	58
France	10.8	4100	35	48		31
Switzerland	8.2	6600	46	31	21	40
Italy	8.5	2800	29	38	49	47
Finland	6.7	3500	28	48	0	33
Greece	2.8	n/a	19	n/a	n/a	n/a
Portugal	n/a	1600		–	–	–
Spain	4.4	2400	14	–	–	–
Poland	3.9	n/a	23	–	–	–
Czechoslovakia	13.1	3500	37	–	–	–
Hungary	9.3	2500	23	–	–	–

Data are as Table 5.3. Left vote is for the period 1945–1950. Spending is from ILO/Eurodata (2001). For most countries the data relates to 1949–1951, although rapid growth in this period means that they should be taken as indicators of development rather than precise levels. The data for Spain are for 1960 and for Hungary 1963. Vote data is from www.parties-and-elections.de.

covers social security in the broad sense including both healthcare and public employee pensions. While there must be considerable questions about the precise comparability of the data that was provided to the ILO by national institutions, the picture available from this data does broadly correspond to the picture we have obtained from the SCIP data.

The 'Christian centrist' group (except the Netherlands) all have relatively high levels of expenditure at over 10 per cent of GDP. The emerging social democratic group is led by the United Kingdom at about 10 per cent of GNP, followed by Sweden and Norway. Denmark and Italy are at about average levels of spending, with Finland, Ireland and Switzerland somewhat below. Of those countries not included in the SCIP, Greece and Spain (when it appears in the data in 1960) all have low level of welfare spending. It is difficult to rely on data for the then state socialist countries, due both to accounting issues and different approaches to welfare support (such as policies of full employment and subsidisation of food and housing). However, the data does suggest that welfare systems in Czechoslovakia were quite well developed, with Poland at a lower level of development.

DETERMINANTS OF WELFARE DEVELOPMENT

ECONOMIC DEVELOPMENT AND INDUSTRIALISATION

Turning to the determinants of welfare development, we find that countries at a high level of economic and industrial development (that is, with an average per capita income of $4,000 in 1985 terms and industrialised workforce of 33 per cent or more) all have well developed welfare states. The exceptions to this are Germany and Austria, whose economies have yet to recover from the effects of the Second World War but whose welfare states remain (relatively) well developed. Finland and Italy, which both have about 28 per cent of the workforce engaged in industry, have comparatively less developed welfare states. Switzerland, particularly in terms of its level of welfare spending, is an exception to this general trend and has a lower level of spending than would be expected for its level of wealth and industrialisation. The southern semi-peripheral countries all have relatively low levels of economic development and low levels of welfare expenditure.

POLITICAL FACTORS

Political factors go only a limited way to explain the level of welfare development. There are countries with well developed welfare states which have had a very limited experience of left rule in the period from either 1930 or the end of the War (for example, Germany) and countries also with a very limited history of left rule (such as Ireland), which spend more than would be expected given their level of economic development. While there are no countries with a long history of left rule which do not have well developed welfare states, the universe of such countries is also very small (Sweden, Norway, the United Kingdom in the post-War period), which makes it difficult to draw too many conclusions about the impact of left rule.

However, political power does have an impact on the type of welfare state. All the 'Christian centrist' nations have been ruled by Christian democratic or centrist parties in the post-War period (albeit that Belgium and the Netherlands were governed by coalitions led by social democratic prime ministers). Equally the three 'social democratic' countries have all experienced long-term social democratic government (at least in the post-War period in the case of the United Kingdom). Similarly, trade union influence (as measured by union density) is generally greater in the social democratic countries (albeit that Austria has a comparably high level of unionisation). No particular relationship is evident for other factors such as the level of trade or female employment.

THE GOLDEN AGE, 1950–1970

The decades after the Second World War up to the oil crises of the 1970s are often presented as the golden age of welfare development. This picture is perhaps over-drawn: there was arguably less consensus about the benefits of the welfare state than is sometimes claimed and many countries still had comparatively limited schemes by 1970. However, it is certainly true that both coverage and benefits expanded enormously over the period from 1950 to 1970. Benefit coverage increased, on average, from about half the relevant group to three-quarters or more (except in the case of sickness insurance where the Continental countries remained stubbornly slow to expand sickness coverage). Replacement rates increased by between two-thirds and three-quarters.

WELFARE STATE GROUPINGS

The two groups of countries identified in 1950 remain clear in 1970:

- First, a Christian centrist group (with Italy arguably joining Austria, Belgium, Germany and the Netherlands), which provides relatively high benefits but with about average scope and average levels of public services.
- Second, a social democratic group with relatively universal scope but more limited benefits. Sweden is now the leader of this group with both universal scope, high benefits and high levels of public services. Norway also had universal scope but more modest benefits. Finland[10] and the United Kingdom achieve similar rankings, with average scope and modest benefits, but whereas Finland is developing into a welfare leader, the United Kingdom is falling back in relative terms (albeit that it still has relatively high levels of public services).

The United Kingdom's decline reflects its fall in economic status from the clear European leader in the early twentieth century (in terms of GDP per capita) to a position where its GDP per capita is below that of many European countries by 1973 (Maddison, 1991). Denmark has more generous benefits than the social democratic group but very

---

10 Albeit that most of the key programmes were established under the Agrarian/Centre party (Kangas, 1991).

limited unemployment coverage. However, its relatively high level of public services perhaps justifies inclusion in the social democratic group. Ireland, paralleling the United Kingdom trajectory both economically and in welfare, has also fallen back in relative terms and now has one of the most limited welfare systems of the countries studied. France and Switzerland remain difficult to categorise. Both countries continue to have welfare states at relatively modest levels given their level of economic development.

Here we can draw on OECD expenditure data in relation to 16 countries. The picture broadly corroborates that drawn from the SCIP data. Both the Christian centrist and social democratic groups are the highest spenders. However, all the Christian centrist countries are spending above 12 per cent of GNP on social security. In contrast, in the social democratic group, while Sweden and Norway are high spenders, we see a similar picture of Finland moving to join them and the United Kingdom falling away rapidly. Again Switzerland spends less than would be expected given its SCIP ranking, suggesting that actual claim loads must be relatively low (perhaps related to Switzerland's immigration-related labour market policy).

DETERMINANTS OF WELFARE DEVELOPMENT

Table 5.5 sets out the relationship between the welfare groupings and the key determinants discussed earlier.

ECONOMIC DEVELOPMENT

The usual relationship between the level of economic and welfare development can be seen with all the countries at a higher level of development having better developed welfare states. While it would be wrong to group them together given that the structure of their welfare systems are quite different, all the more peripheral European countries for which we have data (and assuming it is broadly comparable) are making a much lower degree of welfare effort. There is little difference between the two main welfare groups in terms of levels of GDP per capita (CC: $9,400 v. SD: $9,900) or industrialisation (40 per cent v. 37 per cent). In terms of trade, there is a considerable variation within each group, with both including low (for example, Italy, the United Kingdom) and high trade (for example, Belgium, Norway) countries. Again we must turn to political factors to distinguish the two families.

POLITICAL MOBILISATION

The social democratic countries (except Finland) all have experienced long-term social democratic government, while all the Christian centrist grouping have been ruled primarily by Christian democratic or

Table 5.5   Welfare states c. 1970

	Spending	Income	Industrialisation	Left vote	CD vote	Trade union density	Female employment
Germany	15.4	10100	47	43	46	30	37
Austria	14.1	8600	41	45	47	51	39
Netherlands	17.4	10300	36	32	47	34	27
Belgium	12.7	9400	40	35	36	51	34
Italy	12.4	8500	38	43	39	36	26
	14.4	*9380*	*40*	*40*	*43*	*40*	*32*
United Kingdom	8.6	10100	42	46	0	44	37
Sweden	11.0	11300	37	53	2	75	41
Norway	12.3	9300	33	56	9	52	36
Finland	7.2	9000	34	45	0	45	45
	9.8	*9925*	*37*	*50*	*3*	*54*	*40*
Ireland	9.3	n/a		15	0	n/a	26
Denmark	11.6	10500	33	49	0	50	41
France	17.1	10300	39	37	0	15	37
Switzerland	11.0	13200	45	28	23	27	34
Greece	8.4	n/a	23	14	0	n/a	29
Portugal	3.1	5600	33	–	–	–	22
Spain	8.1	7500	35	–	–	–	23

Income, industrialisation, and voting are as in Table 5.4. Votes refer to the average in the previous decade. Female employment is from Maddison [1991], trade union density from Wallerstein and Western [2000], while spending data is from OECD.

religious centrist parties. The Christian democratic countries all have a substantial left vote (30 per cent+) but an absence of long-term left government. As in 1950, unionisation tends to be higher in the social democratic countries, albeit that female employment is only some-what higher in social democratic countries (40 per cent) than under Christian centrism (32 per cent). The different policy trajectories in both France and Switzerland may be explained by their different political composition with a secular centrist/right government in France and institutionalised power sharing and federalism in Switzerland.

WELFARE CRISIS, 1970–1980

In this section we combine analysis based on the SCIP with expenditure data from the OECD (see Table 5.6). The oil crises of the 1970s took some time to impact on the development of welfare states. Between 1970 and 1980, European welfare states continued to expand in scope and generosity. Almost all countries moved close to universal pension and unemployment coverage, with about 75 per cent

---

11 SCIP data shows a level of about 60 per cent in Ireland, but this appears to understate coverage levels.

Table 5.6   Welfare states c. 1980

	Spending	Income	Left vote	CD vote	Trade union density
Germany	23.0	9349	42	47	41
Austria	22.5	8092	51	43	65
Netherlands	26.9	8837	30	34	40
Belgium	24.1	8639	30	34	77
	24.1	*8729*	*38*	*40*	*56*
Sweden	28.8	9661	49	2	90
Norway	17.9	9706	46	12	65
Finland	18.5	8313	42	3	86
	21.7	*9227*	*46*	*6*	*80*
United Kingdom	17.9	7993	39	0	56
Ireland	17.0	n/a	13	0	63
Denmark	29.1	8820	51	3	86
France	21.1	9095	43	0	20
Switzerland	14.2	10672	24	21	35
Italy	18.4	7874	44	38	n/a
Greece	11.5	n/a	30	0	n/a
Portugal	10.9	n/a	62	1	n/a
Spain	15.9	n/a	40	2	n/a

Data as per on Table 5.5

being the lowest level of cover for the respective schemes.[11] Sickness insurance cover increased to about two-thirds of the relevant population. Average replacement rates for the three main programmes increased to between 60 per cent and three-quarters of average earnings. Welfare spending increased very significantly in this period.

WELFARE STATE GROUPINGS

Unsurprisingly, given the relatively short period involved, many countries saw little dramatic change in their welfare states in the decade of the 1970s. However, Finland and Norway were exceptions to this, with both countries continuing their dramatic growth to convert the 1970s social democratic group to entirely Nordic membership, and with a stagnating United Kingdom dropping out based on SCIP criteria but on the basis of expenditure data arguably remaining a member of that group as late as 1980.

We see three basic groups:

- First, a Christian centrist group of Austria, Belgium, Germany and the Netherlands (with Italy falling away from membership again). France would join this group on the basis of expenditure data, but not on the basis of the structure of its welfare state (as shown in SCIP data).

- Second, a social democratic group of Finland, Norway and Sweden (and possibly Denmark).
- Third, a southern, 'semi-peripheral' group including Greece, Spain and Portugal, with Italy arguably also falling into membership.

Denmark stubbornly refuses to align itself with the social democratic group on an analysis based on SCIP data. In an analysis of sickness and pension insurance, Korpi and Palme (1998, also based on SCIP data) also classified Denmark separately to the other Nordic countries and, as discussed in the next chapter, Denmark's income inequality remained higher than the other three countries. However, its high level of public services perhaps justifies inclusion in the social democratic group. France also shows a distinctive pattern, with benefits which are structured differently and (other than family allowances) less generous than the other continental countries. Switzerland continues to have a theoretically generous but cheap 'in-practice' welfare state. The southern grouping spend less on welfare but follow a broadly similar structure to that of the Christian centrist group, with very lower spending on welfare services.

DETERMINANTS OF WELFARE DEVELOPMENT

Given the relatively short period between 1970 and 1980, we will only discuss here the factors which changed over that time. There remains little difference between the two main groupings in terms of GDP or industrialisation. However, the southern group is generally at a much lower level of economic development and industrialisation.

Both Germany and Austria experienced considerable social democratic government in this period. Otherwise the Christian centrist thesis holds and in no Christian centrist country (other than Austria) has social democracy been in government for more than one-third of the period from 1946. In contrast, the social democratic countries (with the exception of Finland) remain strongly social democratic. The United Kingdom's 'falling out' of the social democratic group can, in large part, be attributed to its limited experience of social democracy. The social democratic countries now also show a significantly higher level of unionisation (80 per cent compared to 56 per cent in the Christian centrist countries).

There are a number of countries which do not fall neatly into any group, including Ireland (peripheral but still showing strong policy legacies of its membership of the United Kingdom and post-colonial policy diffusion) and Switzerland (much less developed than would be expected with a unique political system and strict labour migration policy).

RETRENCHMENT, RESTRUCTURING
OR RESILIENCE, 1980–2000

SCIP data is not yet publicly available for this period and we accordingly rely primarily on the detailed breakdown of expenditure published by the OECD.

WELFARE STATE GROUPINGS

Table 5.7 sets out the levels of spending for those European welfare states for which comparative OECD data is available. It also – in the absence of SCIP data – provides some indication of the relative 'generosity' of welfare states in relation to pensions and family support (broadly defined). Both overall spending and relative spending on pensions and family supports have increased over the period. In only two countries has overall spending fallen (the Netherlands and Ireland). Pension ratios have increased significantly in Christian centrist countries (except the Netherlands) and the Southern countries. Family support ratios have fallen in only three countries (Belgium, Netherlands and Sweden) and increased in 12 – particularly in Southern Europe (except Portugal). The Christian centrist countries have the highest pension ratios while the Nordic group provide most support to families. As can be seen, we can identify three clear groupings of welfare state:

- The Christian centrist (Austria, Belgium, France, Germany, Italy,[12] Netherlands and Switzerland) model, which are high spenders (26 per cent of GDP), heavily focussed on pension and health spending (on average 40 per cent of all spending goes on pensions and one-quarter on health) and spend little on family services and services for older people. While fitting broadly within this grouping in terms of spending, the Netherlands generally spends less overall and less on pensions, and our more detailed examination in Chapter 7 would suggest that it is on a separate trajectory out of the old Christian centrist grouping (or perhaps leading a new trajectory for the group).
- The social democratic family (Denmark, Finland, Norway and Sweden) are also high spenders (26.7 per cent) but spend less than one-third of the total on pensions and much more on welfare services. This group had the highest level of spending on family supports.

---

12 Italy continues to sit somewhere between the Centrist and Southern groups. Its level of spending is closest to that of the Centrist group, but spending structure is closer to the Southern countries.

Table 5.7   Welfare state trajectories, 1980–2000

	1980 % of GDP	Pension	Family	2001 % of GDP	Pension	Family
Austria	22.5	56	15	26.0	69	18
Belgium	24.1	42	15	27.2	52	13
France	21.1	56	11	28.5	66	15
Germany	23.0	64	12	27.4	68	13
Italy	18.4	57	5	24.4	64	7
Netherlands	26.9	62	11	21.8	47	6
Switzerland	14.2	41	5	26.4	75	7
Average	**22.7**	**56.2**	**11.5**	**26.0**	**63.0**	**11.3**
Coefficient of variation	*12.6*	*13.7*	*31.9*	*9.4*	*15.1*	*38.7*
Denmark	29.1	57	14	29.2	56	20
Finland	18.5	43	9	24.8	53	17
Norway	17.9	34	8	23.9	45	16
Sweden	28.8	48	19	28.9	53	16
Average	**23.6**	**45.5**	**12.5**	**26.7**	**51.8**	**17.3**
Coefficient of variation	*26.4*	*21.1*	*40.5*	*10.3*	*9.1*	*11.0*
Greece	11.5	39	2	24.3	76	12
Spain	15.9	30	2	19.6	52	7
Portugal	10.9	42	3	21.1	49	3
Average	**12.8**	**37.0**	**2.3**	**21.7**	**59.0**	**7.3**
Coefficient of variation	*21.4*	*16.9*	*24.7*	*11.1*	*25.1*	*61.5*
Poland	–	–	–	23.0	70	5
Czech Republic	–	–	–	20.1	49	10
Slovak Republic	–	–	–	17.9	59	8
Hungary	–	–	–	20.1	54	15
Average				**20.3**	**58.0**	**9.5**
Coefficient of variation				*10.3*	*15.5*	*44.2*
United Kingdom	17.9	37	10	21.8	52	12
Ireland	18.9	42	4	16.5	28	9
Average	**18.4**	**39.5**	**7.0**	**19.2**	**40.0**	**10.5**
Coefficient of variation	*3.8*	*9.0*	*60.6*	*19.6*	*42.4*	*20.2*

Data are from OECD [2004]. The pension figure gives the average amount of pension spending per person 65 or over compared to GDP per capita. Similarly, the family figure represents family spending per child (under 15) compared to GDP per capita. This should not be confused with a replacement rate as some benefits may be paid to persons outside the group and/or may be more or less evenly distributed. Irish data is corrected for missing unemployment data in 1980 and given as a percentage of GNP for 2001, due to the very large gap which has developed between GNP and GDP.

- Southern European countries (Greece, Spain and Portugal), which are lower spenders (21.7 per cent) but also strongly focussed on pensions and health (40 per cent and 25 per cent of total spending) and spend very little on welfare services.

There is a general trend towards convergence in the social democratic group and (excluding the Netherlands) in the Centrist group, albeit that the southern group does not show any clear trend. Generally there has been an increase in spending overall and in spending on pensions and services for older people (reflecting the ageing population) and health services. Conversely, spending on incapacity benefits has fallen or remained the same in about half the countries. The United Kingdom spends an average amount on social protection (21.8 per cent) and this is strongly focussed on pensions (40 per cent). Spending on welfare services remains rather low. Spending on unemployment and active labour market policies is very low but spending on disability benefits has increased, reflecting the 'parking' of people with low employability on disability benefits in the 1980s. Ireland also does not fit into any particular group; partially due to the very recent rapid growth in GDP (and consequent fall in unemployment) it has one of the lowest levels of spending as a percentage of GDP. Due both to a small older population and low benefits, Ireland's, spending on pensions is the lowest of all OECD Europe.

The OECD data include four CEE countries (Czech Republic, Hungary, Poland and Slovakia) but there is a considerable level of variation in the total level of spending and in the structure of spending so that it would be incorrect to describe them as forming a consistent grouping at this stage.

WHITHER THE WELFARE STATE?

This section has drawn on expenditure data to track the position of welfare states. As can be seen for 1980, this can give a somewhat different perspective from the data on replacement rates and coverage from the SCIP. What can this tell us about the trajectory of European welfare states? On the one hand, expenditure data is important. As opposed to political and policy rhetoric, it shows the amount of cash actually being spent on different aspects of the welfare state at a given time. On the other, expenditure data (even the disaggregated data now available from the OECD) has its limitations. In itself, it does not show *why* this level of spending is occurring. It frequently does not show the effect of incremental policy changes which may only appear in a 10- or 20-year period. In order to get a better picture of the policy dynamics behind welfare spending, we look in more detail at five country studies in Chapter 7.

However, a number of points can be made at this stage. First, the data does not provide support for a thesis of significant or widespread retrenchment or 'permanent austerity'. Of the countries for which we have data, only two (Ireland and the Netherlands) spend less now than they did in 1980 at the end of the golden age of welfare. Many spent very significantly more. As we will see from the detailed country studies, several countries would currently have been spending more again had they retained the policies on benefits rates or coverage in place in 1980. But whether this should be seen as retrenchment or restructuring to make the welfare state affordable is a matter for debate (which is pursued in Chapter 7).

Figure 5.1 Economic and welfare development, 2001

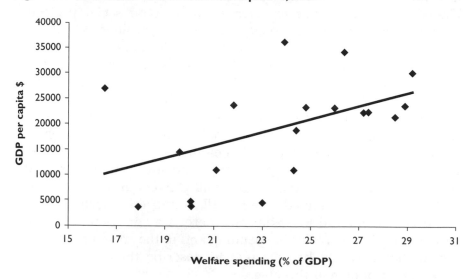

Second, the major growth area has been in old age pensions which increased significantly – particularly in Christian centrist and Southern countries. In contrast, health spending – which rivalled pensions in 1980 – has plateaued in many of the Centrist and social democratic states.

DETERMINANTS OF WELFARE DEVELOPMENT

ECONOMIC DEVELOPMENT

As we can see in Figure 5.1, there remains a strong link between the level of economic development and the level of welfare spending in a country. In fact, the correlation between the level of development (measured in terms of GDP per capita) and the level of welfare spending is a strong 0.69 (excluding Ireland, whose recent dramatic growth makes it an outlier). The level of economic development, however, has little impact on the categorisation of the two leading welfare groups (although it does help to explain the level of welfare in the Southern semi-peripheral countries).

POLITICS

There has been considerable debate about the role of party politics in recent decades. Some have suggested that politics has become less relevant (Castles, 1998); others argue that social democracy continues to support the welfare state (Korpi and Palme, 2003); yet others, to the contrary, suggest that following a 'Nixon goes to China' strategy left-wing parties are most likely to support welfare retrenchment (Ross, 1999). The evidence here indicates that politics continues to play a role in terms of welfare structures, although there is a strong impact of policy legacies. The Centrist countries (with the exception of France) remained under primarily Christian centrist government. Conversely, most of the social democratic countries remained under primarily social democratic government. But even Denmark, which was governed more by conservatism than social democracy in the period, does not show any dramatic change from its existing welfare trajectory. Detailed studies do show battles over retrenchment in Denmark, but then even Sweden – where social democracy remained almost hegemonous – also shows similar struggles. There is no clear support on this evidence for either of the theses that left-wing governments are more inclined to support or attack the welfare state (see Chapter 7).

There is a relationship between welfare groupings and levels of corporatism (using the Hicks–Kenworthy (1998) index) and unionisation, which are highest in the social democratic countries, high in Christian centrist countries (although only moderately so in France and Italy) and low in the United Kingdom. In relation to unionisation, however, studies have suggested that there is an element of reverse causality involved, that is, welfare state structures can lead to high unionisation rates – particularly in those countries which delegate authority to trade unions in paying unemployment benefits (Rothstein, 1992).

GENDER

The influence of gender can be seen in the development of 'new social risks'[13] involving childcare and care for older people. The social democratic countries were amongst the first to recognise these risks and have developed policies on widespread public support for childcare (as indeed did France) (Morgan, 2003). However, the Christian centrist countries also increasingly developed policies in these areas with Germany, for example, introducing social insurance schemes to cover care risks and a number of countries introducing parental leave schemes.

KEY INFLUENCES

This section summarises the evidence in this chapter of the influence of a number of key factors (drawing on the theoretical factors identified in Chapter 2).

---

13 New in the sense that these are newly recognised as being 'social', rather than that the risks themselves are new.

ECONOMIC DEVELOPMENT

This chapter would suggest that the 'logic of industrialisation' argument is more important than is often credited – especially in relation to the link between the level of economic development (whether measured in terms of GDP or industrialisation) and the level of welfare development. The evidence would suggest that there has been a clear link (with very limited exceptions) throughout the twentieth century between the level of economic development and that of welfare development (if not with the precise structure or timing of welfare measures). This macro-linkage might seem to be at odds with the emphasis on process tracing in Chapter 1, as while general arguments can be made as to why increased economic development might lead to higher levels of welfare development (as discussed in Chapter 2) it is difficult, if not impossible, to trace the precise mechanisms through which this effect happens. Nonetheless it is clear that such a relationship does exist. Indeed, a similar relationship can be seen between levels of economic development and democratisation, although again it is difficult to trace the precise processes which relate these two macro-processes (Przeworski et al., 1996; Boix and Stokes, 2003).

POPULATION AGEING

One part of the functionalist arguments relating to the development of the welfare state was that welfare spending was largely driven by population ageing. The level of older people in a society is likely to have an impact on the level of spending at that particular time: the more older people the more pensions will cost – all other things being equal. But this, of course, depends on the level of pensions and all other things rarely are equal. In fact, studies indicate that 'generosity of spending ... is a far more significant determinant of levels of pension spending than the age structure of the population' (Castles, 2004: 129). And obviously the link to total welfare spending is even more indirect. In fact, there is a very low correlation (0.2) between the old age ratio in the EU 15 countries and the level of spending on social protection (excluding Ireland, which has both a low proportion of older people and low overall welfare spending).

POLITICS

The impact of politics can be seen less in terms of levels of welfare spending than in terms of the structure of spending. Thus, amongst economically developed countries, we can distinguish over a long period between a Christian centrist group of countries and a social democratic group in terms of the structure of welfare services. The Christian centrist group tends, in general, to be more focussed on cash benefits, with lower levels of service employment and spending. Its cash benefits tend to be generous but more narrowly focussed and more categorical. In contrast the social democratic group was later to develop. Universalism was always a strong feature of its systems, but benefits were initially moderate in Scandinavian countries. The social democratic group only becomes Nordic in about 1980, with the United Kingdom falling out of the group and Finland becoming a member. The Southern group, however, is distinguished more by economic development than by politics.

In terms of the levels of spending, long-term left government is a sufficient but not necessary condition for high spending, in that all countries which have experienced long-term social democratic government are high welfare spenders – but so are many countries which have been ruled primarily by centrist parties. The caveat to this, however, is that the universe of long-term social democratic countries is very small and this argument could be seen as an example of Nordic exceptionalism rather than a general rule. In other words, one could make the argument that in the particular circumstances of the small, ethically homogenous Nordic countries, social democracy has succeeded in becoming (and remaining) politically hegemenous and building a strong welfare state. However, the failure of social democracy to achieve political hegemony outside four small Nordic countries questions the broader applicability of a social democracy–welfare state nexus. There are obviously detailed processes at work in political systems which impact on the structure of welfare development and these are considered in more detail in the case studies in Chapter 7.

GENDER

Unfortunately there is an absence of long-term data from which one can analyse the impact of gender on the development of European welfare states. The data presented here support the argument (advanced by Huber and Stephens, 2001) that there is a mutually reinforcing relationship in social democratic welfare states between higher levels of female employment and the development of public welfare services. More detailed country studies indicate that Christian centrist and social democratic welfare groupings are structured differently in terms of gender. Christian centrist welfare states tend to be based on the concept of the male breadwinner and to discourage female employment with (relatively generous) support being provided to women through dependency payments rather in their own right. In contrast, social democratic welfare states encourage female employment and the sharing (with both men and the state) of caring responsibilities and fund childcare and related services.

GLOBALISATION

Given the degree to which all countries are integrated into the world economic system, changes in that system can impact on welfare systems – primarily indirectly through factors such as rising unemployment or changes in labour force structures. However, there is little sign that the key indicators of globalisation – such as the level of trade – have a direct impact on welfare. The countries with the highest level of trade openness include Ireland, with the lowest level of welfare spending in the EU 15, and Belgium and the Netherlands, with some of the highest.

LABOUR MARKET CHANGE

Contrary to the findings of Iversen and Cusack (2000), there is little sign of a relationship between labour market change (deindustrialisation) and either levels or structures of welfare spending. There is little difference between the two main groups of countries in terms of average levels of deindustrialisation or levels of change over the period from 1960. Indeed, both Austria and Germany show significantly lower levels of deindustrialisation (and comparable levels of change) than the two smaller Christian centrist countries. The three Scandinavian countries begin with intermediate levels of deindustrialisation and change somewhat more over the period from 1960 to the mid-1990s, but this is not reflected in more rapid welfare growth. Finland's catch-up in terms of welfare spending might be, in part, accounted for by very high levels of labour market change in the 1960s. But the United Kingdom's levels of deindustrialisation broadly parallel its former social democratic partners up to the 1990s, while its welfare trajectory does not. Switzerland shows a lower level of deindustrialisation which might go some way to explain its lower levels of welfare spending, but its apparent convergence towards levels of welfare spending more in line with its levels of economic development is not related to any dramatic change in occupational structure.

However, the argument that welfare spending is related to labour market change is intuitively appealing and it may be that the apparent lack of relationship relates to the somewhat crude measure of labour market change utilised here. For example, costs arising from changes in the labour market may be exported through emigration to another country. Conversely, costs may be met through immigration, for example, the import of workers trained in a new area of expertise. Indeed, detailed studies such as analysis of responses to early retirement would suggest that structural labour market change is directly linked to welfare spending (Mares, 2003).

CONCLUSION

This chapter has summarised the development of European welfare states and has looked at the factors which have influenced that development. In Chapter 7 we will look in more detail at the recent development of welfare in five European countries with different welfare structures. This will allow a more detailed assessment of the micro-politics of welfare reform and will allow more examination of the processes which intervene between macro-level variables – such as changes in labour market structures and changes in the welfare state.

We have looked in some detail at the manner in which welfare states cluster, based on the structure of their welfare system (an issue which is discussed in more detail in Chapter 6). In line with most existing research, we identified Christian centrist and social democratic groupings and, in addition, a Southern group of welfare states.

- First, a Christian centrist grouping which appears in the post-Second World War period and remains in place to date with a core membership of Austria, Belgium and Germany. However, there is a considerable degree of variation amongst the countries of this grouping with both France and Italy only loosely (if at all) attached and the Netherlands appearing to be now on an exit trajectory from the group.
- Second, we found a social democratic grouping – again emerging post-War – led by the United Kingdom and including Sweden and Norway. Over time the United Kingdom drops out of this grouping and is replaced by Finland. Denmark, despite a quite different structure of benefits, arguably joins this grouping on the basis of its high level of services.
- Finally, only identifiable in the recent period for which more comparable data is available but perhaps existing also from the post-War period, we see a Southern European group with levels of spending which somewhat resemble the Christian centrist group but are structured somewhat differently.

There is also a liberal 'group' of one: the United Kingdom in the period from 1980. Ireland, while still showing affinities to the United Kingdom in terms of welfare structure, shows few similarities in terms of levels or structure of welfare spending. The CEE countries (for which data is available) also do not, to date, form any consistent group.

On the one hand we see the impact of policy legacies – such as the consistent clustering of Germany and Austria in the period from the late 1800s and their continued emphasis on a social insurance-based welfare state. On the other, we see considerable variation and movement in and out of groups – with the Netherlands, the United Kingdom and Finland being particular examples of this.

Summary

This chapter has:

- outlined the development of welfare states in Europe with a particular focus on the period from the late nineteenth century to date;
- broken welfare development down into specific periods including: the introduction of welfare schemes, 1880–1920; welfare state consolidation, 1920–1950; the golden era of welfare, 1950–1970; Welfare crisis, 1970–1980; and recent welfare developments, 1980–2000;
- examined the manner in which welfare states cluster and how these change over time;
- looked at the factors which have influenced the development of welfare states (and welfare state clusters) including economic development, politics, unionisation, globalisation and gender; and
- summarised the evidence to date on the influence of the different factors.

Discussion points

1 '[T]he battles behind the welfare state lay bare the structure and conflicts of modern society' (Baldwin, 1990). Discuss with reference to the early development of European welfare states.
2 Which factors do you think have been most important in the recent development of your national welfare state? And why?
3 'The strongest tendency over the past two decades has been a convergence toward what may, perhaps, most appropriately be described as a "steady-state" welfare state' (Castles, 2004). Do you agree?

Supplementary reading

There are a number of excellent studies of the development of welfare states which both outline the factual development and analyse the determinants behind such developments, including Flora and Heidenheimer (1981), Hicks (1999) and Huber and Stephens (2001). More recent debates on welfare retrenchment are set out in Pierson (2001). Pierson's views have been criticised in, for example, Korpi and Palme (2003).

SIX TYPOLOGIES OF WELFARE

This chapter examines the literature on typologies of welfare and looks at how these apply in a European context. It looks at the general debates about 'typologising', at the main typologies which have been proposed (in particular that of Esping-Andersen), at the criticisms which have been advanced of such typologies and at the defences of that approach. It also examines alternative approaches such as the 'families of nations' (Castles, 1993). It examines the extent to which typologies can inform our understanding of European welfare states and the extent to which 'actually existing' welfare states match the typologies.

WHY TYPOLOGIES?

Given the voluminous literature on typologies of welfare state in recent years, a question which has received only very limited attention is that of the precise role and value of typologies. As Arts and Gelissen (2002) point out, a key question is whether typologies based on ideal types have theoretical and empirical value. They argue that ideal types have no value in so far as they are goals in themselves, but only if they are the means to an end.

WEBER ON TYPOLOGIES

Max Weber has stated that 'sociology seeks to formulate type concepts and generalized uniformities of empirical process' in distinction to history which focuses on the causal analysis and explanation of individual actions, structures and personalities (1978: 19). He argues that 'an important consideration in the formulation of sociological concepts and generalizations is the contribution that sociology can make towards the causal explanation of some historically and culturally important phenomenon' (1978: 19–20). In this regard, 'sociological analysis both abstracts from reality and at the same time helps us to understand it, in that it shows us with what degree of approximation a concrete historical phenomenon can be subsumed' under theoretical concepts which are adequate on the level of meaning (1978: 20).

Weber argues that in order to give meaning to these terms 'it is necessary for the sociologist to formulate pure ideal types of the corresponding forms of action which in each case involve the highest possible degree of logical integration by virtue of their complete adequacy on the level of meaning' (1978: 20). However, precisely because of this fact, Weber accepts that it is seldom if ever that a real phenomenon can be found which corresponds exactly to one of the ideal types. He goes on to add that it is often convenient for the sociologist 'to employ average types of an empirical statistical character, concepts which do not require methodological discussion' (1978: 20). It is important to distinguish between these two forms of ideal type or typology: first, a typology which seeks to explain a concrete historical phenomenon in terms of theoretical concepts, and, second, typologies of a statistical nature. The distinction is not perhaps sufficiently made in many studies of the welfare state, and many studies simply produce typologies of a statistical nature which are not explained by any underlying theoretical concept.

WHEN ARE TYPOLOGIES USEFUL?

Having looked at what typologies are, or should be, when can typologies play a useful role? Arts and Gelissen (2002: 140) suggest that they can do so in three circumstances. The first is if the typology is 'a valid and reliable instrument for classifying welfare states' (2002: 140). The second is that the typology 'is a means to an end – explanation – and not an end in itself' (2002: 140). Thus, typologising is useful if it is not simply used to produce clusters of welfare states but to explain cross-national variations in the type of welfare state which exist. Esping-Andersen has argued that 'the point of generalization is economy of explanation – to be able to see the forest rather than the myriad unique trees. The danger is that the resulting forest bears little if any resemblance to reality' (1997: 179). The third condition for accepting the validity of typologising is that welfare state theorising is still at an early stage. We can safely accept this one of the three conditions but, in the concluding section of this chapter, we will return to examine the extent to which some key typologies meet the first two conditions.

TYPOLOGIES OF WELFARE STATE

One of the first typologies of welfare state was drawn up by Richard Titmuss (1974), although it is fair to say that he did not develop this typology in any great detail. As Titmuss put it, 'the purpose of model-building is not to admire the architecture of the building, but to help us to see some order in all the disorder and confusion of facts, systems and choices concerning certain areas of our economic and social life' (1974: 30). Titmuss suggested that three welfare models could be identified. The first, or residual welfare model, was based on the premise that an individual's needs are properly met through the private market or the family. Under this model the state only interfered where these institutions broke down and then only temporarily. The second Titmuss described as the 'industrial achievement-performance model'. This model incorporated a significant role for welfare state institutions as adjuncts of the economy and held that needs should be met on the basis of merit, work performance and productivity. The third, or institutional re-distributive model, saw social welfare as a major integrated institution in society providing universal services outside the market on the principle of need.

THREE WORLDS OF WELFARE CAPITALISM

While there were a number of other attempts at categorising welfare states (for example, Mishra, 1977; Flora, 1986), the *locus classicus* of welfare state typologies has been Esping-Andersen's *The Three Worlds of Welfare Capitalism* (1990). Esping-Andersen's approach is important (not only because it has been so influential) because it did not simply rely on an empirical classification of welfare states but was based on a theory as to why welfare states took on a particular form. Esping-Andersen identified a number of 'welfare state-regimes', a concept which 'denotes the institutional arrangements, rules and understandings that guide and shape concurrent social-policy decisions, expenditure developments, problem definitions, and even the response-and-demand structure of citizens and welfare consumers' (1990: 80).

Welfare state regimes reflect 'historical institutionalisation that differ qualitatively between countries'. Esping-Andersen identified three regime types:

- First, 'the "liberal" welfare state, in which means-tested assistance, modest universal transfers or modest social-insurance plans predominate' (1990: 26). 'Benefits cater mainly to a clientele of low-income, usually working-class, state dependents' and 'progressive social reform has been severely circumscribed by traditional, liberal work-ethic norms' (1990: 26).
- Second, a conservative-corporatist type committed to 'the preservation of status differentials' and to 'the preservation of a traditional family-hood' (1990: 27). Such welfare regimes rely heavily on social insurance, while 'private insurance and occupational fringe benefits pay a truly marginal role' (1990: 27).

- Third, the social democratic regime type under which 'the principles of universalism and decommodification' are extended to the new middle classes. This regime pursues 'an equality of the highest standards' with 'all strata incorporated under one universal insurance scheme, yet benefits are graduated according to earnings' (1990: 27–8).

Esping-Andersen categorises welfare regimes according to the degree of decommodification, the extent of stratification and the public/private mix. By 'decommodification' is meant a situation when 'a service is rendered as a matter of right, and when a person can maintain a livelihood without reliance on the market' (1990: 22).

Kemeny (1995) has made the point that Esping-Andersen's categorisation of welfare regimes into liberal, corporatist and social democratic does not simply refer to types of welfare system but to 'theories of power'. Different types of welfare system (comprehensive, conservative and residual) arise from different welfare regimes (social democratic, corporatist and liberal respectively). A welfare regime is 'the product of a particular constellation of power in society' (1995: 89). A comprehensive welfare system arises from a social democratic welfare regime based on a corporatist compromise driven by a strong labour movement. It is 'the fruit of a class mobilization based on a coalition between working class and farm worker plus white collar interests' – a model of labour movement hegemony (1995: 93). The conservative welfare system is based on a 'corporatist power structure in which the major vested interests are concerted by means of a strong central state' (1995: 93). They are based on 'a less complete mobilization in which middle class loyalties are forged by segmenting welfare into a stratified system' (1995: 93–4). Residual welfare states are 'the product of weak middle class mobilization behind the welfare state, in which their interests are largely met by the market but a much-reduced welfare state is tolerated for the working classes' (1995: 94). A liberal welfare regime is thus one in which working class hegemony is weak or absent.

CRITICISMS OF THE THREE WORLDS

Returning to our earlier discussion, it can be seen that Esping-Andersen's is a theoretical rather than a statistical typology. Nonetheless, as Arts and Gelissen have emphasised, it is important that the theoretically driven typology should be a reliable instrument for classifying welfare states. There have been a number of criticisms of Esping-Andersen's approach, both from an empirical and a theoretical perspective. There have also been a number of proposals for alternative typologies, perhaps most notably the 'families of nations' approach advanced by Castles and his colleagues.

THREE WORLDS AND REAL WORLDS?

From a country point of view, there have been numerous criticisms of the allocation of particular countries to particular worlds and proposals for additional categories. This is, in large part, due to the fact that many countries in the original study fitted loosely if at all into the three worlds. Daly (2000: 53) suggests that seven of the original 18 countries studied by Esping-Andersen were 'obvious outliers'. Even Arts and Gelissen (2002), who defend Esping-Andersen's approach, suggest that consensus about categorisation exists on only three or four countries: the United States of America, Germany, Sweden and Norway.

In a European context, one of the main issues has been the categorisation of the Southern European countries. A number of authors have argued that these countries are sufficiently distinctive to constitute a different category of welfare state (Ferrera, 1996). The Netherlands has also proved a somewhat difficult country to classify. In their re-examination of Esping-Andersen's classification, Wildeboor Schut et al. (2001) argue that the Netherlands (originally categorised as corporatist) is a hybrid, not falling into any one of the three worlds (a position which Esping-Andersen appears largely to accept, 1999: 88), while Goodin et al. (1999) categorised the Netherlands as social democratic. In addition, studies of other areas of social policy have not always found a close match to the three worlds identified by Esping-Andersen, for example in relation to tax policy (Kemmerling, 2002), housing policy (Conley, 2000) or child income support (Wennemo, 1994; Bradshaw and Finch, 2002). Studies of broader social policy issues such as the establishment of children's rights and legislation in relation to divorce have also shown quite different affinities (Castles, 1993).

The criticisms outlined in the previous paragraphs include both theoretical and empirical criticisms of Esping-Andersen's approach. Some, particularly many cross-national studies of particular social policy areas, have formed statistical typologies and simply noted their mismatch with the three worlds rather than calling into account the theoretical underpinnings of the Esping-Andersen's approach. Others, however, including studies in relation to Southern Europe, have suggested that the empirical mismatch may arise because there are more than three theoretical worlds of welfare. Of course a further issue arises in relation to the Central and Eastern European countries which were only emerging into the worlds of welfare capitalism at the time when Esping-Andersen wrote his original book.

CRITICISMS FROM A GENDER PERSPECTIVE

A number of feminist critics have emphasised the extent to which the three worlds analysis ignores issues of gender. Drawing on Esping-Andersen's criteria of decommodification, stratification and the state–market relationship, Orloff (1993a) develops a framework for analysing the gender structure of welfare states. She criticises the decommodification criteria for making implicit assumptions about the sexual division of caring and domestic labour and for ignoring the different effects which so-called decommodifying benefits have on men and women. She argues that the stratification dimension should be expanded to consider the effects of the welfare state on gender relations, especially the treatment of paid and unpaid labour. She also argues for the expansion of the state–market dimension to include the manner in which countries organise the provision of welfare through families. Finally, as we have discussed in Chapter 4, she argues for the addition of two criteria to capture the effects of welfare states on gender relations: access to paid work and the capacity to form and maintain an autonomous household. Unfortunately, there do not appear to have been any studies which have attempted to use these five reworked criteria to categorise European welfare states.

However, Lewis (1992) has adopted a categorisation of welfare state based on the extent to which they are built around the 'male breadwinner concept', that is, the extent to which countries recognise women solely as wives and mothers or the extent to which women are also recognised as workers. She found that the United Kingdom, Ireland and Germany had a strong 'male breadwinner model', whereas France adopted a 'modified' breadwinner approach, facilitating women in employment to a much greater extent. Sweden, in contrast, was a weak breadwinner model, encouraging two-earner households. While this is a valuable attempt to incorporate a gender perspective into the categorisation of welfare states, a telling criticism of this particular approach has been made by Daly (2000: 54, 55, 58–9) who highlights both the conceptual difficulties around a dichotomous treatment of women as either mothers or workers and the practical difficulties created by the fact that most states will be towards the strong breadwinner end of the scale.

Subsequently, Sainsbury (1996, 1999) developed two contrasting ideal types of gender models of social policy: the male breadwinner and the individual models. These models include the state–market–family and stratification dimensions, but Sainsbury also emphasises the importance of gender and familial ideologies as a key variation and highlights whether social rights are 'familialised' or individualised. Sainsbury accepted, however, that an analytical scheme based only on two contrasting types was difficult to apply empirically, and proposed an additional ideal type in subsequent work (1999), which differentiated between women's entitlement as wives and as mothers.

In a recent attempt to incorporate gender into mainstream analysis, Korpi (2000) has sought to combine gender and class in an analysis of patterns of inequalities in different types of welfare states in 18 countries. Korpi outlined a threefold typology of policy institutions likely to be of relevance for gender inequality in terms of labour force participation: a general family support model, a dual earner support and a market-oriented model. The general family support model was found to include most Continental European countries (Belgium, Germany, France, Italy, Austria) as well as Ireland. The dual earner support model included the Nordic countries, while the market oriented model identified those countries commonly identified as liberal (in European terms, the United Kingdom and Switzerland).

However, despite the criticisms from a gender perspective, Esping-Andersen (1999) has largely maintained his original approach and his adherence to the three worlds, albeit now incorporating family policies into his analysis.

FAMILIES OF NATIONS

One alternative approach, which seeks to retain the power of explanatory and theoretically driven typologies, while maintaining a greater degree of sensitivity to both national variations and to variations in typologies in different policy areas, is the 'families of nations' approach advanced by Castles and his colleagues (Castles, 1993). Castles has argued that it is possible 'to identify distinct *families of nations*, defined in terms of shared geographical, linguistic, cultural and/or historical attributes and leading to distinctive patterns of public policy outcomes' (1993: xiii). Thus, this approach is different from Esping-Andersen's, which focuses primarily on the balance of power between different classes in society and the consequent political coalitions.

Castles argues that 'some of the more important policy similarities between groups of nations and their differences from other groups may be attributable as much to history and culture and their transmission and diffusion amongst nations as to the immediate impact of the economic, political and social variables that figure almost exclusively in the contemporary public policy literature' (1993: xv). However, power structures are also recognised as one possible basis for affinity (Therborn, 1993: 336). The families of nations approach is also somewhat more flexible than the three worlds, recognising that 'nations can simultaneously belong to more than one family' (1993: xxi). It questions the 'assumption that all that is particularistic to individual nations or groupings must be set aside, or rather disaggregated into more generalized components' (1993: xiv).

In terms of welfare states, Castles (1998: 8–9; see also Castles and Mitchell, 1993) identifies four families:

• an English-speaking family including, in Europe, Ireland and the United Kingdom, united by language and common political and legal traditions;
• a Nordic family with a closely interlinked history, a common legal tradition and, with the exception of Finland, closely related languages;
• a continental Western European group of Austria, Belgium, France, Germany, Italy and the Netherlands with a historical legacy of dynastic links, cultural and religious similarities and a high degree of policy diffusion; and
• a Southern European family of Greece, Portugal and Spain sharing affinities as part of the Mediterranean cultural world and due to their late economic, political and social modernisation.

DO EUROPEAN WELFARE STATES MATCH THE 'THREE WORLDS'?

Before coming to any conclusions as to the extent to which existing typologies reliably classify welfare states, it may be useful to examine the level and structure of welfare spending and the distributional and poverty outcomes. Details in relation to the level of social expenditure in European countries are set out in Chapter 5. In that chapter, we identified four current groupings of welfare state (social democratic, Christian centrist, Southern and the single-member liberal 'group'). But we saw that these groupings were quite loose, with a number of countries only loosely attached to specific groupings and with changes in group membership over time. In the remainder of this chapter we look in more detail at welfare state spending and outcomes to examine whether these groupings are representative of ideal types.

WELFARE SPENDING

As we have seen, there is a significant variation in social expenditure between European countries. From the perspective of typologies, looking at gross public spending we can see a certain match between low spending Southern countries and higher spending Northern

Europeans. There is, however, little distinction between corporatist and social democratic countries on the basis of spending alone. The similarity in terms of total expenditure is consistent with Esping-Anderson's theory that different welfare regimes will use spending in different ways. However, there is a better match with the three worlds in terms of the structure of spending, that is, the extent to which this is funded by taxation as opposed to social insurance contributions and the extent to which benefits paid are means tested as opposed to paid on a contributory or universal basis (data from Eurostat for 2002). The Nordic countries (with the exception of Finland) are distinctive, with both very low levels of means testing (3 to 4 per cent of all benefits) and comparatively low levels of funding coming from social insurance contributions (with from 47 to 62 per cent of income coming from general taxation). The Christian centrist countries have low to average levels of means testing (3 to 11 per cent) and relied more on support from social insurance contributions (with only about 30 per cent of receipts from taxation). The southern countries were broadly similar with means testing, making up 8 to 12 per cent of spending and tax funding only 31 per cent of income on average. The CEE countries (Czech and Slovak republics, Hungary and Slovenia) have average levels of means testing (8 per cent) and again rely heavily on social insurance contributions. Ireland, and to a lesser extent the United Kingdom, show high levels of means testing (25 and 15 per cent respectively) combined with above average tax funding.

There has been a long-term trend for the importance of funding from the state to fall since the 1930s (particularly in relation to pension funding) (Sjöberg, 2000a). In the EU there has been some fall in the share of funding coming from contributions in the 1990s, from 66 per cent in 1990 to 60 per cent in 2002, reflecting the policy aim of shifting taxes away from labour, but this did not apply in all EU member states (European Commission, 2002: 28). There has not been a significant change in the degree of means testing in EU countries in the 1990s, with different trajectories being seen in different countries. Thus in terms of the structure of welfare spending, we see a broad match with the three worlds, with the social democratic countries generally having low levels of social insurance and means testing, Ireland and the United Kingdom low social insurance but average to high means testing, and continental countries high social insurance and low means testing. But this is unsurprising because most typologising starts from a structural perspective.

WELFARE STATE OUTCOMES

To what extent do welfare state outcomes in terms of income distribution and property reflect welfare regimes? Comparable data on income distribution and poverty are only relatively recently available but, rather than having to rely on welfare state inputs (at a macro or micro level), they provide important information as to what welfare regimes achieve in practice. Comparative studies of income distribution have shown a general tendency for income inequality to fall in line with economic development (at least in developed countries). The comparison of income distribution and GDP per capita for EU countries shows that there is a strong relationship between the level of wealth of a country and its level of income inequality (see Figure 5.1). Mitchell (1991) used data from the Luxembourg Income Study (LIS) for 1980 and 1985 to examine the relationship between income and inequality for 10 OECD countries. She did not find a close correlation between welfare outcomes and the three worlds in terms of income redistribution. While Sweden and Norway generally performed well on a range of indicators and the United States of America performed consistently poorly, a number of countries (in particular the United Kingdom) had outcomes which were not consistent with a three world categorisation.

Table 6.1 sets out data from the LIS for income inequalities (utilising the Gini co-efficient) in countries for which comparative data is available for the period from 1980 to 1995 (or 2000 where this is available). This data looks only at the final outcomes rather than at the redistributive impact of the welfare state. Of course, the welfare state, while a very important factor, is not the only factor to affect income distribution (Bradley et al., 2003).

Box 6.1: The Gini co-efficient

The Gini co-efficient is one of the most commonly used summary indicators of income distribution. The measure gives a value between 0 and 1: the closer to 0 the closer the income distribution is to perfect equality.

The broad picture presented by this data confirms that found independently by the OECD, that is, that while there was no generalised trend in the distribution of income, inequality had risen in about half of the countries and that no country showed an 'unambiguous decrease in inequality' (Förster and d'Ercole, 2005). As can be seen, in 1980 the two social democratic countries for which data is available had the lowest levels of income inequality, followed by a largely indistinguishable group of countries. Switzerland and Spain were the most unequal countries, although in the Spanish case this was related to its level of socio-economic development at that time.

Table 6.1   Income inequality, 1980s to 2001

	1980	1985	1995	2000	2001
Austria		0.227	0.277	0.260	0.27
Belgium		0.227	0.250	0.277	0.28
Denmark		0.254	0.263		0.22
Finland		0.209	0.217	0.247	0.24
France	0.288	0.298	0.288		0.27
Germany	0.244	0.268	0.272	0.264	0.25
Hungary			0.323	0.295	
Ireland		0.328	0.336	0.323	0.29
Italy		0.306	0.290	0.338	0.29
Netherlands		0.256	0.253	0.248	0.26
Norway	0.223	0.233	0.238	0.251	
Poland		0.271	0.318	0.293	
Spain	0.318		0.353	0.340	0.33
Sweden	0.197	0.218	0.221	0.252	0.24
Switzerland	0.309		0.307	0.280	
United Kingdom	0.270	0.303	0.344	0.345	0.31

Source: LIS (1980–2000; data is for the year closest to the date); Eurostat (2001).

By 1985, the social democratic group (except Denmark) remained the most equal but were joined by Austria and Belgium. They were followed by the remaining corporatist countries (except France) and by Denmark. The United Kingdom, Ireland and Italy showed the highest levels of inequality. In 1995, the Nordic countries (again excluding Denmark) showed the lowest levels of income inequality. They were followed by the corporatist group Denmark and Poland. Switzerland, Hungary, Ireland, Spain and the United Kingdom produced the most unequal outcomes.

More recent LIS data are not yet available for all countries. However, data are available for 15 EU countries up to 2001. While the different database does not allow a comparison in trends over time, it does allow for a recent categorisation of welfare states in terms of outcomes. This data shows that the Nordic countries together with Germany, Austria and the Netherlands perform best in terms of income equality. These are followed by a group at about average levels of Belgium, France, Italy and Luxembourg. The remaining Southern countries (Spain, Greece and Portugal), Ireland and the United Kingdom bring up the rear.

Thus, while as Mitchell found with the earlier data, there is some correlation with predicted welfare regimes and welfare outcomes (low inequality in most Nordic countries, high inequality in some Southern and some liberal countries), there is again a considerable number of countries which do not correspond to their ideal type, and there is also considerable movement over the 15 years. In fact, the 'liberal' grouping

Table 6.2   Poverty rates in Europe, 2001

	Pre-transfer	Post-transfer	Reduction %
Belgium	38	13	66
Denmark	36	10	72
Germany	39	11	72
Greece	39	20	49
Spain	37	19	49
France	40	15	63
Ireland	36	21	42
Italy	42	19	55
Netherlands	36	11	69
Austria	38	12	68
Portugal	37	20	46
Finland	30	11	63
Sweden	34	9	74
United Kingdom	40	17	58
EU 15	39	15	62

Source: Eurostat, 2001

only emerges more clearly in the period after 1980 with the widening of the income distribution in the United Kingdom. It is worth reporting the alternative hypothesis of a simple link between income inequality and the level of national income. There is a close negative correlation between levels of income per capita and income inequality for European countries (except Switzerland) in each of the years (1980: –0.79; 1985: –0.66; 1995: –0.67; 2001: –0.66).[1] While the focus here is on European welfare states, it is worth noting that this relationship disappears when Australia, Canada and the United States are included. This finding suggests that, in terms of welfare outcomes, there may be more in the notion of a European welfare state than the three worlds would suggest.

The development of the European Community Household Panel (ECHP) has allowed a detailed examination of the impact of different national welfare regimes and poverty dynamics. As in the case of income distribution, poverty measures tend to be closely correlated to GDP per capita.[2] It is arguable that there is no particularly strong clustering of poverty outcomes when regard is had to a country's level of economic development. Poverty data from the ECHP for

---

1 Switzerland is a noticeable outlier in this relationship and is excluded in the calculation of the correlation.

2 Income poverty and persistent poverty, at 60 per cent of median income, in the period 1994–1997 show correlations of –0.87 and –0.86 respectively with per capita GDP in 1996.

2001 allow us to examine both the pre- and post-transfer levels of poverty and the national effectiveness in reducing poverty. Bearing in mind the fact that the pre-transfer figure is a hypothetical one and can arguably be influenced by taxes and transfers (Kim, 2000), the picture we find for pre-transfer poverty is that poverty would have been highest in Italy and lowest in Finland and Sweden. The remaining countries cluster closely around the EU average. Looking at the post-tax and -transfer position, the Nordic countries, Germany and the Netherlands have the lowest poverty levels (9 to 11 per cent) followed by Belgium and Austria (12 to 13 per cent). France is at the average (15 per cent) while the UK is somewhat above the average (17 per cent) and Ireland, Italy, Spain, Greece and Portugal have the highest poverty levels (19 to 21 per cent).

In terms of poverty reduction, Sweden stands out as the most effective country, reducing poverty by 74 per cent. This is followed by a large group of countries which reduce poverty by between 63 to 72 per cent (Belgium, Denmark, Germany, France, the Netherlands, Austria and Finland). Italy and the United Kingdom reduce poverty by 55 to 58 per cent while Ireland, Greece, Portugal and Spain reduce poverty by less than 50 per cent.

A recent study has looked at the effectiveness of different member states in reducing poverty (Maitre et al., 2002). It did not find any clear relationship between the three worlds and welfare outcomes. As can be seen in Table 6.3, a broadly corporatist group (Austria, Luxembourg and the Netherlands) cluster together with poverty levels of 25 per cent and poverty reduction of over 50 per cent but

Table 6.3   Effectiveness of welfare payments on household income poverty, 1996

Countries	% of poor households before transfers	% of poor households moved out of poverty by transfers
Portugal Italy Greece Germany	<25 per cent	<35 per cent
Austria Luxembourg Netherlands	25 per cent	55–58 per cent
Ireland United Kingdom Spain	28–30 per cent	43–47 per cent
Finland Denmark	25–35 per cent	73–76 per cent

with Germany, the prototypical corporatist state, missing. But, in fact, three 'low spending' countries – Ireland, the United Kingdom and Spain – are quite close in outcomes to this group, having slightly larger initial poverty and reducing it slightly less. Finland and Denmark have quite different initial poverty levels but are brought together by their remarkable effectiveness – reducing poverty by three-quarters. A group involving a number of Southern countries (Portugal, Italy and Greece), but also including Germany, has low initial poverty (less than 25 per cent) but a low level of poverty reduction (one-third or less). Again, while one can see (as one would expect) patterns which would be predicted by the three (or four) worlds approach (high poverty reduction in Nordic countries, low poverty reduction in some Southern countries), there are again a significant number of exceptions.

CONCLUSION

Returning to the issue of typologies, in principle a theoretically informed typology of welfare states (which Esping-Andersen's undoubtedly is) has much merit. Such an approach does not seek simply to cluster together welfare states based on different criteria but, beginning from a theoretical framework as to the factors influencing the development of welfare states, seeks to use typologies to develop these theories. As we have seen in this chapter, the three worlds do highlight affinities in welfare systems in relation to factors such as the extent to which a particular system relies on public as opposed to private spending, social insurance as opposed to tax-based funding, or means-tested and insurance-based entitlement. However, it is arguable that the three worlds approach is over-inclusive. A strong case can be made that the Southern countries take a sufficiently different approach to welfare, both qualitatively as well as quantitatively, to be recognised as a theoretically different regime.

Returning to Arts and Gelissen's three conditions for accepting typologising, it has already been said that we must accept the third condition, that welfare state theorising is still at an early stage. We can also, in the case of Esping-Andersen, accept the second condition, that the typology is a means to an end, that is, explanation, and not an end in itself. However, one could question the extent to which the three worlds are a valid and reliable instrument for classifying welfare states and the degree to which they trade off economy of explanation for the important differences which exist between welfare states.

In addition, the criticisms of the three worlds from a gender perspective have considerable validity. The original construction of the three worlds did not have particular regard to the manner in which gender structures welfare states and the impact that welfare states have in return on the gender division of labour. Nor was Esping-Anderson's (1999) subsequent reconsideration (which took on board the criticisms but ended up with the same answer) very convincing. However, those authors critical of Esping-Anderson have not yet developed a convincing gender based typology of welfare states. Indeed, while it is clear that gender has played an important role in structuring welfare states, it is not necessarily clear that the manner in which it has done so breaks down into typologies that match the class based typologies which underlie the three worlds.

An alternative approach, which retains the theoretical underpinning but allows more flexibility, recognising that 'the kinship of nations is multi-linear, over-layered and subject centred', is the families of nations approach. While this approach is underpinned by theory, it is not really an ideal type in the Weberian sense, falling somewhere mid-way between the strict theoretical construction of an ideal type and the statistical grouping. It may be that a flexible approach, akin to the families of nations, which, while analysing the theories of power and social systems of production underlying particular welfare states, also recognises importance of history, gender and culture, may be a more reliable instrument for classifying welfare states and thus may compensate in validity and reliability for what it loses in economy of explanation.

Summary

This chapter has:

- outlined the role and purpose of typologies;
- discussed key welfare state typologies, in particular the 'three worlds' developed by Esping-Andersen;
- outlined criticisms of this approach and an alternative 'families of nations' categorisation; and
- looked at the extent to which welfare states match the typologies in terms of welfare spending and structure and in terms of inequality and poverty outcomes.

Discussion points

1 Classification is a condition for cognition and not cognition itself; cognition in turn dispels classification (Adorno and Horkheimer, 1972). Discuss.
2 Economy of explanation in Esping-Andersen's *The Three Worlds of Welfare Capitalism* is more important for the study of welfare states than the fact that some welfare states are difficult to classify under this approach. Discuss.

3   How would you classify your national welfare state?
4   What are the key differences between the Three Worlds and the Families of Nations approach?

Supplementary reading

Weber (1978, see also Weber, 1949) provides an important discussion of the role of typologies. The most influential book on welfare typologies is undoubtedly Esping-Andersen (1990, see also 1999). A recent defence of Esping-Andersen's approach is Arts and Gelissen (2002). An alternative approach based on 'families of nations' is set out in Castles (1993).

SEVEN COUNTRY STUDIES

This chapter provides an overview of current welfare regimes in a number of contrasting European countries. Each country system is outlined using a common analytical framework. Building on the description of the development of European welfare states in Chapter 5 and the discussion of typologies in Chapter 6, the purpose of this chapter is to give a more detailed account of recent developments (over the period from about 1980 to 2005) in a number of key European welfare states. These are not intended to be 'representative', but they are intended to be indicative of the different 'families' of welfare state which exist within Europe.

COUNTRIES SELECTED

The countries have been selected to show the range of different types of welfare state and the different approaches to the development of welfare which exist in Europe today. In so far as possible, countries have been chosen from different 'worlds of welfare' and 'families of nations'. The countries which will be outlined in detail are:

- *Czech Republic* While most Central and Eastern European countries share common policy legacies from their period as part of the Soviet Union or, more loosely, the Soviet bloc, there is considerable variation between the different countries and many are in a state of considerable policy flux. One could not, at this time, argue that the CEE countries make up a coherent world of welfare or even, in any strong sense of the term, a family of nations. The Czech Republic is one of the best-documented CEE countries and serves as an interesting example of the type of issues facing CEE (and EU accession) countries.
- *The Netherlands* The Netherlands, as we have seen in earlier chapters, does not fall clearly into any world of welfare. It has sometimes been seen as a hybrid, falling between the conservative-corporatist and social democratic worlds. However, our analysis has highlighted its affinities with the Christian centrist group of countries. Currently it is one of the leading European countries

in the restructuring of the welfare state and has changed its welfare trajectory dramatically in recent decades. Indeed, it could be seen as identifying a new trajectory for other Christian centrist countries. For that reason it warrants particular attention.

- *Spain*   We have argued in Chapters 5 and 6 that Southern countries are sufficiently different – both in qualitative and quantitative terms – to be recognised as a separate family of welfare. However, there is considerable variation between the different Southern welfare states. Spain, as a large, economically less-developed, semi-peripheral country, provides an interesting example of a Southern European approach to welfare.
- *Sweden*   Sweden is the archetypal representative of the social democratic (or Nordic) model of welfare and is included here to provide an overview of developments in this particular family type (albeit that, as in all 'families', the closer one looks the more differences emerge between different countries). Sweden is the largest and arguably the most 'social democratic' of the Nordic family.
- *United Kingdom*   The main (if not only) representative of the 'liberal' world or the Anglo 'family of nations' in Europe. The United Kingdom adopts a significantly different approach to welfare policy to most continental European countries and is perhaps more influenced by US policy debates.

In this section we outline comparative data on the five countries in terms of their demographics, economy and welfare states.

SIZE AND ECONOMIC DEVELOPMENT

Looking first at the size and wealth of the five countries (Table 7.1), we see that the countries range from one of the largest in Europe (the United Kingdom) to the moderately sized Sweden and Czech Republic – although not including any of the many small (2–4 million). From the perspective of economic development, we also have a range from the Czech Republic – one of the relatively poor (albeit one of the more developed) new members of the EU – to countries at the higher end of the European wealth table such as the Netherlands. We do not include either very wealthy countries (such as oil-rich Norway), nor any of the very poor European countries (such as Albania).

DEMOGRAPHICS

There is considerable variation in terms of the old age ratio (that is, the section of the population over 65 as a percentage of the working

Table 7.1   Economy and demography, c. 2002

	Population	GDP	GDP per capita billion $	Economic growth (1990–2003)*	Trade openness	Old age ratio	Fertility rate
Czech Republic	10.3	154.1	15108	2.3	113.4	19.8	1.17
Netherlands	16.1	468.4	29009	2.4	48.7	20.1	1.71
Spain	40.5	908.5	22406	2.7	42.7	24.8	1.25
Sweden	8.9	243.3	27625	1.8	62.2	27.1	1.65
United Kingdom	59.8	1654.7	27948	2.2	39.9	24.1	1.64

*CZ = 1994–2003

Source: OECD; Eurostat

age population) and the fertility rate (Table 7.1). As can be seen, the Netherlands has a comparatively low old age ratio of 20 per cent (only Ireland is lower amongst EU countries), while Sweden is in the upper end of the range with a ratio of 27 per cent (joint highest in the EU with Italy). In terms of fertility we see a split – which is generally representative – between the Northern European countries which have higher fertility rates – albeit below replacement levels – and the Southern and CEE countries which have very low fertility rates. Although fertility rates have fallen generally over the recent decades, in the Southern and CEE countries there has been a particularly sharp fall and fertility rates have dropped from above replacement levels in 1980 to the lowest in Europe. Combined with already ageing populations this gives rise to particular long-term pressures on the welfare state. Births outside marriage vary enormously from about one-fifth or one-quarter in Spain, the Netherlands and the Czech Republic to 40 per cent in the United Kingdom and a high of 56 per cent in Sweden (the highest in Europe with the exception of Iceland).

ECONOMY

Table 7.1 also sets out details of the countries' economies including the level of economic growth and trade openness. As can be seen, economic size varies enormously from the small Czech Republic to the United Kingdom. The economic performance of countries has varied over the recent decade. The Czech Republic saw initial rapid recovery from the transition but turned to negative economic growth in the late 1990s before again returning to reasonable levels of growth. The Netherlands has experienced generally strong growth during the 1990s but has seen low or negative growth in the new Millennium. Spain experienced generally strong growth over the period (with the exception of the early 1990s). Sweden also experienced negative growth in the early 1990s, recovered well, but has again experienced slow growth since 2000. Finally, the United Kingdom has generally experienced reasonable growth over the period (2–3 per cent).

In terms of trade openness, there is a general tendency for smaller countries to depend more on trade than larger population centres and this can be seen in our data (Table 7.1). Both Spain and the United Kingdom have lower levels of trade openness (imports and exports as a percentage of GDP), while Sweden is somewhat higher and the Netherlands and Czech Republic have the highest levels. The Netherlands (with Belgium and Ireland) has a long history of high trade openness, but this is a recent phenomenon in the case of the CEE countries.

LABOUR FORCE

Table 7.2 sets out details on labour force structure and employment levels. As can be seen, Sweden, the Netherlands and the United Kingdom all have typically post-industrial employment structures, with very low numbers employed in agriculture and about three-quarters of the labour force employed in services. The Czech Republic retains a much more industrial workforce, with only half the working population employed in services. Spain falls between the two, with two-thirds now employed in services. It should be noted that several European countries such as Poland or the Ukraine still have a much higher level of the population engaged in agriculture (c. 20 per cent).

Table 7.2   Labour force, 2001

	Employment	Unemployment	Female employment	Services	Industry	Agriculture
Czech Republic	68	7.3	58	55	40	5
Netherlands	74	2.7	66	65	21	3
Spain	58	11.3	43	62	31	7
Sweden	73	4.9	72	73	25	2
United Kingdom	71	5.1	63	73	25	2

Source: OECD; Eurostat, 2001

Employment rates overall are low in Spain at only 58 per cent, with the Netherlands and Sweden at the higher end of the spectrum at 75 per cent. Female employment varies from a low of only 43 per cent in Spain to about two-thirds in the three Northern countries. In Sweden this is largely full-time work, whereas in the Netherlands the high rate of female employment is achieved through high rates of part-time work. Unemployment is relatively low in all the five countries (at or below 5 per cent), with the exception of Spain where it is 11 per cent and the Czech Republic, which has seen unemployment grow to 7 per cent.

TRADE UNIONISATION AND CORPORATISM

There is significant variation in the countries' approach to unionisation and corporatism. Sweden has a high level of both – a long-standing feature of this country. The Czech Republic has a moderate level of unionisation, but as in many CEE countries trade union influence – damaged by its relationship with the former regime – it is weak. The Netherlands and the United Kingdom have rather low levels of unionisation, but Dutch trade unions retain more policy influence than their UK counterparts. Spain has a very low level of unionisation, although this arguably understates the influence of labour unions on welfare state development (Guillén, 1999).

WELFARE STATE

As set out in Table 7.3, there is a significant variation between countries in terms of general government revenue as a percentage of GDP, ranging from a high of 62 per cent in Sweden to a low of about 40 per cent in the Czech Republic, Spain and the United Kingdom. In terms of gross welfare spending, Sweden is clearly the highest spender at about 30 per cent of GDP, followed by the Netherlands and the United Kingdom at 22 per cent and with the Czech Republic and Spain spending 20 per cent. As we can see, there is not a strong relationship between the level of economic development and welfare spending for these five countries, with the richest – the Netherlands – coming in the mid table in terms of spending.

Table 7.3 Welfare state spending and structure, 2001

	Total government revenue	Welfare expenditure	Expenditure in PPS	% social insurance
Czech Republic	41	20.1	2986	75.4
Netherlands	46.5	21.8	6243	66.9
Spain	39.2	19.6	4179	69.2
Sweden	61.7	28.9	7780	52.5
United Kingdom	41.1	21.8	5906	50.0

Source: OECD; Eurostat, 2001

In terms of the structure of spending, the Netherlands and Spain fund most of their spending from social insurance contributions (about two-thirds) rather than general taxation and the bulk of their welfare spending is by way of contributory payments. In contrast, Sweden and the United Kingdom fund much more of their spending from general taxation (about 50 per cent), but only the United Kingdom has a high percentage of means-tested benefits.

Traditionally, social expenditure comparisons have been made on the basis of *gross public* social expenditure and it is on that basis that the above comparison is made. However, the OECD has recently carried out a number of groundbreaking studies to go behind this data and to look at expenditure on a *net* basis, that is, taking account both of tax deducted from public benefits and tax breaks for social purposes, and the inclusion of *private* social expenditure. The OECD looked at spending in 12 European countries where data was available for 1997 (Adema, 2001; see Table 7.4). On the basis of gross public social expenditure Sweden had one of the highest levels at 35.7 per cent (of GDP), whereas the Czech Republic was one of the lowest at 20.7 per cent per cent (the Netherlands 27.1 per cent and the United Kingdom 23.8 per cent – Spain was not included).

Table 7.4   Gross and net social expenditure, 1997

	Czech Republic	The Netherlands	Sweden	United Kingdom
Gross public social expenditure	21.7	27.1	35.7	23.8
Direct taxes	0	4.4	4.4	0.4
Indirect taxes	2.5	2.4	2.8	2.3
Tax breaks for social purposes	0	0.1	0	0.5
Mandatory private social expenditure	0	0.5	0.2	0.3
Voluntary social expenditure	0	3.3	1.9	3.2
Net total social expenditure	19.3	24.0	30.6	24.6

Source: Adema, 2001

Countries deduct, to a greater or lesser extent, direct taxes and social contributions from social benefits. The general trend found was that countries that had higher gross public social expenditure (as a proportion of GDP) deducted more by way of taxes than countries with lower gross expenditure (up to 4.4 per cent in the Netherlands and Sweden). Thus a proportion of the higher expenditure was 'clawed back' by way of taxes, bringing the net level of expenditure closer together. Countries also deduct indirect taxes on consumption purchased out of social benefits, although there was little variation between the four countries in this area.

Some countries put considerable emphasis on the use of the tax system for social purposes (or social-fiscal measures in the OECD's terms). For example, some countries provide for child tax allowances while others have cash benefits. There are definitional issues as to precisely what constitutes a tax expenditure and also a range of methodological issues as to how to cost tax expenditures. These are particularly acute in relation to pensions to such an extent that the OECD does not include pension tax expenditures in their calculations. The OECD found that countries with lower levels of gross public social expenditure tended to have higher levels of tax expenditures, again further narrowing the gap between the countries in terms of net public social expenditure. However, our four countries did not show significant levels of tax breaks (but recall that significant tax spending for pensions is *not* included). To public expenditure was added mandatory private social expenditure and voluntary private social expenditure. Mandatory private expenditure was a relatively small item in most countries. However, voluntary private expenditure was much more significant, varying up to 3.2–3.3 per cent of GDP in the Netherlands and the United Kingdom. Taking all these adjustments into account, the OECD found that the gap between high and low spenders for the total 12 countries narrowed significantly. In the case of our four countries, there was also some narrowing of the differential from 20.7–35.7 per cent to 19.3–30.6 per cent, with Dutch spending falling to 24 per cent and the United Kingdom rising somewhat to 24.6 per cent.

Table 7.5   Gender and household income, mid-1990s

	Gender gap	Income female-headed households containing older person	Gender gap older households
Netherlands	89	90	83
Sweden	86	92	94
United Kingdom	74	72	81

Source: Rake and Daly (2002). Gender gap is income of female-headed households as percentage of male-headed; income female-headed households containing older person is the mean income of this household type as a percentage of the overall mean; gender gap old households is income of sole older females as a percentage of sole males.

There have, to date, been limited studies of the impact of welfare states on gender. Rake and Daly (2002) have carried out a comparative study (drawing on LIS data) which includes three of our five countries. As set out in Table 7.5, there is a significant gap between the income of male- and female-headed households in all European countries. However, there is a significant difference between the Netherlands and Sweden (86–89 per cent) and the United Kingdom (74 per cent). In both the former countries, market income makes up close to 60 per cent of the income of female-headed households while the remaining 30 per cent consists of the impact of tax and transfer policies. In contrast, in the United Kingdom, the market income of female-headed households comes to less than 50 per cent and tax and transfer policies increase this by only 26 per cent (less than any other European country studied). Turning to households including an older person, a similar pattern is seen with female households receiving significantly less (as a percentage of the overall mean) than in the Netherlands and Sweden. In this case, however, this outcome results from both lower pensioner incomes for both genders and an about average gender gap (in terms of the overall countries included).

In the case studies that follow we look in more detail at the changing structures in the five welfare states, looking in particular at pensions, unemployment (and where relevant sickness and disability payments) and family policies. We also look at the gender impact of change but, unfortunately, comparative data is often not available in this area. For example, while it would have been useful to include data on childcare coverage for the five countries, reliable and comparable data on childcare coverage and accessibility are simply not yet available (Eurostat, 2003).

MEASURING WELFARE CHANGE

Before going on to discuss policy change in the period from 1980 to 2005 in each of the five countries, we need to discuss and define what we mean by – and how we measure – welfare change. There has been considerable discussion about the meaning of welfare state change and, in particular, the concept of retrenchment. As we have seen in Chapter 5, in the period to the 1970s, and indeed the 1980s, the trajectory of the welfare state – whether measured in terms of total spending or of SCIP data – was overall one of growth.[1] However, in the period since 1980 the trajectory of welfare development has been much more ambiguous. On the one hand, as we have seen in Chapter 5, welfare spending overall has increased. On the other, as we will see in this chapter, there have been reductions in the level of benefits or in the scope of schemes at some point in almost all European countries. There has been significant debate about the extent to which 'retrenchment' has occurred in European welfare states.

Box 7.1: Definitions of 'retrenchment'

Retrenchment is:

the process of shifting social provision in a more residualist direction (Pierson, 1994: 15)

political decisions which cut back, scale down, or curtail welfare-state benefits (Green-Pedersen, 2004)

---

1 Clearly there were periods – in particular the 1930s – and countries in which there was significant retrenchment.

Welfare retrenchment is much more difficult to define and assess than welfare growth. Welfare retrenchment is generally not universally politically popular and so governments are unlikely to trumpet their achievements in this regard. While most governments will have a financial assessment of changes in their welfare system, these will rarely be published in any systematic fashion. In addition, they are simply estimates which may be incorrect due to errors in calculation or due to a mis-estimate of the impact of the measure (for example, a reduction in spending in one policy area may simply lead to an equal increase in a different policy area). Ex-post facto evaluations of the impact of welfare cutbacks are, unsurprisingly, rarely commissioned by governments and it is difficult to disentangle the impact of a particular measure from the general 'noise' of social and economic change. In addition, welfare cutbacks are often counterbalanced by improvements in other areas which call for difficult judgements as to the overall impact of a range of measures.

Pierson (1996) has argued that an analysis of retrenchment should focus on both quantitative and qualitative changes in programmes (including the long-term impact of changes). He suggests that attention should be given to: significant increases in reliance on means-tested benefits; major transfers of responsibility to the private sector; and dramatic changes in benefit and eligibility rules that signal a qualitative reform of a particular programme. However, it is not clear why either increased means testing or privatisation should per se be considered to be 'retrenchment'. In subsequent work, Pierson (2001) has suggested that we need to move beyond a simple dichotomous notion of welfare change as 'more–less' and that we should focus on three different dimensions of retrenchment, namely re-commodification, control of costs and recalibration. Although Pierson has, in principle, eschewed any reliance on simple expenditure figures, his overall analysis of retrenchment has been criticised by both Clayton and Pontussen (1998), who argue that more attention should be given to the provision of public welfare services (by way of the numbers employed in the area) and by Korpi and Palme (2003) and Allan and Scruggs (2004), who both argue for more attention to replacement rates. All argue that there has been a greater degree of retrenchment on the basis of their preferred indicators than allowed by Pierson. Hacker (2004) has also made the important point that, in looking at retrenchment, we need to examine not only changes in existing policies but the extent to which policies have (or have not) evolved to meet new needs.

Overall, the discussion of retrenchment has raised more questions than it has answered (Green-Pedersen, 2004; Powell, 2004). Much work has suggested that retrenchment can be measured only through very detailed assessment of individual policy changes in national welfare states and the application of somewhat subjective judgements as to what constitutes retrenchment. It may be better to eschew the concept of retrenchment in the first order analysis of welfare state change and to look at what has happened in the aggregate in terms of welfare spending, numbers entitled and welfare outcomes. Having established what has actually happened, judgements can be made as to whether or not the balance of developments can be categorised as retrenchment or restructuring, focussing particularly on policy outcomes (rather than policy inputs) in making these judgements. A distinction has been drawn between 'parametric' reforms which 'aim to maintain the basic structure of the existing system while attempting, through changes in parameters, to influence the costs, financing or incentive structure of the scheme in order to adjust it' and 'more radical systemic reforms' (European Commission, 2001b: 177). While the line between parametic and systemic reforms can sometimes be somewhat unclear, it may be a useful distinction to adopt in assessing the impact of change. This is the approach adopted in this chapter.

COUNTRY STUDIES

In this section we will look closely at the individual welfare state systems of each of the five countries.

CZECH REPUBLIC

DESCRIPTION

The Czech Republic is one of the smaller European countries, with a population of about 10 million. In comparison with the EU15, the Czech GDP per capita is rather low but it has one of the higher GDP per capita levels of the accession countries. As in all the other transition countries, GDP dropped sharply in the early 1990s but recovered strongly after that with comparatively low levels of unemployment for much of the 1990s. The Czech Republic had a number of advantages in the early 1990s in that it started with a relatively large GDP per capita, a very equal income distribution and a relatively high level of state capacity. However, unlike many of its neighbours, the Czech economy ran into difficulties in the late 1990s with unemployment rising to close to 10 per cent.

POLITICAL BACKGROUND

The Czech political system is bicameral, with a House of Deputies elected by proportional representation and a directly elected Senate. The Czech system requires a party to get a minimum 5 per cent of the vote in order to be represented in parliament (a requirement which has, to date, prevented the Pensioners Party from obtaining representation). The first democratic elections in the then Czechoslovakia were won by the Civic Forum. However, the disintegration of this party led to the establishment of a Civic Democratic Party (ODS)-led coalition after the 1992 elections. The ODS – a conservative party led by Vaclav Klaus – coalesced with the Civic Democratic Alliance (ODA) and the Christian Democratic Union–Czechoslovak People Party (KDU-ČSC). The election of quite different political groupings in the Czech Republic and Slovakia, where left-wing parties took power, was one of the factors contributing to the break-up of Czechoslovakia into the Czech and Slovak Republics on 1 January 1993. The Klaus-led government continued in power after the 1996 elections, but as a minority government. Political pressures led to the disintegration of this government in 1997. Following a short-lived technocrat government, the 1998 elections saw the Czech Social Democratic Party (ČSSD) taking power as a minority government with the agreement of the ODS subject to consultation on any major policy changes. In the 2002 elections the ČSSD retained power but this time in a coalition with the KDU-ČSC and a small liberal party, the Union of Freedom (US). The ČSSD has remained in power to 2005 albeit with several changes of Prime Minister and amid considerable political instability.

WELFARE STATE

The 1989 Czechoslovak welfare system shared common features with most of the other CEE transition countries including a tax-funded pension system for all workers with a relatively low pensions age. The Czechoslovak government established a 'Scenario for social reform' which proposed the establishment of a comprehensive health and social insurance system and a means-tested system of social assistance (Potůček, 1997). However, the election of the ODS government in 1992 gradually led to a shift in priorities in many areas.

PENSIONS

The Czech Republic is unlike many other CEE countries in that it has not introduced a World Bank-supported mandatory privatised pension system (Mácha, 2002; Müller, 2002a; 2002b). A number of changes to the existing pension system – including a switch to a contributory system and the abolition of special privileges – were made in the early 1990s. The original 'Scenario' had favoured a classic Bismarckian pension system. However, this began to be questioned under the conservative ODS government. The ODS was never strongly committed to pension privatisation and, unlike many other

CEE countries, there was no immediate fiscal crisis to drive pension change. Vaclav Klaus' preferred strategy was a slow reduction in public pension rates to low levels, thereby encouraging the use of voluntary private pension schemes (Müller, 2002b: 11). Indeed, pension replacement rates did fall in the 1990s and private pension funds were created in 1994. In addition, significant parametric reform of the pension system was introduced in 1995. First the pension age was raised over time from 60 to 62 for men and from 53–58 to 57–61 for women (women's pension age depends on the number of children). In addition the pension was restructured into a basic pension and an earnings related element with the level of the latter to be calculated over a 30-year period (rather than over the best five years). However, the 30-year rule was to be phased in over time in the period to 2016. The 1995 legislation sparked major opposition and street protest from the trade unions movement and, somewhat in contradiction of the original objectives, access to early retirement was eased to compensate for the rise in retirement age.

Pension privatisation was considered by the short-lived technocrat government in 1997–1998 but was quickly rejected by the ČSSD government which came to power in 1998. The ČSSD prepared a proposal for pension reform based on parametric change but this was not agreed in parliament and pension reform did not progress pending the outcome of the 2002 elections. The ČSSD ruled out both privatisation and further significant increases in retirement age (Král, 2004). Instead it relied on parametric reform – such as tightening of early retirement pensions in 2001 – and consideration of a switch to a notional defined contribution basis to be implemented over a period of time. However, different views within the coalition – with the US favouring mandatory private savings – and government instability have made for slow progress.

One of the interesting questions is why the Czech Republic has followed a different path to many of its other CEE neighbours. In the early 1990s, the lack of fiscal crisis meant that key national actors (such as the Ministry for Finance) did not prioritise the issue and international bodies (such as the World Bank) did not have any leverage to press for implementation of its policies (Müller, 2002a; 2002b). In addition, the ODS never favoured pension privatisation (though nor did many of the ruling parties which introduced such policies elsewhere). In the late 1990s when greater fiscal pressures began to develop – due to employment and economic downturn – the ČSSD was in power and had given strong commitments against privatisation. It has also been suggested that the experience of privatisation of industries has made Czech actors (and its public) skeptical about the benefits of capital markets.

Currently notional defined contributions are under serious consideration. These would have the effect of significantly reducing the element of redistribution by reducing the replacement rate for those on lower incomes. It has been argued that this can be counteracted by the establishment of a guaranteed minimum pension but, of course, in so far as this is sufficiently high to compensate for losses, it will not save any money and in so far as it is not, it will reduce the element of redistribution. One of the arguments for the NDC approach is that the current high level of replacement rates means that lower paid persons retire at the earliest possible opportunity, but this would appear to be an argument for a higher retirement age. In 2004 a pension reform process was established involving political parties and government agencies. Their proposals are being examined by a working group whose report will lead to further political debate intended to lead to broad consensus on the appropriate approach. At present, the 'Klaus approach' to pension reform, that is, of allowing public pension rates to fall thereby encouraging greater reliance on private pensions, cannot be ruled out as a default strategy.

UNEMPLOYMENT

Like the other CEE countries, unemployment did not officially exist in Czechoslovakia before 1989 and there was no scheme of unemployment insurance. As in many CEE countries, unemployment insurance was introduced in the early 1990s (1991). However, the initial level of benefit and its duration was cut back over the course of the 1990s, again paralleling the pattern in other CEE countries (Vodopivec et al., 2003). The Czech Republic now has an unemployment benefit duration of only six months which, in comparative terms, is quite short. In general CEE countries have comparatively low levels of expenditure on unemployment and comparatively low replacement rates (Baradasi et al., 1999). A review of unemployment benefit schemes in CEE countries, including the Czech Republic, found 'quite a positive experience', with UB helping to redistribute income, reducing poverty and creating only limited work disincentives (Vodopivec et al., 2003).

GENDER

Czechoslovakia (like other CEE countries) had what has been described as a 'gendered defamilist' approach to labour market and welfare policy. In other words, these countries encouraged female participation in the labour force but, unlike the Nordic countries, without also encouraging a sharing of household responsibilities. Thus women faced a heavy burden of combining both work and household responsibilities, although CEE countries did provide supports such as extensive childcare and compensatory pensions measures such as earlier retirement. A review of the gender implications of social security reform in CEE countries found that, while gender was rarely an explicit issue in formulating reforms, many reforms had important gender impacts (Fultz et al., 2003). For example, pension reforms which more closely linked pensions to contributions would tend to have a disadvantageous effect on women who tended to have lower earnings. The fact that the Czech Republic has, to date, had one of the most limited reforms of the pension system and has only altered redistribution to a limited extent means that there has been little negative impact for women, while retirement ages for men and women have been brought closer together.

In the Czech Republic, family benefits were subjected to an income limit in 1995/6 but not in a 'highly restrictive' manner (Fultz et al., 2003). These restrictions mean that family benefits are concentrated more on low income families but may also contribute to work disincentives for mothers. Equal access to child benefits was granted to men in the 1990s but to little practical effect. Overall a recent study suggested that the Czech Republic was, in comparative terms, a country where the gender impact of reforms had been modest. However, Saxonberg and Sirovátka (2004) point out that there has been a very significant fall in the level of publicly provided childcare and suggest that this constitutes a move away from the 'gendered defamilialism' of the former era towards refamilisation.

IMPACT OF EU ACCESSION

A recent review of the impact of EU accession on social policy development in the Czech Republic suggests that there has been only a limited impact (Potüček, 2004). Given the relatively gender-friendly nature of the Czech system, only limited changes have been made in terms of access to benefits to satisfy equal treatment criteria. In terms of macro-level constraints – such as the Maastricht criteria – Czechoslovakia already had a relatively high level of welfare spending given its level of economic development. This has not changed significantly in the decade since the transition to democracy.

INEQUALITY AND POVERTY

Czechoslovakia, like most other CEE countries, had very low levels of income inequality in 1989. The LIS data (available for 1992 and 1996), indicate that these have risen over the period from 0.207 in 1992 to 0.259 in 1996, but this is still at the low levels of the Nordic countries (albeit that these data are considerably out of date). Similarly in an EU context, income inequality in the Czech Republic is well below the EU average (0.25 compared to 0.28). Of course, trends in income inequality are not driven solely by changes in the welfare state but are also influenced by a range of factors including labour market trends and household composition. Of perhaps more direct relevance to assessing the impact of welfare policy, the same pattern can be seen in relation to the risk-of-poverty indicator (50 per cent of median incomes). In the Czech Republic only 8 per cent of the population was at risk of poverty compared to an EU average of 15 per cent. However, the use of a 'relative' poverty indicator for CEE countries disguises the fact that, in absolute terms, overall living standards (and therefore the incomes of the lowest deciles) are well below those of the EU15.

CONCLUSION

To date, although there has been significant change in the Czech system including the introduction of unemployment insurance, the level of change has probably been less than in many of the other CEE countries. While inequality and poverty levels have risen during the transition, these are still below the EU average and the Czech Republic's relatively high level of welfare spending (for its level of economic development) appears to have assisted in cushioning the impact of the transition, with spending increasing from 17 per cent of GDP in 1990 to 20.1 per cent in 2001. However, it is still very early to come to an assessment of the Czech welfare trajectory. Significant financial pressures are developing for further pension reform and it remains to be seen whether a degree of political consensus can be developed and, if so, whether the direction of reform will remain broadly parametric and whether it will retain its quite positive equality and poverty outcomes.

THE NETHERLANDS

DESCRIPTION

The Netherlands is a medium sized European country with a population of about 16 million people. Because it has one of the higher levels of GDP per capita its total GDP output is in the middle of the European range.

POLITICAL BACKGROUND

The Netherlands has a bicameral political structure consisting of the Eerste Kamer (First Chamber or Senate), which is indirectly elected by provincial councils and the directly elected Tweede Kamer (Second Chamber), which is the main source of legislative power. In contrast to both Westminster and the Swedish models – where power alternates between two clearly defined parties (or blocs of parties) – Dutch history has seen a complicated system of shifting alliances with parties from different political perspectives sharing power at different times. However, the Christian democratic parties have been permanently in government over most of the twentieth century. In November 1982, the Christian Democratic Appeal (CDA), led by Ruud Lubbers took power at the head of a coalition also involving the liberal VVD. This combination was returned to power in 1986. In 1989, with the VVD vote having declined, the CDA formed a grand alliance (representing two-thirds of votes cast) with the opposition Labour party (PvdA). This governed until 1994, when the Wim Kok-led PvdA – despite a sharp drop in its vote – assumed the reins of power in a 'purple' coalition with the VVD and the Democrats 66 party (D66) – the Christian democrats leaving office for the first time since the 1920s. The PvdA continued in power after the 1998 elections. The 2002 elections saw the dramatic rise of the right-wing Lijst Pim Fortuyn, with 17 per cent of the vote and the return of a CDA-led government in coalition with the LPF and VVD. However, this government was short-lived and further elections were called in 2003 which saw a continuation in power of a CDA-led coalition, this time with the VVD and D66 (the LPF vote declining dramatically to 6 per cent). It is worth noting the extent to which the CDA has been involved in the government over the last two decades and that the CDA (and its predecessor parties) played an important role in the original establishment of the Dutch welfare state.

WELFARE STATE

In the late 1970s, the Dutch welfare state consisted of:

- 'people's insurances' covering the long-term risks of old age, disability, survivorhood and child benefit;
- contractual (but effectively mandatory) occupational pension cover (see Haverland, 2001; Rein and Turner, 2001);
- 'workers' insurances' covering unemployment, long-term disablement and sickness; and
- a social assistance, means-tested safety net.

The late 1970s and early 1980s saw dramatic increases in the claim loads and costs of many areas of the welfare state and the 1982 Lubbers government began a campaign of restructuring which has in effect continued unabated ever since under different governments. These policies have been described as following, initially, a 'prices policy', that is, of limiting the amount of benefits paid by deindexation or reducing the replacement rate, and subsequently a 'volumes policy' of attempting to limit the numbers of people qualifying for benefits by stricter qualification criteria (van Oorschot, 1998). However, the failure of these two approaches fully to achieve their objectives led to a further more fundamental reappraisal of the Dutch approach to the welfare state which has led to the Netherlands being engaged in one of the most radical restructurings of the welfare state. Spending has declined significantly from 26.9 per cent in 1980 to 21.8 per cent in 2001.

To summarise briefly the changes which have been made, there have been relatively few changes to the old age pension scheme other than those required to implement the EU directive on equal treatment for men and women. Declines in public pension rates in the 1980s were largely compensated by increased occupational pensions (Rein and Turner, 2001). The Netherlands has one of the lower levels of old age ratio at present and thus pressures in this area are less intense than in some other European countries. In addition, the combination of a flat rate (albeit relatively generous) public scheme and effectively mandatory, funded, occupational cover reaching over 90 per cent of the employed population means that there is less direct financial pressure on the state (van Riel et al., 2002). In the run-up to the 1994 election the CDA suggested that cutbacks in pensions might be necessary, but this was extremely unpopular with the electorate (van Riel et al., 2002; Green-Pedersen, 2002a). The election led to the Christian Democrats' removal from government for the first time since 1917 and the establishment of a PvdA-liberal 'purple' coalition. This government committed itself to guarantee public pensions with indexation for the future. The costs were to be met largely through increased labour force participation. However, the survivors' pension has been limited to people born before 1950 and means tested (effectively phasing down the pension over a long time period). This followed a court decision requiring equal treatment between men and women. Child benefit payments have been restricted (with payments for 18- to 27-year-olds abolished) and the rate of payment reduced (although compensatory study grants were introduced).

UNEMPLOYMENT

In the case of the workers' insurances, the qualifying periods for unemployment benefits have been increased and the rates reduced. This had the effect that the longer-term unemployed must rely on social assistance payments. The Netherlands has also adopted a major market-based reform of employment services (Struyven and Steurs, 2003). The former public employment service has been split into a basic employment services provider, which remains public, and the reintegration services, which have been privatised, and required to compete with commercial bodies for contracts to provide return to work services. It is, however, probably too early to provide a detailed assessment of the outcome of this process in terms of costs and employment impacts.

SICKNESS AND DISABILITY

More radical changes have been made in the area of sickness and disability payments. In the case of disability payments, the Netherlands had been one of the countries with the highest levels of disability claims in Europe, as the disability pension scheme had been used as a quasi-unemployment payment. The qualification conditions were tightened up to prevent the scheme being used to compensate for poor labour market conditions. In addition, employers were required to pay higher insurance premia if they generated higher than average disability claims. This was intended to encourage employers to improve working conditions or adapt work places to accommodate disabled workers. Firms may also opt-out of the scheme and assume direct responsibility for payment of disability benefits.

There has been a major privatisation of sickness benefits (Muffels and Dirven, 2001; Geurts et al., 2000). Responsibility for the payment of sickness benefit (at 70 per cent of previous wages or the minimum wage) was transferred to employers initially for a short period but subsequently extended to 52 and then 104 weeks. Employers may reinsure with a private insurance company, carry the risk themselves or remain insured with the public insurance body where premiums are related to the level of sickness in the firm or sector. About 80 per cent opted to carry their own risk (Muffels and Dirven, 2001). Surprisingly, data indicates that the level of sickness leave is highest amongst this group and lowest amongst companies reinsured with a private insurance company. Employers may now opt-out of the public insurance scheme for the period of up to five years of sickness/disability. These changes are reflected in a major fall in public expenditure on incapacity related benefits from 7.1 per cent in 1980 (the highest in Europe) to 4.1 per cent in 2001 (still well above the EU average).

GENDER

In 1980 the Dutch welfare system was structured around the notion of the male breadwinner. This led to considerable difficulties in the implementation of the EU directive on equal treatment for men and women and to a series of court cases to the European Court of Justice. Unfortunately the gender impact of the more recent restructuring of the Dutch welfare system does not, to date, appear to have received detailed study. Part-time work for women is particularly high. A detailed OECD study of childcare and related policies in the Netherlands found that formal childcare was largely unsubsidised and could be prohibitively expensive for families with more than one pre-school-age child (Adema, 2002). This suggests that the high incidence of part-time work amongst Dutch mothers is related to the absence of affordable childcare.

THE ROLE OF POLITICAL STRUCTURES

Green-Pedersen (2002a) has argued that the political structures in the Netherlands and the position of the CDA as a pivotal party played an important part in allowing the restructuring that has taken place. The CDA began the initial retrenchment drive in the early 1980s. But, in contrast to, for example, the UK Conservatives, the CDA was a centre party which had made a key contribution to the development of the Dutch welfare state. Thus it had more credibility with voters in saying that changes had to be made. In addition it was a pivotal party which was normally involved in government with partners to the left (PvdA) or right (VVD). Again this made it well placed to lead a reform campaign. While the PvdA initially strongly opposed welfare changes, it changed its policies in the mid-1980s and eventually participated with the CDA in a reforming government before leading the more radical restructuring itself in the 1990s. Thus the combination of a clear perception of a 'need' for reform (rising welfare rolls and costs at a time of economic and budgetary difficulties) combined with the particular political structure of the Netherlands allowed radical reform to proceed – although it was frequently a matter of heated political debate both between and within political parties.

GLOBALISATION

There is little sign of a direct link between indicators of globalisation and specific developments in the Dutch welfare state. One might argue that the recent restructuring and reduction of overall spending is a reflection of the pressures of globalisation in a highly open economy. But the Netherlands remains one of the higher spending countries and other open countries – such as Belgium – have not adapted in the same manner. Green-Pedersen (2002b) has argued that the main challenge in the Dutch case 'has been to meet the demands of international financial markets for a macro-economic policy delivering low inflation and only limited budget deficits' (2002a: 143–4). He accepts that this response is partially voluntary as Dutch governments could have chosen alternative options such as floating exchange rates but preferred the discipline which international pressure imposes on labour markets for wage moderation. Green-Pedesen emphasises that this response was not an automatic response but the outcome of a political struggle.

INEQUALITY AND POVERTY

Overall, most authors agree that a fundamental paradigm-shift is underway in the Dutch welfare system. What impact has this had on welfare state outcomes? The outcomes to date support a positive view of the Dutch restructuring. The Netherlands has had one of Europe's lower levels of income inequality and this has changed little in the period from 1983 to 1999 (0.26–0.248). There has, however, been a rise in low income or income poverty (albeit from a low level) from 3.9 per cent in 1983 to 7.3 per cent in 1999. More recent data from the ECHP for 2001 also provide a positive view, with the Netherlands 'at risk-of-poverty rate' of 11 per cent (the lowest apart from Sweden and Denmark) compared to an EU average of 15 per cent and an income inequality level of 0.26 (again one of the lowest) compared to an EU average of 0.28.

CONCLUSION

As can be seen, while, initially, the changes in the Dutch welfare state may have focussed on the traditional approach of cutting back benefit levels and numbers, more recently the Dutch approach has involved a radical change in the policy approach to the provision of welfare. This has been described as 'a shift from solidarity towards selectivity' (van Oorschot, 1998) or a change from 'a social right paradigm to an incentives paradigm' (van der Veen et al., 2000). The changes are based on moving away from (what is seen to be) excessive reliance on the state and towards the encouragement of individual responsibility at the level of both the firm and the individual by making all actors face more directly the costs of social provision.

Overall there has been a mixed academic assessment of the impact of the Dutch changes. Green-Pedersen (2002a) has, for example, highlighted the extent of 'retrenchment' in the Dutch system, arguing that this has been greater than that in Denmark. Van Oorschot (1998) broadly shares this perspective, arguing that ties of solidarity between good 'risks' and bad have been dismantled and that the system has not only lost part of its solidaristic character but also become less collective, leading to an overall decline in the level of citizens' social protection. While accepting that some of the decreases in state provision have been compensated by collective bargaining, he argues that those who have lost out most are people with weak or no ties to the labour market. In contrast, van der Veen et al. (2000) take a more optimistic outlook. While broadly sharing van Oorschot's analysis of what the changes were intended to achieve, they adopt a more positive interpretation of both the objective and the outcome of these changes. They believe that the changes have led to little retrenchment because they have been compensated by legal obligations on employers and collective bargaining. The shift in responsibility to employers and employees should lead to a fall in the use of benefits, but this they argue may not be a bad thing as long as this does not lead to 'underconsumption' (that is, a failure to realise entitlements due to strong disincentives or rigid administrative policies). They also identify the danger that the emphasis on the responsibility of employers may reduce the employment opportunities of persons with disabilities.

SPAIN

DESCRIPTION

Spain is one of the larger European countries, with a population of 40 million people. However, due to its lower level of GDP per capita, its overall economic importance is somewhat smaller. Spain has seen significant economic growth since its transition to democracy in the 1970s and its membership of the EU in 1986.

POLITICAL BACKGROUND

The Spanish system is bicameral but the main powers lie with the Cortes Generales (National Assembly). However, decentralisation is an important part of the Spanish political system, with the establishment of 19 autonomous communities with significant powers. In particular, the communities have authority in relation to minimum income and social services policy and this division of roles has an important impact on the development of Spanish welfare policy. In the first democratic elections in 1977, the conservative UCD (Democratic Centre Union) led the government until 1982. The social democratic Partido Socialista Obrero Español (PSOE) came to power in 1982 and remained there until 1996 (with elections in 1986, 1989 and 1993). However, it was in a minority position in the 1993–1996 period, being dependent on smaller parties for support. In the 1996 elections the conservative Partido Popular (PP) came to power with the support of regional parties and the PP attained a majority position in 2000. However, the PSOE, to the surprise of many commentators, regained power in 2004. Although neither the PSOE nor the PP ever approach a plurality of votes (44 per cent – in

1986 and 2000 respectively – being their best performance) we thus see a reasonably clear two-party alternation of power. However, on occasion the regional parties (such as the Catalan CiU) and the left-wing Izquirda Unida also play an important role.

WELFARE STATE

The Spanish welfare state in the mid-1970s was underdeveloped – reflecting Spain's economic status at the time. In structure it was largely Bismarckian, with expenditure concentrated on pensions and with very limited provision of public services. In line with the Francoist support for *familista* (pro-family) policies, a significant proportion of welfare spending was on family benefits. Welfare spending in 1974 (just before the end of the Franco era) was about 8 per cent of GDP. This grew rapidly to 15.9 per cent by 1980. In the period from 1980 spending has increased further to 19.6 per cent in 2001. However, this overall rise conceals growth to about 1993 and a steady decline in spending since then from a peak of 22.5 per cent. This is related to the Spanish government's intention to meet the Maastricht criteria and join the Economic and Monetary Union.

The overall development of the Spanish welfare state since the mid-1970s falls into three main periods:

- an initial period of catch-up growth which saw an increase in spending but little change in the overall structure of the system (1975–1982);
- a period of general growth and the introduction of significant new policy approaches including the establishment of a national health service (1986–1989) and the decentralisation of social services to the autonomous communities (1989–1993). This period was not, however, one of unidirectional growth. Spending fell in the period 1985–1988 and legislation to restructure the pension scheme was introduced in 1985 (discussed below); and
- a period of restructuring from 1993 to date where the emphasis has been on restricting spending growth, and continuing the restructuring of the pension system through a corporatist process of consultation.

PENSIONS

Spain had a fairly standard Bismarckian social insurance pension system which was occupationally structured and provided relatively generous benefits to those covered. Over the period from 1980, the coverage of the pension scheme has extended from 82 per cent to 92 per cent of the population over 65 (Moreno, 2002). However, in most other aspects policy has focussed on restructuring the pension scheme to reduce future costs. While Spain's current old age ratio is just above the EU average, it is projected to rise sharply in the future – largely due to the very low level of fertility in Spain (see Chapter 9). The initial 1985 reform by PSOE increased the minimum period of contribution required from 10 to 15 years and the period over which the earnings-related pension rate was calculated from 2 to 8 years. This was quite controversial and was followed by general strikes in 1985 and 1988.

However, pressure for reform resumed in the 1990s. In February 1994, a Parliamentary committee of the Budgets Commission of the Cortes was established to maintain and guarantee the future viability of the social security system. This led to the agreement by the government and trade unions of the *Pacto de Toledo*, which proposed a gradual reform of the pension system. In contrast to calls for radical privatisation of the Spanish system, the agreement set out significant but parametric reforms of the existing system including tightening the links between contributions and benefits. This led to a further agreement between government and unions in 1996 which was implemented in legislation in 1997. This legislation, inter alia, further increased the period over which pension rates were calculated to 15 years leading to a reduction in benefits in most cases (estimated at about 10 per cent). Despite this the legislation achieved a high degree of parliamentary and social consensus. The legislation also provided for the establishment of a reserve fund into which surplus social security contributions would be paid to meet future pension costs. In 1987 separate legislation was also agreed, encouraging the development of private pensions.

The Toledo agreement has been renewed by the government, employers and unions, after considerable discussion and debate, in 2001 and again in 2003. Arising from the 2001 agreement, the PP government proposed legislation which would have further increased the period over which pensions were calculated to 35 years. This was projected to lead to a further fall in average pensions of between 12 and 20 per cent and was strongly opposed by the unions, including a general strike in 2002. The introduction of this measure was postponed. Other features of the agreement included improvements in widow's pensions and a relaxation of entitlement to early retirement pensions. In September 2003 the main political parties agreed to further renew the Toledo agreement, publishing a report which agreed a further increase in the link between contributions and pensions. It also included proposals to reduce the use of pre-retirement pensions and strengthening the reserve fund. In 2005, the new PSOE government significantly increased minimum pensions as part of a commitment to raise such pensions by 25 per cent during its term of office.

UNEMPLOYMENT

In the area of unemployment, reform has been less concerted and less successful. Spain has seen extremely high levels of unemployment of about 20 per cent for much of the period from 1980. This has fallen since about 1997 but remains quite high at 11 per cent in 2002. However, more importantly, Spain's levels of *employment* are very low. The overall employment rate is below 60 per cent, compared to the EU target of 70 per cent (see Chapter 9). Female employment and employment of older people is only about 40 per cent, compared to the targets of 60 per cent and 50 per cent respectively. Spending on unemployment has been at comparatively high levels at all stages in recent decades. However, a comparative study indicates that Spanish unemployment benefits are not well targeted, with less than 50 per cent of unemployed persons who are actively seeking employment being in receipt of benefit and less than 50 per cent of those in receipt of benefit actively seeking employment (Baradasi et al., 1999). In this context the lack of significant reforms and the expansion of early retirement schemes as recently as 2001 is striking. In 2002, the PP government, following the failure of negotiations with social partners, amended the unemployment benefit legislation by decree. Amongst other things the decree imposed obligations on unemployed people to give a written commitment to accept measures to help them find work and an obligation to accept 'suitable work'. This led to a general strike in June 2002, following which the government withdrew some aspects of the decree and modified others. The difficulties in identifying a clear policy in this area appear to be related to the broader failure to agree on labour market policy reforms.

FAMILY SUPPORTS

As many commentators have noted, the Spanish welfare state is both heavily reliant on the family as a key source of support and largely devoid of any specific family policies. As we will see in Chapter 9, Southern European countries, including Spain, have quite distinctive household structures, with much higher levels of co-residence and lower levels of one-person households, than Northern Europe. Welfare benefits for families are amongst the lowest in Europe. This is a sharp contrast with the Franco years and it has been suggested that this is, in part, a reaction to the association of generous family benefits with Francoist policies. In 1990, family benefits were made subject to a means test. In addition, the tendency of the PP has been to target child support through the tax system (albeit at very moderate levels).

It has been suggested that this combination of a lack of family policy and a heavy reliance on the family is not necessarily contradictory, but rather that the lack of public involvement emphasises the important role of families (Flaquer, 2000).

The reliance on family support has many positive aspects including the degree of social support and income sharing provided by co-residence. Indeed, Spanish household structures would appear to contribute to the lack of a gender gap in poverty levels compared to other European countries. However, other observers have emphasised the extent to which the Spanish family is not egalitarian but reflects patriarchal structures, with women and younger men being dependent for income on older men. Reflecting this, research indicates that the Spanish welfare system concentrates income from both employment and benefits on older men to a greater extent than other European countries (King, 2002).

DECENTRALISATION AND MINIMUM INCOME

Up to the 1990s, Spain, like other Southern European countries, had no national system of minimum income. However, the delegation of authority to the autonomous communities led to the establishment of minimum income schemes in the Basque country in 1989 and, by 1995, in all 19 communities (Moreno and Arriba, 1999). However, the benefits are quite modest and, with the exception of the Basque country, cover only about 1 per cent (or less) of the population (Moreno, 2002).

GLOBALISATION AND EUROPEANISATION

It has been argued that there is little evidence that globalisation has led to retrenchment of social policies to enhance economic competitiveness (Guillén and Álvarez, 2002). Rather, Guillén et al. have argued that 'significant Europeanization has taken place in Spain' (2002). Membership of the EU is seen as applying positive pressure for welfare improvements in a period of redesign of welfare programmes (see also Guillén and Álvarez, 2004). However, the most obvious impact of EU pressure has been to restrain government expenditure in the context of EMU. Examples of policy diffusion, such as the establishment of minimum income programmes, might well have occurred in any case and, in the overall context, are of limited scope. In addition, local democratisation and decentralisation would appear to have been much more important factors in the development of these policies.

INEQUALITY AND POVERTY

The LIS indicators for Spain show some rise in poverty (after an initial fall) from 12.2 per cent in 1980 to 14.3 per cent in 2000.

Inequality also rose from 0.318 in 1980 to 0.340 in 2000. Figures from the ECHP (European Community Household Panel) show that in 2001 Spain remained the second most unequal EU country, with a Gini co-efficient of 0.33 (compared to an EU average of 0.28) and one with a risk-of-poverty rate well above average (19 per cent compared to an EU average of 15 per cent).

CONCLUSION

Many assessments of Spanish social policy development in the last two decades are quite positive, pointing to pensions reform, the establishment of the national health service and of a nationwide (if not national) minimum income. However, a more critical assessment is also possible. The pension reform has been basically parametric rather than systemic and should help to ensure the future affordability of pensions. However, the failure to reform unemployment and pre-retirement pensions so as to impact on overall employment rates reflects much more negatively on Spanish policy makers. While the family has to date played an important role in providing support, one can only speculate about the extent to which the heavy reliance on families combined with very underdeveloped family support has contributed to the very low level of fertility in Spain. In addition, the low fertility rate means that the current family structure cannot continue. Finally, while Spain's overall economic position has improved relative to its European partners, its levels of income inequality and poverty remain amongst the highest in the EU. So while the approach to pension reform might be considered to be analogous to that of successive Swedish governments (see below), the overall Spanish approach to welfare reform leads to radically different outcomes.

SWEDEN

DESCRIPTION

Sweden is one of the smaller European countries, with a population of only 9 million. It has a relatively high level of GDP per capita and its overall economic output puts it in the middle of the European table. After a series of economic problems in the 1980s and 1990s, its economic performance in recent years has become much more positive.

POLITICAL BACKGROUND

The Swedish legislative system is unicameral with all legislative powers based in the Riksdag. The Social Democratic party has held power for the vast majority of the last 70 years. Having lost office in 1976 (despite winning 43 per cent of the vote), it returned to power in 1979 and won subsequent elections in 1982, 1985 and 1988 (with between 43–45 per cent of the vote). In 1991, its vote dropped sharply to 38 per cent and a centre right coalition ruled until 1994. However, the Social Democratic party returned to office in 1994 and has remained in power to date (despite a fall in its vote in the late 1990s).

WELFARE STATE

The Swedish welfare state is the archetypal Scandinavian (or Nordic) welfare system. This has been described by Abrahamson as:

> ... universal and (therefore) expensive, based on public provision of both transfers and services, emphasising personal social services vis-à-vis transfers; provides high quality provision; has high compensation rates and is therefore egalitarian; and is based on a high degree of labour market participation for both sexes. (2003)

This is reflected in its level of welfare spending, at 28.8 per cent of GDP in 1980 and 28.9 per cent in 2001 – in both cases amongst the highest in Europe. In the early 1990s, Sweden faced very significant economic and fiscal difficulties. In the period from 1990 to 1993, the government balance went from surplus to a deficit of over 12 per cent of GDP. 'Open' unemployment rose to 8 per cent and about 16 per cent of the workforce were not in ordinary employment (Abrahamson, 2003). Reflecting these problems welfare spending rose to 36.8 per cent in 1993. These difficulties have led to significant changes in aspects of the Swedish welfare state, although it arguably retains its commitment to the overall Scandinavian approach.

PENSIONS

In the area of pensions there has been a significant reduction in pension replacement rates in the 1990s. In addition, there has been a significant reform of the basis of the Swedish pension system. This was initiated by the conservative government, carried out by the subsequent social democratic government and done in consultation with the key business and trade union organisations. The key elements of this reform were as follows (Andersen, 2001):

- The benefit formula was altered from the best 15 years of a person's working life to lifetime earnings (although compensatory measures were introduced to take into account time spent in child rearing and education).
- The calculation of pensions was changed from the standard 'defined benefit' approach to a 'notional defined contribution'

basis – the final pension is based on the amount of contributions paid into a fund but subject not to actual growth but the government-defined (and hence notional) value of that fund. Indexation was changed from a link to the CPI to a link to inflation and real wage growth, but this will be altered based on changes in life expectancy.

• The scheme was changed from pure PAYG with the introduction of partial capitalisation.

• Funding was altered from being primarily an employer responsibility to being shared equally by employers and employees (second-tier pension) and coming from general taxation (basic pension).

While these are significant changes and while studies show that a majority of pensioners will receive lower pensions as a result, overall the objective of the pension system remains largely unchanged and this might be categorised as a restructuring rather than a retrenchment. A key issue will be whether capitalisation is allowed to be extended further beyond its current modest limits.

Studies have highlighted different (but not inconsistent) aspects of the forces behind the reform. Clearly the financial pressures facing Sweden, the relative generosity of its pensions and the high level of older people in the population all combined to create financial pressures for reform. Andersen (2001), arguing against Pierson's thesis that politics are no longer central to welfare state reform, has highlighted the fact that political parties, employers and unions were key to the negotiation and acceptance of the reforms. In particular, the fact that the political parties did not make it a contentious political issue and the fact that the trade union confederation (LO) reluctantly accepted the need for reform, facilitated the process. Green-Pedersen and Lindbom (2002), in agreement with Myles and Pierson's (2001) thesis that countries with well-established PAYG schemes will find it very difficult to alter these substantially, highlight the path-dependent nature of the change (see also Andersen, 2001: 1085). They quote from the original Pension Systems Working Group (a parliamentary group established in 1991 to prepare reform) which argued that:

> The most important argument for organising the pension system as a mandatory, state run system is that the present general pension system is mandatory. The promises made within the framework of the current system must be kept. It is therefore impossible to replace the current system with an entirely voluntary system by a certain date. (2002)

Green-Pedersen and Lindbom argue that 'path-dependency does not mean that political factors such as the colour of the government become irrelevant but that they work within paths already laid out' (2002: 23).

UNEMPLOYMENT AND SICKNESS

There have also been changes in the unemployment scheme, with replacement rates being significantly reduced and a requirement of five waiting days introduced. However, in this area, the conservative government planned more sweeping changes including removing the administration of the scheme from the trade unions. They, in fact, legislated for this but the legislation was repealed by the Social Democrats. One of the key differences here was that, in contrast to its reluctant acceptance of the need for change in pensions, the LO would not agree to the removal of its role in benefit administration (which has been shown to have significant membership benefits to trade unions) (Andersen, 2001). In 2004 the Social Democrat government proposed a range of measures to reduce the high sickness absence rate including incentivising employers to reduce long-term absence. These proposals have been strongly opposed by both employers and some trade unions.

GENDER

The Nordic welfare states – and Sweden in particular – have long been held to have amongst the most gender-friendly welfare systems, in the sense of policies which support women and men both to participate in the labour market and in care work (Sörensen and Bergqvist, 2002). For example, all parents in Sweden have been entitled to substantial parental leave rights since 1974. In recent years there have not been substantial changes in the supports provided for care. The number of children in day care institutions or family day care has fallen slightly in the period from 1995 to 2001 and responsibility for the costs has been shifted somewhat from the state to parents (Morel, 2003). However, Sweden still has one of the more extensive childcare networks. In contrast to Norway, where a home care allowance was introduced by the Conservative government, a similar scheme was provided for by the Swedish Conservative government but abolished by the Social Democrats. In terms of broader labour market outcomes, research indicates that Sweden had one of the lower gender gaps in terms of male–female earnings in the mid-1990s (Sörensen, 2002).

INEQUALITY AND POVERTY

The Swedish data on income inequality and poverty show the reverse picture to the Netherlands, with a rise in income inequality (albeit from a very low level) but no rise in poverty levels. National research indicates that the rise in income inequality 'was more a consequence of changes at the top than at the bottom of the income distribution' (Welfare Commission, 2002: 94). Overall, the Gini index rose from 0.197 in 1981 to 0.252 in 2000 with the bulk of the increase coming in the late 1990s. In contrast relative income poverty has remained quite stable, beginning at 5.3 per cent in 1981, rising slightly before falling back to 6.5 per cent in 2000. EU data also shows Sweden in a very positive light with the lowest 'at risk-of-poverty rate' of 9 per cent and one of the lowest Gini coefficients at 0.24.

Unusually the Swedish government appointed a public commission – chaired by academic Joakim Palme – to analyse changes in welfare in the 1990s (Welfare Commission, 2002). The Commission defined welfare in terms of 'individual resources that allow citizens to control and consciously steer the direction of their own lives' (2002: 9). It found that – despite improvements in real wages and mortality rates – the most noticeable change in the 1990s was 'the increase in the proportion of the population that encountered various kinds of disadvantage or illfare' such as unemployment, poorer working conditions, financial difficulties and a decline in mental wellbeing (2002: 9). Single mothers, people born outside Sweden and young adults were identified as vulnerable groups. However, it found that 'women were not generally hit harder than men by the economic crisis and the changes in the welfare system in the 1990s' (2002: 95). Gender differences remained but did not increase. Overall the Commission felt that these developments represented 'a significant challenge to welfare policy' (2002: 13).

Academic assessments of the extent of change in the Swedish system are somewhat mixed. One the one hand, Kautto and Kvist (2002) argue that a distinct Nordic welfare model can still be identified and that the last 20 years of development have not led to the dismantlement or 'Europeanisation' of Nordic welfare states. In contrast, Abrahamson finds that these welfare states are still distinct but less so than they were a decade or two ago and concludes that 'welfare in Scandinavia is undergoing a process of Europeanisation' (2003). To some extent, this depends on one's perspective. Looking closely at the Swedish welfare state, it has indeed seen cuts in replacement rates and shifts towards pension capitalisation which can be seen to bring it closer to other European models. Overall, however, in terms of structure and outcomes, the Swedish (and Nordic) welfare state remains quite distinctive in Europe.

UNITED KINGDOM

DESCRIPTION

The United Kingdom is one of the biggest and most economically important European countries, with the third largest population (59 million people) and one of the largest economies in terms of total GDP. In terms of GDP per capita, however, the United Kingdom has seen a long-term decline over the twentieth century from a position in the early twentieth century where it was the clear European leader. Over the period 1990–2000, United Kingdom GDP has grown at a modest 2 per cent per annum.

POLITICAL BACKGROUND

The United Kingdom political system is relatively unusual in European terms, being based on a 'first past the post' system of single member constituencies (also know as simple majority voting). This results in a high level of disparity between votes cast for and seats won by a party (leading to significant under-representation of smaller parties) and also means that, in practice, a party can (and has) obtained a significant overall parliamentary majority with much less than 50 per cent of the total votes. The United Kingdom parliamentary system is a bicameral one, with the head of government elected (in practice if not in theory) by the House of Commons (the lower house). The upper house (the House of Lords) has relatively limited powers to alter or delay government legislation. Despite the limited recent devolution of powers to the Scottish Parliament, the Welsh Assembly and (sporadically) the Northern Ireland Assembly, the United Kingdom remains a unitary state in relation to most aspects of the welfare state and the main welfare provisions apply across the United Kingdom. All of this means that the United Kingdom is a state in which the governing party (in most cases) effectively controls parliament (without having to rely for support on smaller groupings) and adopts and implements laws for the entire country.

Compared to most other European countries, the political make-up of the United Kingdom can be very simply outlined for the last two decades. In 1979 the Conservative party was elected to power (with a total vote of only 44 per cent) and remained in office through four elections (until 1997) under two prime ministers: first Margaret Thatcher and, from 1990, John Major. This was a particularly long period of single party government even by United Kingdom standards. The Conservative party is a secular right-wing party and part of its stated agenda was the restructuring of the welfare state. In 1997 the Labour party and its leader Tony Blair was elected to office (with a vote of 43 per cent). Labour retained power in the 2001 elections, and again in 2005, now becoming the longest serving Labour government in the history of the United Kingdom. The Labour party would traditionally be categorised as social democratic and remains part of the social democratic grouping in the European Parliament. However, it would be somewhat difficult to categorise many of New Labour's policies as 'left of centre' and in European terms it is probably best categorised as a secular centre party.

WELFARE STATE

In the United Kingdom overall public social expenditure has, in fact, increased from 17.9 per cent in 1980 to 21.8 per cent in 2001, driven largely by an increase in pension expenditure. However, the United Kingdom is widely seen as having carried out significant welfare retrenchment in recent decades and its level of social expenditure per capita (using purchasing power standards) is now one of the lowest in the EU15 (ahead only of Ireland and the three Southern European countries). In the late 1970s, the UK system consisted of a mixture of insurance based and means-tested payments with a separate universal national health system. The UK pension system was based on a relatively low basic insurance pension topped up either by a private occupational or personal pension or by the State Earnings Related pension. Low-income pensioners would also receive means-tested support.

PENSIONS

There have been significant changes in United Kingdom pension policy over the last two decades. Indexation of the basic United Kingdom social insurance pension was changed from wage indexation to price indexation in 1982 by the Conservative government and this policy has been continued since. This has resulted in the basic pension falling from 20 per cent of average earnings in 1979 to 15 per cent in 1999. It has also resulted in an increase in the number of older people dependent on means-tested pensions. Labour policy has focussed on increasing the means-tested pension which, it argues, focuses resources on those who need them most and which, of course, is also significantly less costly.

Occupational pensions have always played an important role in the UK system and the United Kingdom only introduced a comprehensive State Earnings Related Pension (SERPS) in 1975. However, SERPS was never allowed to mature to the extent intended. The Conservative government made various changes in the structure of the pension, which had the effect of reducing pension payments and, instead, encouraged people to take out personal pensions to provide support in old age. More recently, the Labour government has broadly continued this approach. Current UK policy is based around a means-tested minimum income guarantee (or pensions credit) for pensioners with no (or limited) other incomes, a Second State Pension (which replaced SERPS in 2002) but which is only to be updated in line with consumer prices, and occupational and personal pensions cover. Labour policy has attempted to meet the twin goals of addressing pensioner poverty through increases in the means-tested pension (variously dressed up as a 'guarantee' or 'credit') – and a strong commitment to encourage private provision for pensions and to shift costs away from the state. Unlike the Republic of Ireland, which adopts a broadly similar approach but relies on a contributory pension as a base, this approach is inconsistent. In so far as the pension credit moves significant numbers of pensioners out of poverty, it will obviate the need for them to save for their own pension. In so far as it strongly relies on private provision, it will inevitably mean that the level of the means-tested pension must be kept low so as not to discourage private provision. The Labour government has appointed a Commission (the Turner Commission) to advise on future pension options. In its first report (Pensions Commission, 2004) the Commission highlighted the difficulties of the current approach and the inadequate level of savings overall which will lead to inadequate pensions in decades to come.

Overall, there has been a significant cut-back in state supports for older people in the United Kingdom compared to the position which was intended in 1979. This highlights the risks of an analysis based only on macro data for programme expenditure. OECD data indicate that the United Kingdom is, in fact, spending significantly more resources – as a percentage of GDP – than it was in 1980. Spending on old age pensions has increased significantly from 5.5 per cent in 1980 to 8.1 per cent in 2001, which accounts for the bulk of the increase in total public social expenditure in the period. This increase is not accounted for by a rise in the old age ratio (that is, the population aged over 65 compared to the population of working age) which has remained broadly static over the period (23.5 per cent in 1980 and 24.1 per cent in 2000). Thus the macro data indicate that spending on old age pensions has risen, while a more detailed examination of policy measures indicate that it would have risen significantly more had the policies in place in 1979 not been altered over the period.

WORKING AGE

There have also been significant changes for people of working age in the United Kingdom. One of the biggest changes has been the introduction – by the Labour government – of the concept of people of working age. Previously working age people had been categorised as unemployed, sick, disabled, and lone parents and many of these groups had not been seen as having a (possible) relationship to the labour market. While the Conservative government introduced a policy of activation aimed at the unemployed – now reconstructed as 'jobseekers' – their Labour successors expanded this to the broader working age population on benefits.

For the unemployed, the rate of benefit has been cut significantly from a comparatively low 24 per cent (OECD summary measure) in 1981 to 17 per cent in 1999. In addition, the Conservative government introduced a new job seekers allowance (JSA) to replace contributory unemployment benefit and means-tested income support (for the unemployed). The effect of JSA has been significant. The main evaluation findings (Rayner et al., 2000) are that:

- JSA resulted in significant increases in movements off the claimant count. The greatest changes have occurred in areas of low unemployment and amongst longer-term clients.
- Both before and after JSA, two-thirds of people who left benefit moved into work. The majority of return-to-work jobs were stable, especially for those who had experienced only a short spell of unemployment.
- Former jobseekers were less likely to return to benefit after the introduction of JSA, and those who had left benefit for work were less likely to return to unemployment-related benefit when they lost their jobs.

The new Labour government continued this approach through its introduction of a series of 'New Deals', initially for the young and long-term unemployed. These have been basically activation measures to provide motivation, training and work placement for unemployed people.

The focus on reform of the unemployment system had certainly kept down the level of recorded unemployment (of which the United Kingdom has one of the lowest levels in Europe) but allowed a very significant rise in the number of people on long-term disability payments (that is, disguised unemployment). While spending on unemployment declined from 1.1 per cent of GDP in 1980 to only 0.3 per cent by 2001 (having initially risen up to the mid- 1980s), spending on disability cash benefits increased from 1 per cent to 2.5 per cent. This, amongst other factors, has led to a broadening by the new Labour government of the focus to the entire working age population including lone parents and people on disability payments and the introduction of New Deals for both these groups. It is in areas such as these that the concept of retrenchment is most limited. It would be difficult to find many people who would agree that keeping lone parents or disabled people on relatively low benefits for a long duration was a positive measure. In so far as the new system attempts to reduce expenditure on benefits, it might be seen as retrenchment but, in so far as its objective is to increase the employment rates (and thereby the incomes) of this group of people, it is difficult to see it as other than a restructuring of the system with potentially positive results. Indeed, evaluation of the New Deal for Lone Parents does indicate a positive outcome both for public expenditure and for individual participants (Evans et al., 2003).

In the area of sickness and disability, responsibility for short-term sickness benefits was transferred to employers beginning in 1982. In an effort to address the continuing high levels of people on long-term disability benefits, qualification conditions have been tightened up. In 2005, further measures were announced which aim to prevent people drifting into long-term reliance on disability payments by requiring those with 'manageable conditions' to attend work focussed interviews and take steps to return to work.

A further area of reform has been the introduction and subsequent expansion and conversion into 'tax credits' of in-work benefits. Originally introduced in 1971 (as family income supplement), these in-work benefits have been expanded significantly by New Labour and have recently been developed into a general employment tax credit applicable to all low-income workers. The United Kingdom is one of the few, if not the only, European country to rely heavily on such benefits, although the Netherlands is also increasing its reliance on in-work benefits. The reliance on in-work benefits is combined with the introduction of a statutory minimum wage in 1998.

CHILD SUPPORT

Public expenditure on family cash benefits has remained fairly static in the United Kingdom. Over this period the youth age ratio (population aged under 15: population of working age) has fallen somewhat from 33 per cent in 1980 to 29 per cent in 2000, indicating some increase in relative generosity. Unlike the other areas outlined above, there was a lack of clear policy direction in relation to child support under Conservative governments and a change in policy direction under the Labour government from 1997. The Conservative government was largely unenthusiastic about universal child support and expenditure declined somewhat by 1990. Subsequently, however, expenditure regained its former levels and since the election of the Labour government there has been both a much greater investment in child support and a restructuring of focus, with a switch from payment through the social security system to the introduction of child tax credits payable through the income tax system.

GENDER STRUCTURE

Directly discriminatory provision in the United Kingdom social security system (that is, provisions which provided for different rules for men and women) still existed well into the 1980s. These were largely removed as a result of the implementation of the EU directive on equal treatment for men and women in social security, in some cases following legal challenges. One remaining area in which different rules still apply is in relation to pension age, where pension age for men is 65 and for women 60 (this area is excluded from the scope of the EU directive). However, the UK government has decided to move to an equal pension age of 65 by 2020.

GLOBALISATION

It is difficult to identify any clear relationship between the various indices commonly used to measure globalisation (as discussed in Chapter 3), such as foreign direct investment or trade levels and the development of the welfare state in the United Kingdom. The United Kingdom has, for example, comparatively low levels of international trade. However, the United Kingdom has been one of the countries in which the policy discourse has focussed most of the impact of globalisation and on the need for restructuring of the welfare state to retain competitiveness (Swank, 2002a). It is thus a good example of the manner in which the impact of globalisation is not automatic but rather is mediated, or indeed shaped, by the particular policy approach which a government adopts in response to the perceived challenges arising from globalisation trends.

INEQUALITY AND POVERTY

There has been a long-term trend of rising inequality in the United Kingdom, with a rise in the Gini index from 0.27 in 1979 to 0.345 in 1999 (most recent LIS data). More recent national data indicates that this trend towards a widening of the income distribution has continued, albeit at a much slower pace (Brewer et al., 2004). There has also been a long-term rise in the numbers below low income or relative income poverty lines from 9.2 per cent in 1979 to 12.5 per cent in 1999. In EU terms, the United Kingdom has one of the highest levels of both poverty and inequality, with a Gini coefficient of 0.31 (compared to an EU15 average of 0.28) and a risk-of-poverty rate of 17 per cent (compared to an average of 15 per cent).

CONCLUSION

As has been seen, the UK welfare system has changed significantly in the last two decades. From a situation where the basis of its pension system was a social insurance payment with an (albeit recently introduced) earnings related pension, it has been changed to a largely means-tested system with a reliance on occupational and private pension for earnings-related support. Of course, these tendencies have existed in the UK system from the 1940s, but there is nonetheless a significant systemic shift in the UK system over that period. While there have been some changes in the New Labour approach – in particular in its development of active labour market policies and in-work benefits – the fundamental approach has not changed significantly. This is indicated by the fact that the United Kingdom, which is one of the wealthier of the EU15 (not to mention the EU25), has one of the highest levels of poverty and inequality in the EU15 (not to mention the EU25).

DISCUSSION

In this section we first summarise key developments in the five countries. Second, we look at the factors that influenced these developments. Finally, we compare welfare inputs and outputs. Our detailed examination of the five countries highlights a number of common points and also a number of divergences between welfare states.

KEY DEVELOPMENTS

PENSION REFORM

First, there are a number of areas in which most of the countries are prioritising reform. All countries (except the Netherlands) have undertaken or are debating extensive reform of their pension systems. Sweden and Spain have introduced extensive but largely parametric reform[2] led in one case by a Social Democratic government and in the other a Conservative, but with a degree of (often hard fought) cross-party agreement and with the involvement of the social partners. In both cases, the reforms will reduce average replacement rates but will obviously make such pensions more sustainable and should still leave in place adequate levels of pension.

The United Kingdom, in contrast, under both Conservative and New Labour governments, has radically changed from a system based on a basic insurance pension and a state earnings related second-tier pension (albeit with contracting out for those covered by private pensions) to a scheme based on a means-tested pension, a limited state second pension (which looks likely to diminish in importance over time) and reliance on voluntary private pensions. It is striking that the United Kingdom is the only country in which pension costs are predicted to fall despite a rise in the old age ratio, and even the World Bank suggests that the problem with the UK pension system is not its cost but its adequacy (Holzmann et al., 2003).

---

2 This assessment depends to some extent on one's assessment of whether a change from a defined benefit approach to a notional defined contribution system is parametric or systemic. In my own view, the level of 'notionality' in the defined contribution approach (which basically means that the amount of pension is ultimately a political decision) means that the change is parametric.

The Czech Republic has identified pension reform as a key issue, but to date actual reform has been limited. In contrast to other countries, this would appear to be related to the inability to date to build a political consensus around a direction for reform. However, it is early days in the Czech Republic and the coming years are likely to see increased pressure for decisions. In contrast, the Netherlands, which is one of the relatively few European countries already to rely heavily on funded occupational pensions, has not seen reform as a priority due to its lower level of public pension costs. However, it has been suggested that reform is more urgent here than has been identified to date (van Riel et al., 2002).

UNEMPLOYMENT BENEFIT REFORM

The area of employment–unemployment has also been a key area for reform, with a generally greater emphasis on active labour market policies in all countries (although the extent to which this policy has changed in practice is always difficult to determine). The Netherlands and the United Kingdom have been leaders in this policy area. In the Netherlands, which was faced with very high levels of sickness and disability payments, there has been widespread privatisation of these benefits with a view to 'responsibilising' employers and employees and encouraging a reduction in claim levels. These reforms are still ongoing but have resulted in a major shift in the Dutch system, away from state responsibility to a broader sharing of responsibility for sickness and disability.

In the United Kingdom the emphasis both under the Conservatives and (to an even greater extent) under Labour has been on active labour market measures for those of working age (in particular the unemployed and lone parents). All studies to date indicate that reforms such as the jobseekers allowance and the various New Deals have been successful both in reducing costs and in increasing employment and income levels. To date, the United Kingdom has not adopted such a comprehensive (or successful) approach to its high levels of disability benefits and it remains to be seen if recent reforms will be more succesful.

The Czech Republic has introduced an unemployment benefit scheme where none existed before. In contrast, in Sweden and Spain reforms have been more limited and, in part, blocked by political differences. The Swedish unemployment system was already quite active and implemented reforms have focussed on issues such as reducing replacement rates and increasing waiting days. In contrast, the Spanish unemployment system could hardly be described as one with a successful record, but here also reforms have been limited by the inability to identify a common path. Spain's high level of unemployment has no doubt contributed to this difficulty.

EARLY RETIREMENT

Despite the broadly shared commitment to active policies, the extent to which, in practice, governments and social partners are *still* prepared to facilitate early retirement is striking. As we have seen in both the Czech Republic and Spain, governments have – somewhat inconsistently – agreed to easier access to early retirement as a trade-off for pensions reform. Herbertson and Orszag (2003) have estimated that the current cost of early retirement at between 5 per cent (Sweden) and 11 per cent (Czech Republic, the Netherlands) of GDP. This is predicted to rise to 8–16 per cent of GDP by 2010 in the absence of a rise in older employment rates. This is based on the (somewhat optimistic) assumption of an older employment rate equivalent to that of the younger age group. But even making some allowance for a lower rate due to age-related disability, the costs involved are still very significant.

GENDER AND CARE

Despite the significant degree of academic attention given to issues of gender and care in recent years, it is clear that (with the exception of Sweden) these issues have rarely been central in the policy reform process in our five countries. Although reforms such as pension reform, privatisation of sickness and disability pensions or the introduction of active labour market policies have clear gender implications, these implications have rarely been discussed in detail in the establishment and implementation of policies. Thus it is often difficult to predict the precise gender impact of many reforms. In addition, despite the growth in literature, there remains a lack of comparative data both on the gender structure and outcomes of different regimes, and on the provision of care. While there have been a number of different country studies, much material remains descriptive and – given the complexity of care provision and the different ways in which care can be provided (both for older people, people with disabilities and children) – it remains very difficult to obtain a clear comparative picture of recent trends in the five countries.

The provision of care appears to have followed different trajectories in different countries. In Spain care provision seems to be a low priority, while in the Czech Republic it would appear that childcare services are now significantly less accessible than they were over a decade ago. Sweden has, of course, had a long tradition of providing a high level of care supports and has continued this approach over the recent decade. The United Kingdom, with its policy of increasing employment rates, has also given much more priority to childcare, but starting from a low base. As we have seen, the Netherlands has, in practice if not in theory, prioritised part-time work for women rather than care services to allow women to work full-time. Given the limited amount of spending in this area, it could not generally be said that issues concerning care have been central to the development of welfare states in the five countries.

Most social security systems remain based on participation in the paid labour market (for social insurance entitlements) and on a 'household' assessment of means (for means-tested benefits). Given that men are more likely to participate in the labour force and more likely to have resources than women, this inevitably means that women are less likely to qualify for most social insurance payments in their own right and, unless they are living alone, less likely to qualify for means-tested benefits. However, while specific aspects of this system remain under legal challenge, the EU directive itself is based on participation in the paid labour force and so, in principle, this approach is compatible with EU law.

WHAT ARE THE FACTORS BEHIND THESE DEVELOPMENTS?

What factors have influenced the development of welfare states in these five countries? In this section, we draw on the discussions in previous chapters to identify some of the key factors.

ECONOMIC DEVELOPMENT AND DEMOGRAPHY

In contrast to the more general analysis in Chapter 5, a more detailed and short-term analysis shows little sign of a direct relationship between levels of economic development and welfare state development. However, there does appear to be a relationship between factors such as labour force change and welfare development, which is discussed below. Demography, that is, the ageing of the population combined with a falling fertility rate (exacerbated by economic difficulties), has been a critical factor in prompting pension reform in the Czech Republic (albeit with limited results to date), Spain and Sweden. In contrast, it is difficult to make the case for this in the United Kingdom where pension costs are predicted to fall despite demographic changes. Rather, it is the commitment of successive right-wing and (nominally) social democratic governments to minimising public pension costs which has driven policy.

LABOUR FORCE CHANGE

If demography has been important for pensions change, structural labour force change has been important for overall welfare state reform. In 1974, agricultural employment ranged from a low of only 3 per cent in the United Kingdom to a high of 23 per cent in Spain. Industrial employment ranged from 36–42 per cent, while Spain still had only 40 per cent of the labour force in services. All countries have seen a significant growth in service employment in the period, with a fall in industrial employment and a sharp decline in agricultural employment in Spain. In addition, unemployment (and non-employment) levels rose dramatically in the United Kingdom, the Netherlands and, particularly, Spain in the 1980s and 1990s (in the Czech Republic, of course, official unemployment did not exist before 1989). The rise in non-employment led to both a rise in the numbers of unemployment payments as well as – and to differing degrees in different countries – to an increase in the numbers on disability and early retirement pensions.

There has also been a major increase in the proportion of the labour force who are women. In 1974, the proportion of the labour force who were women ranged from a low of 26–27 per cent (the Netherlands and Spain) to 42 per cent in Sweden. By 2000 this had risen from 39–48 per cent (with Spain and Sweden having the highest and lowest levels). This has led towards greater formal equality in terms of welfare systems, with an increase in the number of women participating in the labour force and paying social insurance contributions (and qualifying for benefits) and, as we will see in Chapter 9, a change in the old male breadwinner model. These developments have also, obviously, created pressures for reforms such as childcare, parental leave and extended maternity leave.

Related to these issues, there has been a change in the structure of labour force participation (although reliable data over time and space is lacking). There has been a growth in the levels of atypical employment in most countries over this period – although the extent of this again varies greatly across countries with the Netherlands being by far the leader in terms of part-time (mainly female) employment. This has also had implications for welfare change such as an expansion in social insurance cover for atypical workers.

POLITICS

It is difficult to identify a strong impact for left–right political parties based on the analysis of these five countries, thus supporting the thesis that party politics have become less salient (Pierson, 2001). Pension reform was driven in Spain by a conservative government and in Sweden by a Social Democratic government. And in both countries the relevant opposition party also played a broadly supportive role in this reform. The most retrenching pension policy has been continued by the New Labour government in the United Kingdom. This is not to say that political ideologies make no difference. The

Social Democratic party in the Czech Republic has been much more committed to parametric reform than have some of the smaller right-wing parties and, as we have seen, the Swedish Social Democrats rejected (some of) the Conservative government's proposals on unemployment reform and home care payments. But while *party* politics may have become less salient, it is clear that 'the nuts and bolts of social policy' still 'testify to the heated struggles of classes and interests' (Baldwin, 1990).

In working through reforms, political structures remain critically important. We have seen how the role of the CDA as a pivotal party in the Netherlands facilitated the adoption of a consensus around change by parties to its left and right. In contrast, the absence of a similar party has led to a reform roadblock in the Czech Republic, with political parties pursing their own objectives and being unable (to date) to agree a consensus. In contrast again, the (effectively) two-bloc countries (Sweden and Spain) were over time able to develop a consensus around parametric policy reform between the Scylla of increasing pension deficits and the Charibdis of systemic reform. Governance structures are also very important. As we have seen in the United Kingdom, the first-past-the-post system of parliamentary supremacy means that the party of government has significant power to implement policy change. When the parties are of different political complexions, as in the 1970s, this can lead to a stop–start policy process (for example, that concerning the introduction of a state earnings related pension). However, when the parties broadly agree about welfare reform, as in the 1990s, this has allowed one of the most significant shifts in the structure of the welfare state.

GLOBALISATION

There is no clear link between globalisation and welfare reform. All governments do operate in the context of the current world economy (although the extent to which they have always done so is perhaps understated by many current analyses of globalisation). As we have seen, the different countries considered here are integrated into the world economy in different ways and to different degrees. But there is little direct link between indicators of globalisation and welfare changes. Rather, the cases studied here tend to support Swank's (2002a) findings that the key impact is the manner in which integration into the world economy is operationised by national policy makers.

GENDER

As it has always been, gender is central to the policy changes which are being made in many of the welfare states. Welfare states are organised around different economies of care from the Swedish dual earner–publicly funded care model to the Spanish single earner–familial care approach. Yet, while the changes discussed have (and will have) a key gender impact, these have rarely been explicitly debated. While there have been significant reforms in terms of the provision of care (for example, in the United Kingdom), these have rarely been of such a scale as to be central to welfare state change (and indeed some countries may have adopted one approach in one care area and a somewhat different approach in another).

PATH DEPENDENCY

A number of researchers have highlighted the importance of path dependency in constraining welfare reform (for example, Pierson, 2001). The notion of path dependency basically means that decisions made at one point in time, often for rather minor reasons, have a lock-in effect over time and constrain the reform options for future policy makers. To the extent that this implies that decisions made at one point in time (may) have an effect in the future, it is correct but some have advanced a much stronger version of path dependency (Pierson, 2000). One example of this is in the area of pensions where it has been suggested that it will be very difficult to reform long-established PAYG pensions and much easier to reform recently established systems where the lock-in effect has yet to develop (Myles and Pierson, 2001). The cases outlined here – of parametric reform in the long-established Spanish and Swedish pension systems compared to systemic reform of the 1970s UK SERPS – might appear to support this theory.

However, the concept of path dependency has been criticised as not having sufficient regard to the reasons behind the original decision (Schwartz, n.d.). Thus, in the United Kingdom, the original reason why a SERPS was not established until the 1970s was not happenstance but rather reflected political and economic forces in British society. The reason it was possible to gut the embryonic pension system reflected those same forces. Clearly there are lock-in effects once a particular type of welfare system has been established. But path dependency theorists often overstate these effects – which are, of course, highlighted (as we saw in the Swedish case) by those who do not wish to see systemic reform – and do not give sufficient weight to underlying economic and class struggles.

WELFARE INPUTS AND OUTCOMES

Finally, let us compare welfare inputs and outcomes. Welfare inputs are measured in terms of public spending on welfare both as a percentage of GDP and in terms of purchasing power standards (PPS)

Figure 7.1   Welfare expenditure (PPP$) and risk of poverty (percentage), 2001

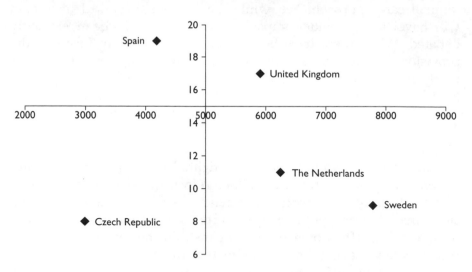

per capita. Welfare outcomes are measured in terms of income inequality (Gini co-efficient) and poverty (EU at risk-of-poverty data). In fact, both inputs and outcomes are closely correlated for the countries concerned.

Figure 7.1 shows a number of different combinations of incomes and outputs. First, we have the Swedish approach, which invests a lot in social protection to achieve low poverty and inequality. The Netherlands also broadly adopts this approach, although its fall in welfare spending in recent years is matched by some rise in poverty (but not inequality) levels. At the opposite end of the spectrum we have Spain, which spends relatively little (even less in terms of PPS than GDP terms) and has relatively high poverty and inequality. Spain is one of the poorer counties involved and, as we have seen (in Chapter 6), there is a linear relationship between poverty and inequality outcomes and levels of economic development. However, its recent economic growth appears to have had little impact in reducing relative poverty and inequality. The Czech Republic spends little in terms of PPS but, reflecting its lower level of economic development, quite a lot in terms of GDP per capita to achieve quite good outcomes in terms of poverty and inequality. Whether it can maintain both welfare inputs and outputs in the coming decade will be a key question. Finally we have the United Kingdom. Despite its significant retrenchment in qualitative terms, it still spends about average levels on social protection. And it 'achieves' some of the worst poverty and inequality outcomes in Europe.

RETRENCHMENT OR RESTRUCTURING?

To what extent do these case studies indicate retrenchment or restructuring of European welfare states? First, all welfare states indicate restructuring over the past two decades. But this is not surprising. Welfare states have always been changing and the extent to which a stable and consistent 'Keynesian national welfare state' existed from 1950 to the 1970s has been greatly overstated. In some cases, the restructuring has been of a broadly parametric nature. Changes to the Spanish and Swedish welfare states have, I would argue, not changed the fundamental objectives nor the basic policies used to achieve those objectives (although in the Spanish case some change might be desirable). In the Czech Republic, there has been systemic economic and societal change. Despite the significant changes in the welfare systems, it is perhaps the degree of continuity which is surprising. In the Netherlands, there has been systemic change: policies have been changed with the aim to devolve greater responsibility to key actors, leading to cost avoidance. But I would argue that this should not be described as retrenchment. While some of the policies of the welfare state have been changed, the fundamental objectives in terms of poverty and inequality have not (to date) been significantly altered. Finally, the United Kingdom is a clear case of retrenchment. In almost any area one cares to examine – with the exception of care services – policies are less generous now than they were in 1980 and, unlike the Netherlands, outcomes have also consistently worsened. Overall we do not see any clear trend towards convergence. Some welfare states have got better in some areas – particularly in their treatment of women and support for services. Others have restructured in order to contain costs but without significantly affecting their outcomes. Others again (or to be more accurate, one other) has retrenched welfare policies.

CONCLUSION

In summary, the discussion in this chapter has highlighted a number of key findings:

- all the welfare states have seen significant levels of change over the last two decades;
- most (with the exception of the Netherlands) have or are engaging in extensive reform of their pensions systems;
- unemployment–employment policies have also been reformed, but the extent to which this has occurred has varied significantly from countries such as the Netherlands and the United Kingdom,

with extensive reform to Spain where reform has been much more limited; and

- there is no clear trend in relation to policies on gender and care support and quantitative data in this area is still lacking.

In terms of the factors driving these changes, we saw that while there was no simple link between the level of economic development and welfare change, structural factors (such as population ageing and labour market change) have been important. Party politics may have become less salient but economic and class struggle and the manner in which this is mediated through state and parliamentary structures remains central to welfare state change. These findings indicate that there remains considerable divergence amongst European welfare states. The extent to which these are reflected in or reflect public opinion is discussed in Chapter 8. As we have seen, welfare states are faced by a number of common challenges. We look at these in Chapter 9. Finally, drawing on both international and national experience, we look at possible future directions for welfare policy in Chapter 10.

Summary

In this chapter we have:

- looked at five particular case studies of national welfare development in the period 1980–2004, looking in particular at:

  - pensions,
  - unemployment,
  - gender, and
  - family issues;

- examined the common features between welfare change in the different countries and the factors behind those changes; and
- discussed the concepts of retrenchment and restructuring and examined the factors that lie behind these developments.

Discussion points

1 What do you feel have been the most important factors influencing the development of European welfare states?
2 Do you agree that there is limited evidence of convergence amongst European welfare states?
3 Has there been significant change in European welfare states in the last decade or is continuity more apparent? If there has been change, should this be described as retrenchment or restructuring?

Supplementary reading

Debates on the concepts of retrenchment are set out in Pierson (2001), Green-Pedersen (2004) and Powell (2004). Up-to-date statistics on European countries' economic and social situation and welfare systems are available from the Eurostat and OECD websites. The *Social Protection in Europe* reports published by the EU are particularly useful, while the Eurostat *Statistics in Focus* series provides more up-to-date data on welfare spending in EU countries. Given the recent expansion of the EU, this will become an increasingly important source of data including the CEE countries. Up-to-date material on the development of welfare states in Europe is, by its very nature, constantly changing. The most up-to-date references are included in the relevant sections of this chapter.

EIGHT PUBLIC OPINION AND EUROPEAN WELFARE STATES

This chapter looks at public opinion, opinion polls and welfare state legitimacy in Europe. It outlines the research which has been carried out to date on the determinants of 'public opinion' about the welfare state. In contrast to much of the work to date, which either assumes that public opinion shapes welfare policy or tries to identify the factors which shape public opinion, we examine the extent to which comparative data in selected European countries show a relationship between public opinion (as identified by opinion poll evidence) and welfare state trajectories. It is suggested that – in a number of countries – there is a significant divergence between public opinion on the welfare state and developments in practice. This chapter looks at the theoretical issues relating to public opinion in the broad sense and at opinion polls and the extent to which public opinion can help to explain welfare state developments.

STUDIES OF PUBLIC OPINION AND THE WELFARE STATE

Although there is a considerable body of work on public attitudes concerning welfare states, this research remains at a fairly early stage both theoretically and empirically. This is, in part, due to the lack of comprehensive data over time on public attitudes to the welfare state. While detailed data is available for a number of individual countries going back over a number of decades, comparable international data is much more limited. Both the International Social Survey Programme (ISSP) (since 1985) and the European Value Study (EVS) (since 1990) have included a limited number of questions on issues related to support for the welfare state (and inequality). These questions are of a very general nature and can be criticised for a tendency to over-estimate support for the welfare state. The European Union's *Eurobarometer* series has also carried out a number of studies which are relevant to this area – specifically two studies looking at support for the welfare state carried out in 1992 and 2001. Unfortunately, while the data contained in these studies was much more detailed than in the ISSP and EVS data, there was no consistency between the questions asked in both *Eurobarometer* surveys and so it is difficult to get a clear picture over time.

In addition, while the geographical coverage of most surveys is now reasonably extensive, it is much more limited for the period before 1990 (or indeed the mid-1990s). Accordingly, much of the work to date has had to rely on snapshots of opinion at one particular point in time rather than being able to draw on a consistent series of data over a considerable period. Much of the analysis has approached the issue from two perspectives.

THESIS I: PUBLIC OPINION SHAPES WELFARE POLICY

First, some studies have assumed that public policy is a function of public opinion and that public attitudes shape welfare policies. The World Bank, for example, from a fairly instrumental perspective, has studied attitudes to the welfare state in order to understand how (what it would see as) appropriate social policy measures might better be implemented (Graham, 2002; see also Boeri et al., 2001). We will examine below the extent to which public opinion does appear to shape welfare policy.

THESIS 2: PUBLIC OPINION IS SHAPED BY …

Second, and much more commonly from an academic perspective, studies have attempted to identify the determinants of attitudes to welfare states at an individual level. It is not easy to summarise (let alone reconcile) the findings which have emerged from the studies to date. This is, in part, because studies have drawn on individual survey data in isolation (or different aspects of different survey data). Understandably, this can lead to somewhat different findings, particularly in relation to the weight to be attached to different factors. In general terms one can say that most studies in this area have suggested that the determinants of individual opinion can be analysed under two headings: those factors which are personal to the individual, and factors specific to the country in which the person is living (Heien and Hofäcker, 1999). Factors relating to these determinants are discussed below.

SELF-INTEREST

One of the most important factors under the heading of personal characteristics is that of self-interest. The argument is that people are more likely to be in favour of the welfare state if this is in their personal interest. This is largely common sense and, indeed, studies have tended to find support for self-interest as a key determinant of attitudes to the welfare state. Old age pensioners are, for example, generally found to be more in favour of increased pensions than are non-pensioners; unemployed people are generally more in favour of increased support for the unemployed than are people who are at work. This thesis would also predict that those contributing to the welfare state by way of taxes are more likely to have negative attitudes towards public spending. However, support for this argument is much less clear. While a number of studies have found that, all other things being equal, persons with higher incomes are less likely to support the welfare state (Heien and Hofäcker, 1999; Arts and Gelissen, 2001), other studies have not found any statistically significant difference between the degree of support from such persons and those with lower incomes (Boeri et al., 2001; Mau, 2001). A number of studies have broadened this approach slightly to take account of the fact that peoples' self-interest may also take account of their recent experience or expectations for the future. Thus it has been suggested that people who have recently been unemployed or who anticipate becoming unemployed may also, from self-interest, support higher payments to the unemployed and support has been found for this. However, self-interest, while an important factor, obviously does not account fully for opinions in relation to support for welfare states.

INDICATORS OF MORAL COMMITMENT

This heading is intended to account for the views personal to an individual which can lead to support for the welfare state independent of self-interest. However, in contrast to the clarity about the rationale behind self-interest, a number of quite different explanations have been put forward as to why a person might have a moral commitment to the welfare state. These include factors such as: 'deeply held norms of reciprocity and conditional obligations to others' (Bowles and Gintis, 2000); legitimacy or 'the beliefs according to which the authority of the central power is justified in the eyes of those who are subjected to it' (Peillon, 1995: 8); and individual socialisation processes (Heien and Hofäcker, 1999). As can be seen, these concepts are somewhat imprecise and can be difficult to operationalise in an opinion poll study. Nonetheless, a number of studies have found support for the thesis that indicators of moral commitment help to explain support for the welfare state. For example, Gelissen (2000) found that people with higher educational attainment, members of a trade union, people with a leftist political orientation and a post-materialist value-orientation were more supportive of a welfare state. However, it should be noted that, particularly in relation to educational attainment, a number of findings have come to the opposite conclusion (Heien and Hofäcker, 1999; Arts and Gelissen, 2001) or have found no statistically significant difference between those with higher and lower levels of education (Boeri et al., 2001). In general, studies have found that women are more inclined to have supportive values than men, but this has not been a universal finding (Gallie and Paugam, 2002; Blekesaune and Quadagno, 2003).

THE ECONOMIC SITUATION OF THE COUNTRY

Moving on from individual characteristics to those specific to the country in which the respondent lives, it has been suggested that persons living in a country with a higher level of economic development will be likely to show relatively lower levels of support for the welfare state and, conversely, that those in less developed countries (with less developed welfare states) will be likely to show higher levels of support. A second argument in this area is that in times of economic recession there will be an increased demand for social policies to protect individuals from the negative effects of economic change and a consequent rise in unemployment. Therefore it is predicted that a declining economic situation may lead to a rise in support of the welfare state (Heien and Hofäcker, 1999). However, it has been argued that, to the converse, a declining economic situation may make people less likely to support increased taxation in order to fund the welfare state and may, in fact, reduce support for welfare state spending. Again the findings in this area are mixed. On the one hand, Heien and Hofäcker (1999) report that the economic situation of a country seems to have no decisive influence on public opinion in relation to welfare other than in relation to specific labour market programmes. (Although they do report evidence from Germany alone in relation to reduced support for the welfare state in times of declining economic growth.) On the other hand, Arts and Gelissen (2001: 292) found that countries which were at a lower level of economic and social development were more inclined to report relatively high scores in relation to solidarity.

NATIONAL WELFARE CULTURES

Finally, it is argued that the cultural, structural and institutional characteristics of a country form dominant welfare ideologies which influence the opinions of persons living in those countries (Heien and Hofäcker, 1999). Again the findings in this area are somewhat mixed. On the one hand, it is clear that there are significant differences between the attitudes to inequality and redistribution between the former socialist countries of Central and Eastern Europe and those of Western Europe (for example, Suhrcke, 2001), with people living in CEE countries significantly more egalitarian than those living in Western Europe, to the extent that they express less tolerance for existing income inequalities even after the actual level of income inequality and other determinants of attitude are taken into account. Suhrcke (2001) argued that these attitudes do not appear to be driven by the recent rapid rise in inequality during the transition but rather arise from an attitudinal legacy carried over from socialism.

On the other hand, considerable effort has been given to attempting to identify attitudinal differences in line with Esping-Anderson's *The Three Worlds of Welfare Capitalism*. Logically, it can be argued that if these 'three worlds' do indeed constitute different welfare regimes they should also develop similar dominant welfare ideologies and, consequently, have broadly similar public attitudes to welfare. The best that can be said for this argument is that the studies to date provide very limited support for this thesis (and that with considerable interpretative effort by the authors concerned). In general, the studies find that the grouping together of European states in regime types does not explain the variation in attitudes satisfactorily (Arts et al., 2003) or that there is little or no evidence for the thesis that there exists a relationship between the type of welfare state and levels of popular support (Gelissen, 2000; Svalfors, 2004).

THESIS 3: WELFARE STATE DEVELOPMENT IS NOT DIRECTLY SHAPED BY PUBLIC OPINION

This section looks at the relationship between the level of public support for the welfare state and the actual changes which have taken place in welfare states in recent years. In other words, we look at the extent to which public attitudes *do* shape welfare policy. In doing so, we focus in particular on the cases which have already been discussed in Chapter 7 (adding France and Germany as further representatives of the Christian centrist grouping and Denmark where data for Sweden is not available). Unfortunately, there are considerable limits to the extent to which comparable opinion poll evidence is available over time even for these countries. The details of the studies drawn on are set out as follows:

1   A detailed poll of public attitudes in relation to European welfare states carried out by *Eurobarometer* in 1992 (Ferrera, 1993). This study focuses on the then 12 member states of the EU and, as a consequence, only includes Denmark from the Nordic countries and, of the former socialist countries of Central and Eastern Europe, only the former East Germany is included. While this study does provide a very detailed range of evidence in relation to support for different aspects of the welfare state, it can be criticised on the basis, common to many opinion polls, that it may tend to overstate support as it does not specifically probe the extent to which people are willing to pay additional taxes in order to fund welfare improvements.

2   A 2001 *Eurobarometer* report in relation to social precarity and social integration (Gallie and Paugam, 2002). This covers the then 15 EU countries, thereby extending coverage to Sweden and Finland (and again reports evidence separately for the former East Germany). Unfortunately, however, while this study does probe the extent to which people are willing to pay additional taxes in order to fund welfare improvements, it provides a much more limited range of questions in relation to support for the welfare state and, somewhat surprisingly, does not replicate any of the questions from the 1992 study which would have allowed a comparison of trends over time.

3   Indicators from the ISSP and EVS. While the questions asked in these studies are of a very general nature and can again be criticised as tending to overstate support for welfare states, we can draw on summary indicators of support for welfare states in order to provide a comparison with the Eurobarometer data.

4   A detailed study of opinions in relation to the welfare state which covers three of our countries (France, Germany and Spain) (Boeri et al., 2001).

5   Finally, given the lack of comparable data for Central and Eastern European countries, a comparative study which included both the Netherlands and the Czech Republic (Sirovátka et al., 1998). Given that the Netherlands is included in most of the other studies utilized here, this does at least allow us to situate the Czech Republic in relation to that country.

The data provided by these studies is outlined below. However, given the different sources of data, considerable caution should be utilised in making comparisons between the different studies.

Table 8.1 sets out selected data from the *Eurobarometer* study for 1992 in relation to our chosen countries. In particular it provides data for:

Table 8.1 Attitudes to the welfare state, 1992 (percentage responses)

	The Netherlands	United Kingdom	Denmark	France	West Germany	East Germany	Germany	Spain	Average
Minimalist	50	44	54	41	30	15	27	47	41
Maximalist	53	79	58	65	57	68	59	71	65
Costly	40	17	41	46	27	68	36	48	36
Not costly	54	73	56	51	66	75	68	48	55
Continuist	16	11	16	21	18	7	16	8	13
Contractionist	15	4	16	11	8	6	8	9	9
Content	21	8	11	6	10	2	8	8	6
Discontent	5	33	16	24	21	39	25	51	33

Source: Eurobarometer (Ferrera, 1993)

- those supporting a minimalist as opposed to maximalist approach to welfare states,[1] the percentage agreeing or disagreeing with the proposition that 'social security is too costly for society. Benefits should be reduced and contributions should be lowered';
- those supporting a contractionist and continuist approach to the welfare state;[2] and
- the percentage who agreed or disagreed with the proposition that they personally thought that the unemployed, the old, the sick and the disabled, those who have a work-related illness or accident and the poor were 'sufficiently well protected' in their country.

As can be seen there is a considerable variation in the attitudes, with the United Kingdom and the former East Germany generally providing most support for the existing or an expanded welfare state, and these two countries and Spain being the most dissatisfied with the current level of support provided. In contrast respondents from the Netherlands were the most satisfied with the current level of support provided and amongst the most likely countries to support a roll-back of the welfare state (albeit that this remained a minority position in the Netherlands). A more detailed discussion of the findings in relation to individual countries is outlined below.

Table 8.2 provides evidence from the European Value Study for 1996–1997 in relation to respondent's views as to whether the government was doing enough to respond to poverty.

The results reported for the countries we focus on are broadly representative of the findings of the study. In general, in Western European countries, about two-thirds of the population (60 to 66 per cent) believed that governments were doing too little in response

---

1 Those taking a minimalist approach agreed with the proposition that 'the government should provide everyone with only a limited number of essential benefits and encourage people to provide for themselves in other respects', while those taking a maximalist approach agreed with the proposition that 'the government must continue to provide everyone with a broad range of social security benefits even if it means increasing taxes and contributions'.

2 Those identified as contractionists agreed with the proposition that 'the government should provide everyone with only a limited number of essential benefits – such as healthcare or minimum income – and encourage people to provide for themselves in other respects' and that 'social security is too costly for society. Benefits should be reduced and contributions should be lowered' and disagreed with the proposition that 'the government must continue to provide everyone with a broad range of social security benefits even if this means increasing taxes or contributions' while continuists took the opposite position on these items.

Table 8.2   Attitudes to government action on poverty, 1996/7 (percentage responses)

	Sweden	West Germany	East Germany	Spain
About right	29	26	16	26
Too little	60	62	77	64

Source: European Values Study

Table 8.3   Attitudes to solidarity, 1996–2001

	EU 01	ISSP 96	EVS 99
The Netherlands	4.20	–	4.54
United Kingdom	4.5	3.98	4.62
Sweden	4.5	3.96	4.54
Denmark	4.0		4.05
France	4.7	4.02	4.66
West Germany	3.8	3.76	4.48
East Germany	4.9		
Spain	5.0	4.42	4.61

Source: ISSP, 1996; EVS, 1999; Eurobarometer, 2001

to poverty, while about 25 per cent believed that the government response was about right.[3] In contrast, in the countries of Central and Eastern Europe and Turkey there was a much higher negative response, with from 77 to 90 per cent of respondents believing that their government was doing too little.

Table 8.3 reports data from a number of different sources: the International Social Survey Programme for 1996, the European Value Study for 1999 and the *Eurobarometer* for 2001, which provide broad indications of support for welfare state measures.[4] While the questions vary somewhat from one study to another, there is a high degree of correlation between the responses, which would tend to indicate that the questions do provide a valid measure of something. Whether this is the degree of national solidarity, the level of support for public action on social policies or the extent to which individuals from different countries are inclined to provide what they perceive

---

3 Norway was an exception to this, with only 53 per cent feeling that the government was doing too little and 41 per cent about right.

4 The ISSP and EVS measures are composite indicators of support for broad 'welfare' policies (Arts and Gelissen, 2002); the *Eurobarometer* measure is also a composite index (Gallie and Paugam, 2002). In all cases, the higher the score the greater the level of support.

Table 8.4   Willingness to pay more taxes to reduce poverty, 2001 (percentage responses)

The Netherlands	United Kingdom	Sweden	Denmark	France	West Germany	East Germany	Spain	Average
54	54	54	50	42	28	35	52	50

Source: Eurobarometer, 2001

Table 8.5   Attitudes to welfare reform, 2001 (percentage responses)

	France	Germany	Spain
Maintain	41.4	55.3	38.50
Reduce	28.3	25.2	11.50
Increase	11.2	13.1	22.30
D.K. (don't know)	19.1	6.5	27.70

Source: Boeri et al., 2001

the right answer to the question, is perhaps more debatable (see Blekesaune and Quadagno, 2003).

Table 8.4 provides the responses from the *Eurobarometer* 2001 study in response to the question 'I would be ready to pay more taxes if it were definitely used to improve the situation of the poor'. The EU average for this question is around 50 per cent (which is only significantly exceeded by Greece). As can be seen, the lowest proportion of the population who would be prepared to pay more tax is found in the former West Germany. This is followed relatively closely by the population of the former East Germany with most other countries being close to or around the average. Gallie and Paugam (2002: 121–3) carried out an analysis of the national impact on responses to this question (holding all other factors equal) and with the United Kingdom as a reference case found that Denmark, Germany and France were statistically less likely to support paying additional taxes. No statistical significance was found for the responses from Sweden, Spain and the Netherlands.

Finally, Table 8.5 reports responses from the Boeri et al. (2001) study of attitudes to welfare state reform. Specifically this table reports the response to the question: 'In your opinion, should the state (a) reduce taxes and compulsory contributions, cutting pensions and/or transfers to households, (b) maintain taxes and compulsory contributions at current levels, or (c) increase pensions and/or transfers to households, by raising taxes and/or compulsory contributions?'

As can be seen, the largest group in all countries favoured maintenance of taxes and contributions at current levels. Only in Spain did the number supporting more taxes and transfers outweigh those supporting less. However, the Spanish response is not representative of a general 'Southern' response as Italy was the only country in the study where the largest proportion supported a reduction in transfers and taxes.

COUNTRY-SPECIFIC RESPONSES

In this section we look at the overall picture in relation to the specific countries we have looked at.

THE NETHERLANDS

In the case of the Netherlands, the 1992 *Eurobarometer* study indicates that respondents are, compared to the average for the EU12, more in favour of a minimalist approach, slightly more likely to see social security as costly and support reductions (albeit that this is a minority position), more in favour of contraction of the welfare state and significantly more content than other EU countries. The results for the broader 'solidarity' type questions in 1999 and 2002 and in relation to willingness to pay more taxes indicate about average levels of support for the welfare state. This combination of low levels of dissatisfaction with benefits paid and comparatively high (albeit overall minority) support for the restructuring of the welfare state may be seen as not inconsistent with what actually has happened in the Netherlands over the last decade. As we have seen in Chapter 7, the Netherlands can be seen as one of the leading countries in terms of restructuring of the welfare state, with the focus being very definitely on restructuring rather than a neo-liberal type retrenchment.

UNITED KINGDOM

The United Kingdom, on the basis of the 1992 data, is much more supportive than average of a maximalist approach, opposed to reductions in welfare state spending and reports relatively high levels of dissatisfaction with the current level of spending. In each of the other measures for which we have data, the United Kingdom is at or slightly above the average in terms of support for the welfare state. This picture is, of course, completely inconsistent with the high levels of retrenchment of the welfare state which have in fact occurred in the United Kingdom over the period since 1979.

DENMARK

In the case of Denmark, the 1992 *Eurobarometer* study finds attitudes which are very similar to that of the Netherlands in terms of relatively high levels of support for a minimalist approach and roll-back in welfare state spending (albeit, as in the case of the Netherlands, that these are minority views). Subsequent studies indicate that Danish respondents report somewhat lower levels of support for the welfare state than do the Dutch. Thus the response from opinion poll surveys would tend to suggest that we should find a higher level of retrenchment in Denmark than we do in the Netherlands. However, comparative studies of the two countries in the relevant period indicate a significantly higher degree of retrenchment and refocusing in the Netherlands and considerably more opposition to retrenchment in Denmark (Green-Pedersen, 2002a).

GERMANY

In the case of Germany (data for post-unification Germany as a whole), there is perhaps a lack of a strong opinion in any particular direction. In the 1992 data, there is a significantly higher proportion of people in favour of a maximalist approach, but both maximalist and minimalist respondents are below the EU average. An above average proportion of the population are, however, against a roll-back of the welfare state and the number of continuists as opposed to contractionists is at about the EU average. Similarly, there is neither a high level of dissatisfaction nor satisfaction with the level of current benefits. In the subsequent indicators in relation to solidarity, German respondents are at or below the average for the countries reported here and, as we have seen, German respondents are the least willing of EU nations to agree to pay additional taxation in 2001. Gallie and Paugam suggested that 'the large-scale transfers from Western Germany to the Eastern region after unification, which resulted among other things in a sizable increase in direct and indirect taxation, may in the end have made the Germans somewhat more lukewarm about redistributions towards the poor' (2002: 121). It is, however, unclear when this change in attitude (if such it is) took place. Data from the ISSP over the period from 1985 to 1996 do not show any significant decline in support for welfare state policies over this period. In the Boeri et al. (2001) study, German respondents were those most in favour of maintaining the existing position. This general lack of enthusiasm for or against changes in the welfare state may be interpreted as being consistent with what has actually happened in Germany over the last decade, with considerable opposition to attempts to retrench or restructure the German welfare state. However, it is not consistent with the recent outcomes of pension reform which have been forced through against strong public protest.

FRANCE

The picture for France is not dissimilar to that for Germany. In the 1992 study, French respondents report attitudes which are very much in line with the overall EU average in terms of support for the welfare state. Subsequent studies in relation to solidarity indicate that French respondents are at or above the average for the countries studied, albeit that they are somewhat less willing than the average to pay additional taxes (in the 2001 study). This might be hypothesised as being consistent with the difficulties which have arisen in France in implementing significant retrenchment or refocusing of welfare state provisions. Again, however, recent pension reform has been implemented despite considerable public opposition.

SPAIN

In Spain, in contrast, there is a very high level of support for a maximalist approach (albeit that there is also a high level of support for a roll-back of benefits as being too costly). There is a very significant level of dissatisfaction with the current level of benefits. Ferrera (1993: 7) suggests that the apparent disparity between the high number in favour of a maximalist approach and the high number in favour of a reduction in benefits may be explained by the fact that the objective of sound public finances and spending control ranked high on the political agenda at the time, particularly in terms of faster EC integration, and that this may have created an ambivalence in public discussion on the welfare state, which propelled popular attitudes in contrasting and inconsistent directions. The apparent division may also be an artefact of this particular poll as it does not appear in subsequent studies. Subsequent data in relation to solidarity polls indicate that Spain is ahead (significantly so in some cases) of average levels of support and is somewhat more willing than average to pay additional taxes to support the poor. In the Boeri et al. study (2001), Spain reports the lowest portion of the four countries studied in favour of reductions in the welfare state and the highest level of support for increases in taxes and welfare state spending. In general, the level of support for the welfare state in Spain would not seem to have been borne out in practice in the developments reported in Chapter 7. While there has been some level of increase in welfare state spending in Spain, this could be largely explained by a catch-up from low levels of initial spending and it might be suggested that public expectations in relation to increased levels of welfare expenditure have not yet been met (as indicated by the 2001 results).

CENTRAL AND EASTERN EUROPE

Finally, turning to Central and Eastern Europe, the only country for which we have data over time is the former East Germany. Here, respondents have generally reported a much more positive attitude to the welfare state than West Germans and a much higher level of support for egalitarian policies. However, it is difficult to suggest any direct link between the attitudes of the former East German respondents and the current welfare state, given that the existing West German welfare state was extended en bloc to East Germany on reunification. We do not generally have any consistent time series of data on attitudes to the welfare state before about 1990 for the former socialist countries (and significantly later in many cases). Given the dramatic changes which have occurred in the economic situation in these transition economies, it is, at this point in time, very difficult to disentangle the effects of economic and political change from the limited data we have on attitudes to the welfare state.

CZECH REPUBLIC

We are fortunate to be able to draw on one detailed comparative study which compares data from the Czech Republic in 1998 with a similar public opinion survey carried out in the Netherlands in 1995. In general, studies report a much higher level of support for egalitarian policies in the former socialist countries (albeit that, at least on some indicators, the Czech Republic shows significantly lower levels of support for such policies than do other Central and Eastern European countries). The comparative study of welfare state solidarity and support in the Czech Republic and the Netherlands (Sirovátka et al., 1998) reports that compared to the Netherlands, the Czech public perceived that income differential in their society was too great and were more supportive of reductions in income inequality. Czechs reported much higher levels of discontent with the system of social security than did the Dutch, albeit that both countries reported high levels of support for the necessity of a social security system. Czechs were also much more likely to have a negative view of the effect of social security, with comparatively low levels of respondents (compared to the Dutch) perceiving the social security system as reducing poverty, reducing social unrest or distributing wealth more justly. In addition, significantly more Czech respondents regarded levels of social security benefits as being insufficient and supported higher levels of social security spending (particularly in relation to child benefit). Related work has looked at changes in public attitudes to the welfare state in the Czech republic, drawing on national data (Sirovátka and Rabušic, 1998). This study, which utilised national data over the period from 1991 to 1998, indicates that 'significant ideological shifts took place in Czech public opinion, showing a very clear trend of gradual movement away from liberal to social democratic values' over that period (Sirovátka and Rabušic 1998: 17).

DISCUSSION

On balance, we see somewhat of a mismatch between public attitudes to the welfare state and actual developments in welfare state policies. In the case of the Netherlands, we see a combination of significant (if minority) support for retrenchment combined with low levels of dissatisfaction with the current level of benefits. This might be seen as facilitating the type of retrenchment and refocusing which has taken place in the Netherlands. However, in the case of Denmark with quite similar attitudes towards public support for the welfare state, we see higher levels of political opposition to welfare state retrenchment and lower levels of change. The levels of support for the maintenance of existing policies in France and Germany and the absence of strong levels of support for either improvement or retrenchment of the welfare state may also be seen as consistent with the somewhat 'frozen' nature of these welfare states in the past decade but inconsistent with more recent pension reforms. The relatively high levels of support for improvements in the welfare state and the high levels of dissatisfaction with current levels of benefit in the United Kingdom must be seen as inconsistent with the also high levels of retrenchment which have taken place in that country. In the case of Spain, one might question whether the apparently high levels of support for additional welfare state spending have been realised in practice. Finally, in the case of the Czech Republic, dissatisfaction with the level of benefits and support for additional spending may reflect the lower income levels in that country. National data suggest that Czech public attitudes may have initially been more favourable to retrenchment but later moved to a more supportive position. In this case it would appear that public attitudes may have been shaped by public policies rather than the other way round.

LOOKING AGAIN AT PUBLIC OPINION AND THE WELFARE STATE

But why is there a mismatch between 'public opinion' (as expressed in opinion poll evidence) and actual welfare state change? In order to answer this question, we need to examine the concepts of legitimacy, public opinion and opinion poll evidence.

LEGITIMACY

Ringen adopts a highly instrumental approach to legitimacy. He argues that:

> ... the problem of legitimacy is a question of how people react to the experience of re-distribution; do they accept social policies and play along with them or do they oppose these policies and try to beat the system? The legitimacy of the welfare state does not depend on theoretical fashions but on the opinions and behaviour of the population. (1987: Ch. 3)

Thus he argues that the legitimacy of the welfare state is basically dependent on the support of public opinion. Public opinion, in turn, can be established through the use of opinion poll evidence (1987: 51).

Other authors have, however, interpreted legitimacy in a more nuanced way. Peillon argues that:

> ... legitimacy refers to the beliefs according to which the authority of the central power is justified in the eyes of those who are subjected to it. The concept of legitimacy applies only when acquiescence to, and compliance with, the rule of the central power rests on a belief in the adequacy and fairness of established political institutions. (1995: 8)

There are, however, practical difficulties in measuring legitimacy by way of opinion poll evidence. It cannot, for example, simply be assumed that support for the welfare state not accounted for by self-interest represents support arising from legitimacy. In addition, it seems likely that people are more likely to believe in the adequacy and fairness of established political institutions if those institutions support their own interests. The 'crisis of legitimacy' theories would suggest that where the legitimacy of a welfare state is strong, the welfare state will be maintained or will continue to grow and that the basis of the welfare state will not be radically undermined. In contrast, these theories suggest that if the legitimacy of the welfare state is weakened, then substantial changes are more likely to occur. So one can suggest that the legitimacy of the welfare state is likely to be related to what has happened in practice over the period in question. If the structure of and investment in the welfare state has remained broadly intact, then one can suggest that its legitimacy may have been reasonably strong. In contrast, if the structure of or investment in the welfare state has changed substantially, this suggests that legitimacy was weak.

PUBLIC OPINION AND OPINION POLL EVIDENCE

Several authors assume that public opinion can be gauged with reasonable accuracy from opinion poll evidence (Ringen, 1987). In contrast, Habermas argues for a concept of public opinion as 'the critical reflection of a public competent to form its own opinions' rather than as a collection of individual opinions (1989: 90). While Habermas accepts that the notion of the public opinion is a fictional one, it is arguably useful to conceptualise public opinion as something more than simply a collection of individual un-debated opinions. Taylor-Gooby (1985: 72) argues that peoples' initial attitudes may not correspond with their ultimate actions and that mass opinion is only one of the factors which influences public policy, with pressure groups and elites also having a key role.

Ringen highlights a number of criticisms of opinion poll data:

> It can be argued that opinion data do not necessarily reveal 'true' public opinion: The survey situation is artificial, questions may be leading or not precisely formulated, respondents are free to express opinions without having to stand by what they say. It can also be argued that individual opinions are merely the raw material for collective preferences and that the latter are developed in a process where opinions are tested against counter-arguments and where those who express opinions must be prepared to accept, challenge and to motivate and defend their views. (1987: 51)

Ringen quickly adds that he does not agree with these criticisms and argues that modern survey techniques are sufficiently sophisticated to monitor opinions with reasonable accuracy. However, it is arguable that the criticism Ringen sets out are more telling than he is prepared to accept. It may be useful to adopt Habermas' concept of public opinion as 'the critical reflection of a public competent to form its own opinions' and to see opinion poll evidence as simply one input into the formulation of this public opinion (1989: 90). Public opinion would then be seen as something more than simply a mass collection of individual opinions and would take on board the views of different interests (to the extent to which these entered into the public debate). In summary, one can develop a hypothesis which sees legitimacy as being related to the acceptability of the welfare state to a broad public opinion. Mass individual opinion can be seen as one (but only one) input into the formation of pubic opinion and opinion poll evidence as an indicator of mass individual opinion.

A RECONSIDERATION OF THE ISSUES

PUBLIC OPINION

In relation to public opinion, we have suggested that this should be seen as something broader than a simple collection of individual opinions. Such a broader concept of public opinion might be measured through an analysis of official publications, books in widespread circulation, newspapers, television and radio programmes, public protests, political party policies, the activities of social movements and so on. To take the case of the United Kingdom as one example; it is clear from general observation that the public discourse in relation to the welfare state is much more critical and challenging than public attitudes as contained in opinion poll evidence suggest. The opinions of key sections of the media and political party platforms (from the mid-1990s in the case of the Labour party) have been supportive of a retrenchment of the welfare state. Thus one could suggest that positive individual opinion in the United Kingdom has been overwhelmed in the formation of a broader public opinion by the creation of a more critical welfare state discourse by the state, by political parties and by the opinions of business. The failure of positive individual opinion to translate into positive public opinion can also be seen as arising from a failure to mobilise individual opinions in a collective manner so as to influence public opinion in relation to the welfare state. This has led to split public opinion, which has weakened the legitimacy of the welfare state thereby allowing the retrenchment which we have seen to have occurred.

POLITICAL STRUCTURES

A further argument would suggest that the different political structures in different countries allow public opinion to be mediated in different ways with different impacts on the welfare state. Thus, for example, in the United Kingdom, with its first-past-the-post electoral system, which allows a party to achieve a significant overall majority with much less than 50 per cent of the total vote, it is possible for political parties to ignore significant levels of opposition to welfare state retrenchment (obviously as long as there are also significant numbers in favour of such retrenchment). In contrast, Green-Pedersen has argued that the higher level of retrenchment in the Netherlands as opposed to Denmark occurred 'due to a broad party consensus about socio-economic policy emerging in the mid-1980s because of the way party competition works in a system with a pivotal centre party' (2001). Green-Pedersen argues that 'governments will only retrench if they do not face a strong opposition' and that such a lack of opposition can emerge 'either if parties of the left are in government or if parties of the left for strategic reasons desist from using retrenchment in inter-party competition' (2001: 23).

CONCLUSION

We have outlined the limited evidence to date as to the basis of support for the welfare state. We have also argued that there is a mismatch between public attitudes towards the welfare state (as reported in various opinion polls) and actual welfare state developments in the past decade or so. While developments in a number of countries can be seen as broadly consistent with public attitudes to welfare, there are also a number of countries where there is apparent inconsistency in this regard. In other words, we suggest that public attitudes do not (or do not always) shape welfare policies. We have argued that this arises for two reasons. First, public opinion is only partially informed by individual opinion and other key interests (such as the opinions of business and the state) play an important role in the formation of a general public opinion. Second, this analysis suggests that the ability to mobilise individual opinion in a collective manner so as to influence public opinion may vary according both to country and to social class. Where public opinion is split, this may weaken the legitimacy of the welfare state sufficiently for retrenchment to occur. In particular, we have argued that the manner in which public attitudes impact on actual welfare state developments depends in part on the political and electoral system which exists in different European countries (Green-Pedersen, 2001, 2002a). Different types of electoral system and different types of party competition facilitate or hinder the extent to which public attitudes can shape welfare policies.

This chapter suggests that we need to take a broader approach to the concepts of legitimacy, public opinion and opinion poll evidence. In particular, it suggests that we need to examine the extent to which individual opinion has been able to influence broader public opinion and to look at factors other than individual opinion poll evidence as being of relevance to the shaping of broader public opinion.

Summary

This chapters has:

- discussed existing studies of the determinants of public support for the welfare state, including self-interest, a moral commitment to welfare, the national economic situation and national welfare cultures;
- examined what we mean by public opinion and opinion poll evidence;
- looked at detailed evidence on public support for welfare in a number of key welfare states;
- studied the extent to which popular support corresponds to welfare developments; and
- suggested reasons for divergences between opinion poll evidence of support for the welfare state and welfare state outcomes.

Discussion points

1   Is Habermas's concept of public opinion as 'the critical reflection of a public competent to form its own opinions' rather than as a collection of individual opinions useful in welfare states studies?

2   What are your views on European welfare state reform? To what extent are they shaped by self-interest and/or moral beliefs?

3   Do you agree with Ringen's concept of legitimacy as 'how people react to the experience of redistribution'?

4   Do you tell opinion pollsters your real opinions?

Supplementary reading

A number of studies present evidence from opinion polls in relation to support for the welfare state, including Ferrera (1993), Gallie and Paugam (2002) and Boeri et al. (2001). Findings from the European Values Study can be accessed directly at http://nds.umdl.umich.edu. There are a considerable number of studies which draw on particular data for particular countries at particular times – many of which are referred to in this chapter – but an absence of a current overview of the findings. Turning to our broader look at 'public opinion', Habermas (1989) provides a useful historical account which sets out a broader understanding of public opinion.

PART THREE
THE FUTURE

NINE CHALLENGES FACING EUROPEAN WELFARE STATES

This chapter looks at the current and future challenges facing European welfare states. In particular, it looks at five key areas: demographic changes – especially the ageing of the population and fertility decline; economic and labour market change; budgetary limitations; changes in gender roles and household composition; and EU (and EMU) membership and further expansion. These issues are all, to a greater or lesser extent, interlinked and changes in one area may contribute to (or cause) changes in another. Likewise changes in one area may exacerbate or alleviate changes arising in another. This chapter outlines the issues that arise. The key responses that have been put forward or which are under discussion are outlined in the next chapter.

DEMOGRAPHY

There are two key demographic changes facing European welfare states. The first is the ageing of the population and the rise in the old age ratio. The second is the sharp decline in fertility.

POPULATION AGEING

At present about one quarter of the EU15 adult population is over the age of 65 (often known as the old age ratio or, perhaps less felicitously, the age-dependency ratio). By 2050 older people will make up almost half of Europe's adult population. In short, this is the population ageing challenge facing European policy makers and it will have significant implications for welfare states, particularly in relation to pensions, health care and caring services.

The rise in the old age ratio is caused by two factors: a greater number of older people in absolute terms and a fall in the number of people of working age. These figures are obviously based on projections and, as such, the one thing we can say for certain is that they will be incorrect. Population projections in the past – particularly in the long term – have often been widely inaccurate because population developments can be affected by a very wide range of factors (such as economic development and war) which are impossible to predict. However, projections in relation to the rising number of older people are likely to be quite accurate. We already know the number of people approaching retirement age and likely mortality rates, so it is relatively easy to project these numbers forward.

The rise in the number of older people stems from two factors: the 'baby-boom' generation born after the Second World War are now approaching retirement age, and continued increases in life expectancy. There was a significant increase in the number of children born after the Second World War in the period up to about 1970. These people will reach the age of 65 over the next few decades, so there will be more older people than there have been in recent decades. It is predicted that by 2050 Europeans will live four to five years longer than we do today. Today's average life expectancy at age 65 is about 15.5 years for men and 19.5 years for women, so an increase of 5 years will increase pension costs by 25 to 30 per cent (European Commission, 2002: 11). In particular, there will be a rise in the very-old population group who are more likely to be in need of health and care services.

The increase in the older population is accentuated by the fact that it is projected that the working age population will fall, due largely to falling fertility rates. Projections in this area are somewhat more speculative as it is difficult to predict whether fertility will continue to fall, stabilise at its current levels, or rise. In addition, migration levels play a very important role in determining the size of the working age population, so increased migration could play an important role in reducing ageing problems. However, studies indicate that the level of migration required to offset population ageing would be 'extremely large and in all cases entail vastly more immigration than occurred in the past' (UN, 2000). A UN study took the view that 'maintaining potential support ratios at current levels through replacement migration alone seems out of reach because of the extraordinarily high number of migrants that would be required' (UN, 2000). The European Commission (2003b: 16) also took the view that using immigration to compensate *fully* for the impact of ageing 'is not a realistic option' due largely to the challenges of integration from a social cohesion perspective. However, migration can contribute significantly as *part* of an overall policy approach.

There are a number of important points which need to be highlighted in relation to population ageing. First, in terms of definition, estimates choose a somewhat arbitrary age of 65 to distinguish between working age and old age. In fact, as we will discuss further in Chapter 10, many people retire from the workforce before the age of 65. Equally if, in future decades, people retire at a later age, this, while not affecting the numbers above or below 65, will affect the numbers who require pensions as opposed to the numbers of 'working age'.

Second, the current and projected level of the old age ratio varies greatly from one country to another (Table 9.1). Ireland currently has the lowest old age ratio (17 per cent) while some of the Southern European countries (Italy, Spain) and Sweden have the highest rates. The CEE countries generally have low old age ratios (c. 20 per cent), but this is not a good indicator of their level of pension pressure as they also have low effective retirement ages, giving rise to high pension claims. It is projected that by 2050 the Czech Republic, Greece, Spain, Italy and Austria will all be over the EU average old age ratio of 50 per cent. Conversely, Denmark and Ireland will all be well below average at 40 per cent or under. So the extent to which countries are facing policy challenges varies across Europe.

Third, this level of population 'ageing' is not, in fact, dramatically different to that experienced in the past. As Castles (2004) points out, over the period from 1960 to 1998, the old age ratio rose by 5.3 per cent compared to a projected 9 per cent further increase in the period to 2030. In addition, in OECD countries in the period from 1960, life expectancy rose by about four years and the age of retirement decreased by about three years, leading to an increase in the average duration of pension payment by some seven years. Of course, the fact that welfare states have coped with this increase in the past does not mean they can cope with a similar increase in the future. However, all these factors do mean that the issue of ageing is one where the precise level of population ageing is not automatically set at this stage, varies greatly from country to country and is not dissimilar to past experiences. This all warrants considerable caution when referring to population ageing as a demographic 'crisis' or 'time bomb'.

It should also be noted that the young age ratio has fallen significantly in the last 20 years (from 34.5 per cent in EU countries in 1980 to 26 per cent in 2000). This is projected to fall further in the medium term. This should mean that the higher costs of pensions is, to some extent, offset by a fall in the costs of child support although, in practice, this 'demographic dividend' is always difficult to convert into Exchequer savings. A fall in class sizes, for example, gives rise to calls for a reduction in the pupil–teacher ratio, leaving the cost the same.

Policy proposals to address population ageing both parametric (for example, reducing pension levels and increasing the effective retirement age) and systemic (for example, privatising pensions) have been advanced by a range of bodies and are discussed in Chapter 10.

Table 9.1 Demographic data

	Old age ratio, 2000	Fertility rates (total fertility rate), 2002	Household size, 2001	Lone parent household (%) C. 2001	Divorce rates (per 000 marriages), 2000	Dual earner households, 2000
Belgium	26	1.64	2.4	9	59.8	67
Denmark	22	1.73	2.1	6	37.5	–
Germany	24	1.40	2.2	8	44.3	65
Spain	25	1.25	3.0	3	16.5	43
France	24	1.88	2.4	9	40.9	66
Greece	26	1.25	2.6	4	15.4	50
Ireland	17	2.01	3.0	7	–	48
Italy	27	1.26	2.6	4	12.5	46
The Netherlands	20	1.73	2.3	11	39.3	69
Austria	23	1.37	2.4	8	49.8	67
Portugal	23	1.42	2.9	4	30.0	70
Finland	22	1.72	2.1	9	53.2	–
Sweden	27	1.65	2.1	22	53.9	–
United Kingdom	24	1.64	2.4	17	52.7	75
Czech Republic	–	1.17	2.6	–	53.7	–
Hungary	–	1.30	2.7	–	49.9	–
Poland	–	1.29	3.1	–	20.3	–

Source: OECD; Eurostat, 2001

FERTILITY

The second area where there has been significant demographic change is in relation to fertility rates. In fact, a number of authors have suggested that change in this area is more significant than population ageing (Sleebos, 2003; Castles, 2004). In short, in the period since 1970, fertility rates in European countries have fallen well below the level needed to replace the population (about 2.1 children). If current levels of fertility in Southern and CEE countries continued – at given mortality and migration rates – the population of these countries would shrink to about one-third of what it is today in less than one century (Sleebos, 2003). This fall in population – particularly the working age population – would in turn be likely to lead to a fall in the levels of economic growth and exacerbate problems arising from the ageing population. In addition, such a fall in fertility would have important impacts for household structures as there would be increasing numbers of people without immediate family, which would have implications for the provision of care services.

As in the case of population ageing, different trends can be seen in different countries, although almost all European countries are now below replacement rates. The Nordic countries, which originally had lower fertility rates, saw their levels of fertility fall first, but these have now recovered to some extent (see Table 9.1). In contrast, Southern European countries generally had high levels of fertility, but these fell precipitively in recent years to the lowest levels in the EU at about 1.3. CEE countries, which had fertility rates at about replacement level in the mid-1980s, also have seen sharp falls to about 1.3. In contrast, Ireland, where fertility has also fallen from high levels, is still close to replacement levels at 1.9.

What is not clear to date is the extent to which the fall in fertility rates to below replacement levels is a long-term phenomenon or to which it is caused by women having children at a later age. This is one factor that has contributed to lower fertility, with the mean age at first birth in OECD countries rising from 24.1 in 1970 to 27.1 in 2000. However, the extent to which this means that women have fewer children or simply the same number of children at a later age is unclear. The evidence to date for 'completed fertility rates', that is, over the lifetime of a woman, is that these rates have declined in most OECD countries but that, in a number of countries, reductions are relatively small (Sleebos, 2003).

While there is considerable debate about the causes of fertility decline, studies have yet to locate clear determinants of fertility trends. Data in relation to women's employment and education in 1980 appear to indicate a negative correlation between fertility and employment and education levels, that is, women in employment and with higher education were likely to have lower fertility. However, these correlations have reversed direction currently, so that now it appears that women in employment and with higher levels of education are likely to have *higher* fertility levels. Changes in fertility are also likely to be affected to macro-level changes in economy and society, as we have seen in CEE countries in recent years.

The lack of clarity about the causes behind changes in fertility makes it difficult for public policies to influence fertility levels. A recent careful review of the research on the effect of policies such as child benefits, childcare and maternity and parental leave found that findings of the research were mixed, being often inconclusive or contradictory. At best they seemed to suggest 'a weak positive relation between reproductive behaviour and a variety of policies' (Sleebos, 2003: 38). Indeed, given the cost of raising a child – including the opportunity cost of the parent's (particularly the mother's) time – it is hardly surprising that even generous child benefits would have limited effect on decisions. Sleebos also found that policy measures are likely to show an effect only in the long-term and that policy makers probably should not expect too much from pro-natalist policies. However, the research does suggest that a combination of measures which make it easier to combine employment and child rearing and strategies which impact on society at large (rather than only on individuals) would seem to be the best approach (Sleebos, 2003). The recent Nordic experience would seem to indicate that higher (if not high) levels of fertility can be facilitated by gender-friendly policies (in the absence of other over-riding factors which reduce fertility).

ECONOMIC AND LABOUR MARKET CHANGE

Economic growth in itself is not sufficient to achieve welfare objectives such as low poverty rates and income inequality. However, economic development is a necessary condition for the establishment and maintenance of high levels of welfare services. There are few, if any, less developed countries which match developed European welfare states in terms of their low levels of poverty and inequality.[1] Thus continued economic growth is essential for the continued well-being of the welfare state. The impact of globalisation and economic integration and structural changes in the labour market have been discussed in previous chapters (Chapters 2 and 3), and this discussion will not be repeated here. Suffice it to say that while these issues have an impact on the overall integration of national states

---

1 The former 'socialist' countries did achieve this at significantly lower levels of economic development but, clearly, at high costs in other areas.

into the world economy and on the structure and size of their labour markets, their impact on welfare would appear to be primarily indirect and to be mediated by political structures.

Economic growth can be broken down into employment growth and productivity change. In relation to productivity, one important issue has been what is known as the cost disease model (or Baumol's disease). As we have seen, there has been a large shift from industrial to service employment in Europe in recent decades. Baumol argues that the expansion in the share of GNP constituted by services is not composed of services generally, but is accounted for largely by the stagnant services – those that have experienced relatively little productivity growth. The basic argument is that services – such as, for example, hairdressing – are highly labour intensive and that there is little scope to improve productivity significantly over a sustained period. This gives rise to two problems for the welfare state. First, it implies a general slow-down in economic growth with consequent implications for the revenue available for welfare spending (Pierson, 2001, discussed in Chapter 2). However, at least this aspect of the Baumol's discase has been questioned by recent research – in the United States of America – which finds a broad acceleration in service productivity in recent years, in part attributable to IT investment (Triplett and Bosworth, 2003).

A second aspect is that welfare state services are generally seen as being amongst the highly labour intensive services in which only limited productivity improvements are possible. This means that the cost of these services increases more rapidly than costs generally, as wages will rise broadly in line with wages in the economy generally while productivity will not. Iversen (1998) has identified a 'trilema' arising from this growing reliance on service sector employment in an era of international economic integration, which means that welfare states cannot achieve simultaneously the three goals of full employment, income equality and budgetary restraint. Given that there is limited scope for growth in industrial employment, in order to achieve full employment governments have to rely on the expansion of service jobs. But the growth in public service employment is constrained for budgetary reasons, while the growth in (generally low skilled and low pay) private sector employment threatens income distribution goals. Welfare states which both apply budgetary restraint and do not allow an increase in wage inequalities are likely to see low employment growth.

EU POLICY

In recent years the EU has played a much more active role in the development of employment policy, having acquired specific policy competences in the Treaty of Amsterdam. The Lisbon Council in 2000 set the goal of becoming by 2010 the most competitive and dynamic, knowledge-based economy in the world capable of sustaining economic growth with more and better jobs and greater social cohesion. Arising from this the Council set a number of key employment goals (the EU's activities in this area have focussed on employment rather than productivity growth). These are:

- an overall employment rate of 67 per cent by 2005 and as close as possible to 70 per cent by 2010;
- an overall female employment rate of 57 per cent in 2005 and more than 60 per cent in 2010; and
- an employment rate for older workers (aged 55–64) of 50 per cent in 2010.

However, a recent study by the Employment Taskforce (2003) (known as the Kok Report after the former Dutch social democratic prime minister who chaired it) found that the EU was at risk of failing to meet this goal unless member states step up their efforts significantly.

OVERALL EMPLOYMENT TARGET

Only Denmark, the Netherlands, Sweden and the United Kingdom had so far achieved employment rates of over 70 per cent. Rates in many Southern (Greece, Spain, Italy) and some Christian centrist (Belgium) countries were still below 60 per cent and growth in Germany was stalled. In the CEE accession countries, the employment rate had fallen over the past decade and for many years was at or below 60 per cent.

FEMALE EMPLOYMENT TARGET

Overall the female employment rate grew significantly in the EU15 from 50.8 per cent in 1997 to 55.6 per cent in 2002, but significant gaps between the level of male and female employment remain in all member states (on average female employment rates are 17 per cent lower). Only the Nordic countries had a gender gap of less than 10 per cent, while the Southern countries (Greece, Spain and Italy) had a particularly large gap between male and female employment of nearly 30 per cent. In general, the CEE countries had historically rather high levels of female participation and, while these have fallen, many (with the exception of Hungary and Poland) are close to the 60 per cent target.

OLDER WORKERS

Only four member states – Denmark, Sweden, Portugal and the United Kingdom – had reached the 50 per cent employment target for older workers. Many of the Christian centrist counties (Belgium, France and Austria) had particularly low levels of older people at work (30 per cent or less). Many of the CEE countries had rather low effective retirement ages and this, combined with economic restructuring, has left them (except Estonia) with low (40 per cent or less), and in some cases very low (below 30 per cent), levels of employment for older workers (with Hungary, Slovenia and Slovakia falling into the latter category).

EDUCATIONAL ATTAINMENT

The Kok Report (Employment Taskforce, 2003: 16) also highlights the link between educational attainment and employment. Only half of low-skilled people are in work compared to 83 per cent for those with high skills. Women with low skills were even less likely to be in employment (37 per cent).

WORK QUALITY

In terms of the quality of work, there is a widespread perception that the old model of long-term stable employment is gone for ever (see, for example, the Third Way document discussed in the next chapter) and that there is an increased tendency towards insecure, poor-quality work with high levels of employee stress. However, this perception is only loosely, if at all, related to actual trends. While survey evidence shows that employees increasingly feel that their jobs are insecure, data on job tenure does not indicate any significant change in most European countries over the period from the mid-1980s to 2000 (OECD, 1994; European Commission, 2001a). Average hours worked have, of course, fallen significantly since the invention of welfare states. Recent studies show that most European countries have experienced a gradual reduction in working hours over the past two decades, although this has been accompanied by the introduction of different working time arrangements and a different dispersion of work (Boisard et al., 2002a). Work deaths and accidents have also fallen significantly in recent decades and physical work effort has also generally declined. Studies of work intensity, on the other hand, do show an increase in recent years (Boisard et al., 2002b). This, in turn, is related to increased levels of reported work-related stress. However, in the longer *durée*, it is perhaps difficult to believe that today's service sector workers (including authors of books on the welfare state) are subject to greater insecurity and stress than, to take just some literary examples, Dickens' (1850s) Coketown industrial workers, Zola's (1880s) striking (and starving) French coal miners, Roth's (1920s) occasionally employed war veterans or Kataev's (1930s) shock-brigading construction workers (*Hard Times, Germinal, Rebellion* and *Time, Forward* respectively).

The Kok Report and a range of other policy documents have put forward proposals for increasing the employment rate in European welfare states and for welfare state reform in this area. These are discussed in Chapter 10.

BUDGETARY LIMITATIONS

As we have seen in previous chapters, in most European countries welfare spending – as a percentage of GDP – has continued to grow in recent decades and now averages 27.5 per cent (EU15). Although these is no pre-determined limit on the level of welfare state expenditure, given that states also spend money in other policy areas, this would suggest that there is a considerable element of truth in the thesis that the welfare state has 'grown to limits' (Flora, 1986). Globalisation has not had any clear downward effect on welfare state spending and, as we have seen, many countries with lower levels of public spending compensate for this to a significant extent through private spending (see Chapter 7). Nonetheless, most governments and international bodies are agreed on the need to at least restrain welfare spending at its current levels (if not to reduce it). In addition, policy measures agreed by the EU as part of Economic and Monetary Union have set specific limits on the level of government budget deficits.

The Treaty on European Union and Economic and Monetary Union (EMU) – agreed in Maastricht in 1991 – provided for the replacement of national currencies by a single European currency (the euro). In order to participate in this process, countries have to meet a number of fiscal conditions. The most important of the 'Maastricht criteria' is that the country's budget deficit cannot exceed 3 per cent of its gross domestic product (GDP) for more than a short period. In addition, public borrowing must not exceed 60 per cent of GDP. Prices and interest rates must also remain stable over a long period, as must exchange rates between the currencies concerned. These conditions provide a legal basis for the political consensus around financial stability apparent amongst European governments of all political complexions and, in principle, have important implications for welfare state spending. The practical impact of these limits can be seen in recent developments in a number of EMU countries such as Italy, France and Germany. Given that EMU (unlike most national 'limits') sets specific and, at least in theory, binding budgetary limits, its impact is discussed in more detail below (pages 207–8).

CHANGES IN GENDER ROLES
AND HOUSEHOLD COMPOSITION

As we have seen in previous chapters, welfare systems have been structured around the concept of different roles for men and women and around particular household structures. Most (if not all) systems were originally based on the concept of the male breadwinner and this remains the case, to a greater or lesser extent, in many current systems despite the removal of formal gender discrimination. This means that welfare systems were designed on the basis that their primary task was to provide insurance against the risk faced by adult male workers such as unemployment, disability, old age and death. 'Female risks' such as care were provided for only to a very limited extent – primarily through short maternity payments. The risks of lone parenthood – which has been one of the key causes of reliance on the welfare state throughout its pre-history and history – was rarely treated as an insurable risk. But gender roles and household composition have and are changing significantly in Europe. In many cases this is related to the changes in demography and the labour force, which we have discussed earlier in this chapter. These changes raise important new challenges for the welfare state.

The key changes are in the areas of:

- household size (and the growth of single earner households);
- the rise in the number of lone parents;
- linked to this, the increase in divorce rates; and
- changes in the earning structure of households (that is, the growth of dual-earner households).

CHANGES IN HOUSEHOLD SIZE

There has been a significant fall in the average size of European households from about 3.3 persons in 1960 to about 2.5 today (Table 9.1). This does not just reflect the falling number of children but is also driven by the fact that more and more people – many older people – are living alone in single-person households. The proportion of people living in single-person households has doubled from about 14 per cent in 1960 to 29 per cent today. Eurostat projections indicate that this may rise further (to as high as 40 per cent) if current trends towards individualisation continue.

It is important to note that there are significant variations between countries, with Southern Europe having significantly larger households and the Nordic countries below average (Table 9.1). Similarly, the Nordic countries have the highest percentage of people living alone, while this is lowest in the South. Children are also more likely to live with their families in Southern Europe (and Ireland) and least likely to do so in some Nordic countries and Germany.

LONE PARENTHOOD

There has been a significant increase in the number of lone parent households (living alone) as a percentage of all households to 9 per cent today (Table 9.1).[2] About 90 per cent of lone parents are women, in all countries except Sweden, where one-quarter of lone parents are men. Again there is significant cross-country variation. Sweden and the United Kingdom have the highest proportion of 'living alone' lone parents (22 and 17 per cent). Conversely, the Southern countries are the lowest at only 3–4 per cent. Perhaps surprisingly, 70 per cent of lone parents (aged between 25 and 49) are working, of which over 80 per cent work full-time (only in the Netherlands does part-time work dominate). While, from a policy perspective, widows are often considered separately from 'lone parents', in the early days of the welfare state the bulk of lone parents were widows with dependent children. However, as a result of falling early mortality, the number of younger widows (and widowers) and therefore those with dependent children has fallen significantly.

DIVORCE

Looking at a crude indicator of divorce rates per thousand of the population, there has been a very rapid increase from 0.6 per thousand in 1960 to 1.9 today. Turning to the more reliable indicator of divorces per thousand marriages, we also see a significant rise from about 14 per 100 marriages in 1970 to over 40 today (Table 9.1). Most European countries – both East and West – fall at or above the average, with particularly high rates in Belgium, the Czech Republic and Sweden (over 50 per cent). As can be seen, there is little relationship between divorce rates and welfare 'groups' and the same groups which have high rates also have countries with low rates (Denmark, Switzerland and Slovakia are somewhat below average).

---

2 This figure includes only those lone parents living alone with their children and, for data reasons, excludes lone parents living, for example, with their own parents. While widely used, this data looks at only a subset of lone parents and, given different levels of co-residence in Europe, can potentially distort the comparative picture. In addition, some countries show significant differences between the numbers of lone parents recorded in household surveys and censuses and those recorded in administrative statistics.

The only clear distinction is a group of 'Catholic' (or Orthodox) countries (Greece, Ireland, Poland and Spain), which have much lower divorce rates (at or below 20 per cent).

DUAL-EARNER HOUSEHOLDS

There has been a strong move away from the single-earner household model on which the welfare state was originally designed. Today about two-thirds of working couple households (aged 20–59) are dual earners (Eurostat, 2002). The most common form of dual-earner household is for both to work full-time (except in the Netherlands, where it is most usual for the man to work full-time and the woman part-time). As we have seen in previous sections, there is again a North–South divide, with single-earner households still more common in Greece, Spain and Italy (but not Portugal). Ireland has recently moved rapidly from a single-earner to dual-earner model, reflecting its dramatic economic and employment growth. However, time use studies indicate that, across Europe, employed women still spend significantly more time on household and family care than do employed men (Eurostat, 2003).

IMPLICATIONS OF THESE CHANGES

All these changes have implications for welfare systems. The greater proportion of older people living alone will, assuming that living alone gives rise to extra costs, lead to higher pensioner 'need'. Probably more significantly, it may contribute to a reduction in informal networks of care (although, to some extent, modern technology which makes it easier to keep in touch may counteract this trend).

The rise in lone parent families – given that lone parents tend to have high rates of poverty – also creates further pressures on the welfare state. The fact that lone parents are normally supported by way of means-tested payments rather than through social insurance schemes means that a rising proportion of lone parents in the claim load has implications for the structure of welfare schemes. The falling numbers of 'dependent' widows and the increase in female participation in the labour force means that widows' pensions in their traditional form are somewhat obsolete and, indeed, we have seen in Chapter 7 that a number of European countries have responded to this trend by reforming (or abolishing) their pension schemes for widows. Others, such as Ireland, however, have not. The rise in divorce, in addition leading to a rise in the number of lone parents, also creates issues concerning entitlement to pension for former wives. As many welfare schemes are constructed around the notion of the male breadwinner, protection for spouses on old age or widowhood is also provided on a 'derived' basis, that is, the right to a payment is derived from the contributions of the (male) worker rather than being a personal entitlement. The rising incidence of divorce raises questions – which apply to both statutory and private pensions – about how pension should be allocated on divorce. For example, a division of pension entitlements between two 'spouses' may leave both with an inadequate level of pension.

Finally, the fact that dual-earner households are now the dominant model in Northern Europe (and increasingly prevalent in the South) means that welfare systems based around the male breadwinner model no longer reflect employment realities. This can lead to unintended consequences, such as disincentives for spouses to take up employment. The rise in female employment also arguably reduces the time available for informal care work.

DISCUSSION

All these issues create new challenges for the design of welfare states and many are interrelated. For example, we have seen that the number of older people is increasing. At the same time older people are more likely to live alone and the availability of informal carers is probably decreasing due to the rise in female employment. Arriving at European solutions to these issues is made more complicated by the fact that there are considerable variations in gender roles and household structures across Europe. Proposals have ranged from greater support for individualisation to support for 're-familisation'.

Overall, it makes intuitive sense that the welfare state has had an impact on household structures. It is, for example, frequently argued that the welfare state has reinforced the gendered division of labour. However, identifying the precise impact of welfare measures is more problematic. Some econometric studies have, for example, found evidence that social security cover has a negative impact on fertility (Cigno et al., 2000). However, it is very difficult to trace precisely how and why such an effect occurs and to be sure that it is not a statistical artefact (Gauthier, 2001). Contrary to popular belief, there is limited evidence that welfare benefits have a strong impact on births outside marriage (see the studies summarised in Gauthier, 2001).[3] While some impacts are reasonably clear – such as the negative effect of means-tested benefits on female participation – the more complex relationship between welfare and living alone, lone parenthood, divorce and overall levels of female labour force participation

---

3 It is unwise to rely on studies from the United States of America in this regard, given the very different social and ethnic context of lone parenthood; unfortunately this disqualifies the bulk of research in this area.

is more difficult to disentangle. This, in turn, makes it more difficult to develop appropriate policy responses.

EU (AND EMU) MEMBERSHIP AND FURTHER EXPANSION

While this chapter focuses on the *challenges* facing European welfare states, it is important to remember that the overall purpose of European integration (including EMU) is to *improve the economic and social welfare of Europe and its people*. EU integration, through the establishment of a large free trade area and significant increases in competition, should on balance lead to a more dynamic European economy. Examples of the European success story are not hard to find. Much of the factors behind Ireland's recent dramatic economic boom relate to its membership of the EU whereby large, highly productive Trans-National Corporations (TNCs) locate in Ireland in order to have an EU base. Similarly, the eastward expansion of the EU (and EMU) is also predicted to have overall beneficial effects on the new (and old) EU countries.

CHALLENGES FOR THE EU15

We look first at the existing challenges posed to the EU15 by membership of the EU and then expand the discussion to look at the implications of expansion. The intention is not to assess the overall impact of membership of the EU – which has been discussed in other chapters – but rather to look at specific current challenges posed by EU membership.

Given the limited remit of EU social policy (in a binding form), the challenges posed by its implementation are rather limited. In the social security area, the legislation is largely confined to the Regulation on social security for migrant workers and the EU directive on equal treatment for men and women. The former poses ongoing challenges of implementation because of its highly technical nature, but these are generally of an administrative nature. The latter posed significant problems for certain member states in the 1980s and 1990s, leading to much litigation before the European Court of Justice (ECJ). However, the implications of this directive have now largely worked their way through the system and, perhaps, this episode has made member states less willing to agree to (what might have appeared to some to have been) aspirational commitments only to find the ECJ (correctly) imposing legal obligations on member states.

One of the key (albeit indirect) challenges facing member states is the Maastricht criteria imposed on members of EMU (and which have a significant impact on non-EMU countries as well). These set specific limits on government deficits of 3 per cent per annum (over a maximum three-year period). In addition, the EU adopted a Stability and Growth Pact (SGP) to provide a mechanism for monitoring and implementing these obligations. The main objective of the SGP is to enforce fiscal discipline on member states. In the long run, price stability and macro-economic certainty should contribute to economic growth. In the short-term, however, it has been argued that the SGP is overly rigid. Requiring member states to make cuts in welfare state budgets in the face of a short-term economic downturn may be harmful from both an economic and a social viewpoint. As has been seen recently, member states faced by short-term financial difficulties are reluctant to embark on significant expenditure cuts and the larger states have the political clout to ensure a more flexible interpretation of the SGP than would otherwise have applied. It is, therefore, difficult to predict the likely impact of EMU limits on the welfare state in any detailed manner. First, the likely impact of the limits is inversely related to economic growth. Where a country is experiencing a reasonable rate of economic growth, it is likely to see revenue growth and only limited growth in welfare 'demand' (for example, for unemployment benefits). Conversely, where a country is experiencing economic difficulties, it is more likely to see stagnant revenues and rising expenditure, thereby increasing the likelihood of hitting EMU limits. Second, as recent experience shows, these limits have proved to be somewhat politically flexible and have been modified to some extent by the member states in 2005 to allow governments to run higher deficits in certain circumstances.

The impact of EMU on labour market reform – and more indirectly on welfare state reform – remains a matter of debate. In theory, the currency union is intended to create increased competition between countries and to generate pressure for structural reforms to facilitate this competition. EMU tightens fiscal policy, thus putting pressure on labour market policies to get people back to work rather than paying them benefits, removes the possibility of devaluation of national currencies, and integrates product and capital markets in a common currency area, leading to greater transparency and competition between firms. While there has been considerable theoretical debate about the impact of EMU, it has been argued that 'the channels from monetary union to labour market reform are difficult to anticipate' and that, so far, 'little impact could be seen in terms of making Western European labour markets more flexible' (Kemmerling, 2003: 11–12).

EXPANSION

Turning to EU expansion, again the implementation of the EU social *acquis* (at least in the areas of social security) is unlikely to create major difficulties for the new member states. The implementation of regulations on free movement will, no doubt, be administratively complex, but new member states – which have a history of more gender-friendly policies – are likely to have less difficulty in implementing equality of treatment.

In relation to EMU, most (if not all) of the CEE accession countries wish to join EMU and this is likely to impose significant constraints on their ability to expand welfare state spending in the absence of above-average economic and tax growth. Again, while the long-term aspects of EU and EMU membership are predicted to be positive, there are likely to be short-term transition costs and greater regional disparities. This would require efficiently operating labour markets in order to smooth the impact of these transition costs. However, given their very different labour market backgrounds, it is arguable that many CEE countries do not yet have sufficiently flexible labour markets (as discussed earlier in this chapter) or labour market institutions and, as we have seen, it is not clear that EMU in itself will lead to appropriate reforms.

CEE economies are small compared to the EU15, but their labour markets constitute a large pool of potentially migrant labour. Because of this the impact of labour markets is likely to be the most important impact for Western Europe. This is of particular concern in Germany and Austria, where 80 per cent of current CEE10 population in the EU15 reside (Kemmerling, 2003: 5). However, earlier alarmist predictions of large labour flows have been significantly reduced and, driven by trade union and populist concerns, all the EU15 have, to a greater or lesser extent, introduced some restrictions on labour market migration or access to welfare benefits for the new member states. Thus the impact on Western Europe is likely to be limited. Conversely, the limited level of migration and the possible limited impact of EMU on structural labour market reform may mean that labour market polices will be insufficient to compensate for other policy challenges, leading to slow convergence in terms of income.

Overall a recent review of the evidence suggests that 'neither labour markets nor social policies of CEE countries will be able to fully absorb the costs of adjustment' of the expansion of EMU (Kemmerling, 2003: 24). However, this study also does not find support for any of the 'catastrophic scenarios sometimes attached to the prospects of enlargement' (2003: 35). Expansion does create pressures for greater linkages between the economic policies of the EU which are set primarily at EU level and the social and labour market policies which remain a national competence.

CONCLUSION

In this chapter we have outlined a range of new policy challenges facing European welfare states including those arising from demography, changing economic and labour market structures, budgetary limitations, changing gender roles and household structures and the eastward expansion of the EU and EMU. As we have seen, many of these challenges are interrelated. However, it is important to recall that many of these challenges arise from factors which are positive overall (such as increased longevity) and/or which also create positive opportunities for the improvement in the welfare of Europe's people (such as the expansion of the EU). In the final chapter we will look in detail at proposals for welfare state reform which have been developed in the light of the challenges and opportunities discussed in this chapter.

Summary

This chapter has outlined a number of key challenges facing European welfare states including:

- demographic changes – especially the ageing of the population and fertility decline;
- economic and labour market change;
- budgetary limitations;
- changes in gender roles and household composition; and
- EU (and EMU) membership and further expansion.

In particular, it has discussed the extent to which these challenges are likely in practice to impact on the development of the welfare state.

Discussion points

1   The demographic 'time bomb' is largely a creation of the marketing departments of pension companies. Discuss.
2   Eastward expansion of the EU, from a social policy point of view, brings as many risks as opportunities for both the old and new member states. Do you agree?
3   Which of the challenges discussed here is the most important for your chosen European welfare state? Why?
4   The manner in which risks are politically interpreted and responded to is as, if not more, important than the original risk. Discuss.

Supplementary reading

The issues of population ageing are addressed in a report from the European Commission (2003a) and in a range of studies from the OECD. Trends in fertility and the impact of public policies are discussed in Sleebos (2003). The current state of employment and employment policy in the EU is discussed in Employment Taskforce (2003). Up-to-date information on changing gender roles and household structures is available from Eurostat (particularly the series *Statistics in Focus*) and in the OECD on-line publication *Society at a Glance*. Kemmerling (2003) provides a useful discussion of the future expansion of the EMU from a social perspective.

TEN FUTURE DIRECTIONS FOR EUROPEAN WELFARE STATES

This chapter looks at the future directions of European welfare states. In particular, it examines current important philosophies of welfare; new technologies of welfare which may play a role in the development of welfare states; policy options in three key areas of working age policies, pensions and gender and care; and EU developments such as 'open co-ordination'. In conclusion, this chapter examines developments at an EU level and, in the light of EU expansion, assesses the extent to which a European welfare state may be developing.

PHILOSOPHIES OF WELFARE

In this section we look at a number of 'philosophies' of (or approaches to) welfare. Rather than examining the classic 'social democratic' or 'Christian democracy' philosophies which have been discussed in detail elsewhere and which have been referred to throughout this book, we focus on current welfare policies from a number of different and important perspectives – although as will be seen there is a high level of commonality on certain points in all mainstream approaches. The approaches we have chosen to outline are those of:

- the World Bank – often considered to represent a right-wing (if not neo-liberal) perspective on welfare reform, with an emphasis on pension privatisation and means-tested safety nets;
- the EU Commission – representing a much more centrist position, with an emphasis on the role of social protection as a productive factor; and
- the 'Third Way' – purportedly a new social democratic approach to the reform of the welfare state.

This section does not attempt to provide a comprehensive account of the different approaches to the philosophy of welfare – one could write a book on each of the approaches. Rather, drawing on a small number of significant texts in each area, it seeks to highlight the key points of each approach and the differences between them. It should be noted that this approach will overstate the extent to which, for example, a coherent EU position exists. In all cases there tends to be considerable divergence between different sections within key organisations (for example, between the Commission and Council in the EU, between the social and economic Directorates General within the EU Commission). Nor should it be assumed that the approaches set out in these policy documents are always (or fully) reflected in the actions of these organisations. For a variety of reasons there is often, if not always, a significant difference between the stated policy approach and policy outcomes.

FROM SAFETY NET TO SPRINGBOARD (WORLD BANK)

The World Bank has been seen as one of the leading, and most influential, purveyors of a broadly neo-liberal approach to welfare policy as part of the 'Washington Consensus'. The Bank has, and still does, argue strongly for pension privatisation through a multi-pillar approach and for the importance of targeting welfare through means- tested 'safety nets'. Nonetheless, while the fundamental approach may not have changed significantly, in the last decade the Bank has perhaps become more sensitive to national particularities and has developed a more coherent framework for its social protection policies. In particular, its recent Social Protection Sector Strategy paper – unimaginatively titled *From Safety Net to Springboard* – has developed the concept of *social risk management* as a conceptual framework for its work on social protection.

The concept of social risk management argues that, in response to both natural and manmade risks, individuals, households and communities have developed elaborate mechanisms of 'self-protection' such as asset accumulation, diversification of income sources and informal family and community 'risk-pooling' arrangements (World Bank, 2003). However, these are often 'expensive and inefficient' (or perhaps simply inadequate), giving rise to the need for public intervention. Social risk management involves making an assessment of the most appropriate risk management strategies (prevention, mitigation and coping) and arrangements (informal, market and public) in any given situation.

The concept of social risk management is an interesting one, particularly in the many less-developed parts of the world in which the Bank operates, which still rely strongly on informal risk management strategies. While it is also applicable in a European context, it perhaps has less immediate implications for welfare state policies in these countries with already highly developed welfare systems. Certainly the implications of the broader approach in a European context are not readily apparent in the World Bank Strategy (World Bank, 2003), nor in the strategy for social protection in Transition economies (World Bank, 2000). Both focus on CEE countries – given that the Bank has limited direct impact on Western Europe – and argue for a traditional list of policies including improved labour market flexibility, low minimum wages, linking benefits to contributions, multi-pillar pensions, and minimum pensions and means-tested social assistance to address poverty (World Bank, 2000: 7–9, 2003: 74).

In the area of pensions, the World Bank has long been a leader in highlighting issues concerning the ageing population and the need for pension reform (World Bank, 1994). The Bank has argued for the need to increase employment rates and effective retirement ages (policy measures agreed by almost all commentators), but has also strongly argued for a diversification of investment through the establishment of multi-pillar pensions. A recent review of pension reform in Europe, while noting progress on employment rates, argues that there is still a need for 'major changes in pension schemes' (Holzmann et al., 2003: 5), including the need for paradigmatic change with the introduction of multi-pillar schemes. The arguments for and against this approach will be discussed later in this chapter. While the Bank has developed some increased degree of awareness of the need for sensitivity to local conditions (primarily in an effort to increase the uptake of its recommendations), it has not altered its basic policy approach despite evidence that paradigmatic reforms in a number of CEE countries have led to difficult implementation issues and often left important parametric issues (such as special concessions for specific groups) in place (Müller, 2002a; 2002b).

On the one hand, the World Bank approach is based on a large amount of serious policy research which engages with policy issues and criticisms of its approach. Its position is considerably more sophisticated and evidence-based than many of the neo-liberal think tanks in the United States, which argue for large-scale privatisation of welfare, disregarding evidence which does not suit their arguments. It has also developed an interesting new philosophical underpinning for its approach – that of social risk management – which may have an important effect in developing future Bank policies, particularly in less-developed countries. However, the Bank has also adhered to a fundamentally neo-liberal approach in a European context, arguing consistently for policies such as multi-pillar pensions and means-tested assistance across the board and, arguably, without full regard to the criticisms of these policies or to whether alternative policy measures might have equal or greater success.

MODERNISING SOCIAL PROTECTION –
EU COMMISSION

The current approach of the European Commission (1999) on social protection policy is set out in its Communication *A Concerted Strategy for Modernising Social Protection*. This document identifies the need for member states to respond to common challenges while balancing European citizens' 'clearly expressed wishes' for continued high levels of social protection against the requirements for more efficient public services and budgetary discipline. It identifies four key objectives within the overall challenge of modernisation:

* making work pay;
* making pensions safe and pension systems sustainable;
* promoting social inclusion; and
* ensuring high quality and sustainable health care.

The Communication highlights the importance of social protection systems in supporting people in times of need and in allowing them to 'accept and embrace economic and social change'. It sees strong social protection systems as 'an integral part of the European Social Model', which is based on the conviction and evidence that economic and social progress go hand in hand and are 'mutually reinforcing factors'. Thus it sees social protection not only as providing 'safety nets for those in poverty', but also contributing to social cohesion by protecting people against social risks, facilitating adaptability in the labour market and contributing to economic performance. 'Social protection,' argues the Commission, 'is a productive factor' (1999).

The Communication identifies a number of issues relating to European integration which give rise to a new context for welfare reform. These include, first, deepening European economic integration arising from the internal market and single currency. In this context the Broad Economic Policy Guidelines established under EMU have, in recent years, emphasised the need to review and in some cases reform pension and healthcare systems. Second, it highlighted the importance of the European Employment Strategy (EES). On the one hand, implementation of the EES (and now of the Lisbon objectives) requires an important contribution from social protection in terms of activation measures and policies to reconcile work and family life. On the other, increasing the employment rate in line with the EES can make a very important contribution to the sustainability of social protection. Third, the Communication highlights the challenge of enlargement and argues that modern social protection systems will facilitate integration of the new member states by smoothing the process of economic transition and maintaining political stability.

Drawing on this analysis, the Communication highlights the four broad objectives listed above. Gender aspects are stated to be an important cross-cutting theme across all four areas. In the area of making work pay, the Commission highlights the need for tax and benefit policies to ensure that it pays to take up work; for social protection systems to reflect and respond to new 'atypical' working arrangements; to provide necessary income support and active help during transitions between jobs; and to contribute to reconciling work and family life (see also European Commission, 2004a). In relation to pensions, the fundamental objective identified is 'to provide people with a securely funded and adequate pension' (European Commission, 1999). This requires a pension system which is both sustainable and guarantees a decent replacement income for pensioners. The Commission suggests that this *may* involve an appropriate balance between funded and PAYG systems. A range of policies are required including measures to discourage early retirement, encourage flexible retirement and promote active participation by older people. The Commission also highlighted the need to pay particular attention to the problem of poverty amongst older women. On promoting social inclusion, the Commission emphasises the role of social protection in promoting social inclusion through, in particular, minimum income benefits, access to housing and health services and active measures to facilitate the broadest possible participation in society. Finally, the Commission emphasises the importance of universal access to healthcare and a reduction in health inequalities; strengthened support for long-term care for older people, and a focus on illness prevention and health protection. However, given rising healthcare costs, it also highlights the importance of efficiency and effectiveness of health systems.

In each of these areas, the Commission has engaged in a process with member states which led to a Communication in the case of making work pay. In the other three areas the Commission has established a process known as the 'open method of co-ordination', building on reports from each member state which are compared and benchmarked and ultimately leading to Joint Council/Commission reports outlining progress and suggesting further policy measures. These, however, are not legally binding on member states (see below for further discussion).

THE THIRD WAY (*NEUE MITTE*) – EUROPEAN SOCIAL DEMOCRACY

The 'Third Way' is a somewhat vague concept advanced by a number of – but not all – European social democratic parties (that is, parties which claim to be social democratic) as a label for their approach, which is a third way between 'old-fashioned' social democracy and neo-liberalism. The extent to which the Third Way exists as a real basis for policy (outside different national contexts) may be open to question. However, it has been argued that the Third Way is 'more than a new slogan' and represents a fairly coherent set of ideas and policies based on job creation, active labour market policies and high employment rates (Green-Pedersen et al., 2001).

In this section we draw on the famous Blair–Schroeder document on the Third Way (Blair and Schroeder, 1999), which sets out a programmatic statement of the aims and objectives of the Third Way (or what is referred to in Germany as the *Neue Mitte* (or new centre)). As the Third Way does not represent the official policy of any particular government or international body, it is more difficult to identify a coherent textual corpus setting out its detailed aims and objectives but – although it has been described as imprecise, intellectually shallow and politically thoughtless – this document is quite specific about welfare objectives.

The overall objective of the Third Way is to retain the social democratic values of 'fairness and social justice, liberty and equality of opportunity, solidarity and responsibility to others' while renewing its ideas and modernising its programmes to achieve those objectives. In terms of specific social policy objectives, it refers in particular to the importance of equality of opportunity (while rejecting imposed equality of outcomes), decent public services (but not measured in terms of the level of public expenditure), the importance of balancing rights and responsibilities, and recognises the importance of markets – the weaknesses of which 'have been overstated and their strengths underestimated'.

The role of the state must be refocused: it should 'not row, but steer'; 'public sector bureaucracy at all levels must be reduced'. There must be no return to the '1970s-style reliance on deficit spending and heavy-handed state intervention'. And this new role for the state does not mean a return to traditional corporatism. While the Third Way seeks to strengthen 'partnership and dialogues between all groups in society and develop (...) a new consensus for change and reform', it supports only 'modern trade unions protecting individuals against arbitrary behaviour and working in co-operation with employers to manage change and create long-term prosperity'. The focus is very much on increasing labour market participation and labour market flexibility and reducing labour costs. 'Having the same job for life is a thing of the past'; 'the tax burden borne by working families and workers should be alleviated'; 'we must make work pay for individuals and families'.

In the area of welfare spending 'public expenditure ... has more or less reached the limits of acceptability' but 'minimum social standards' must be maintained. Poverty is 'a central concern' but with the qualifier that this applies 'especially among families with children'. The social security system must open up 'new opportunities and encourage initiative, creativity and readiness to take on new challenges'.[1] The focus is on welfare-to-work programmes to improve the incomes of those who are out of work and to improve labour supply. And the top priority is stated to be 'investment in human and social capital' through 'lifetime access to education and training'. Tax and social security contributions must be reduced, particularly on low-paid jobs, targeted programmes will be introduced to give the long-term unemployed and other disadvantaged groups the opportunity to integrate into the labour market, and all benefits recipients will be assessed for their potential to earn. References to classic welfare state areas are much more muted: in order to 'improve life chances, encourage self-help and promote personal responsibility' ... 'the health care system and the system for ensuring financial security in old age are being thoroughly modernised in Germany ... without sacrificing the principle of solidarity'. And the same approach is stated to apply to the pension and disability benefit reforms in the United Kingdom.

Green-Pedersen et al. (2001) have argued, drawing on the Dutch and Danish[2] cases, that the Third Way constitutes 'a fairly coherent set of social democratic ideas and policies' which are different to both old style social democracy and neo-liberalism. The core of this thinking is about the creation of employment and high rates of labour market participation. They suggest that the Third Way 'represents more of a break with social democratic *policies* of the past than with the *basic principles* of social democracy'. However, an assessment which sees less continuity is also possible and, perhaps, more accurate. The Third Way does present a fairly coherent set of ideas about the creation of employment and high rates of labour market participation but, arguably, these do little more than reflect commonly held views such as those expressed in the OECD *Jobs Study* (OECD, 1994) or the EU *White Paper on Growth, Competitiveness and Employment* (European Commission, 1994). New 'social democracy' is committed to welfare as a productive factor. In contrast to old social democracy, what is clearly lacking is a strong commitment to redistribution and decent living standards. The Third Way

---

1 Like the World Bank, the Third Way document also refers to the need to 'transform the safety net of entitlements into a springboard to personal responsibility'.

2 Despite, as they point out, the fact that Danish social democrats have never officially supported the Third Way, arguing that there is too little focus on equality.

document abounds with references to an undefined 'social justice' but has only negative references to equality of outcomes and while poverty is 'a central concern' there is no attempt to explain how poverty is to be overcome for those unable to work. The extent to which the Third Way constitutes a genuine project which transcends national borders (as anything more than a catch phrase) must be open to question. Despite their co-signing of the Third Way document, the German and UK governments adopt quite difficult welfare policies (in their quite different welfare states).

TECHNOLOGIES OF WELFARE

This section looks at a number of new technologies of welfare which have been put forward as policy options, including privatisation, individual welfare accounts, refundable tax credits and basic income.

PRIVATISATION

WHAT IS PRIVATISATION?
Privatisation can take place at a number of different levels:

- An area of risk may be privatised, for example, an existing sickness benefit scheme could be abolished and it could be left to individuals to obtain (or not) alternative cover through the market.
- The provision of cover for a risk could be privatised. Again using sickness benefits as an example, the existing scheme could be abolished but employers could be required to provide alternative cover for their employees meeting certain minimum standards.
- The administration of protection for a risk could be privatised, for example, sickness benefits might be maintained but the administration passed to individual employers.
- The funding of protection could be privatised, for example, the funding of sickness benefit could be placed solely on employers and/or employees.
- Market elements could be introduced into the provision of a social service (sometimes referred to as 'marketisation'). One of the most common examples is the introduction of competition and market based principles in the health services. To pursue the sickness benefit example, a (public or private) organisation could be contracted to provide rehabilitation services to claimants with payments being made on results funded from savings in expenditure from people returning to work.

In practice, of course, most reform proposals will involve change at a number of different levels.

THE PROS AND CONS OF PRIVATISATION

Recent debates on welfare reform have emphasised the advantages of privatising welfare, for example, by separating service purchase from service provision through the creation of internal markets in health and social services. The objectives cited for such reforms include: to stimulate efficiency, to obtain better returns, to reform governance, to secure better value for money, to strengthen capital markets, savings and investment, and to increase competition and offer greater choice to consumers by involving private agencies in the administration of public policies. For governments that are ideo-logically committed to minimising public spending and to countries, such as some of those in Central and Eastern Europe which are faced with the need for structural adjustment, there is the advantage that privatisation removes spending from the public balance sheet.

On the other hand, there are arguments against privatisation. First, those opposing privatisation argue that these perceived benefits can be very limited or non-existent. For example, as discussed below, it is argued that investment returns are not higher when account is taken of transition costs and different levels of risk. Second, there is the prob-lem of market failure. The concept of market failure relates to the fact that there are social needs for which it is unlikely that a private market solution will emerge. Of course, market failure is a somewhat circular argument, as once a public system is introduced because of market failure, it will tend to crowd out any possible private measure, thereby confirming the market failure thesis. However, while it is clear that there are areas (such as unemployment) where private markets are unlikely to have any interest in becoming involved in social policy, there are also many areas where such involvement is possible. The third argument against privatisation applies more broadly. This is that markets are likely to provide a less equal outcome than public ser-vices. Market based principles, such as an actuarial approach, are, for example, likely to disadvantage women or people with disabilities. Indeed, there is considerable support for this argument at the macro level in that while highly privatised countries such as the United States of America spend almost as much in total (public and private) on social spending (Adema, 2001), the outcomes whether in terms of income distribution, child mortality or educational attainment are much infe-rior. However, it seems likely that this owes more to broader political choices made in different countries than to the impact of privatisation per se. Whether or not a regulated market can produce acceptable outcomes from an equality perspective can really only be studied in a concrete case.

As we discuss later in this chapter, the World Bank has been a lead-ing advocate of partial privatisation of pension systems though the introduction of multi-pillar systems. In addition, a number of European countries, including the United Kingdom and the Netherlands, have introduced an element of privatisation of sickness benefits.

INDIVIDUAL WELFARE ACCOUNTS

Individual welfare accounts (or personal savings accounts) are an interesting new approach to social insurance. While many privatisation proposals involve the establishment of individual, actuarial accounts, the proposed individual welfare accounts combine 'a savings account into which people save when they can, and out of which they draw when they need to' with 'insurance elements and a possibility of over-drawing the accounts in certain situations' (Fölster, 1996).

The arguments for this approach include the fact that, in contrast to the frequent interpretation of the welfare state as a broad redistributive mechanism, research in Sweden estimates that 75–80 per cent of spending on social transfers smooths income over the individual's life cycle, while only 20–25 per cent involves redistribution between individuals (Fölster, 1996). Thus, it is argued, the savings element of the welfare state is, in practice, much more important than the redistributive effect and that 'there could be substantial efficiency gains from a reform that focuses public welfare provision on the 20–25 per cent of current expenditure devoted to the achievement of interpersonal redistribution and social insurance against adverse economic circumstances ...' (Fölster et al., 2002: 4). Privatisation proposals which favour a more actuarial approach face a number of difficulties. Higher earners generally already pay more than an actuarial amount and thus a shift to a more actuarial approach would involve a revenue loss. Conversely, any attempt to introduce a more actuarial approach for the lower paid faces the combined problem that higher contributions could affect employment creation while lower benefits might increase poverty rates. The individual welfare account 'addresses this problem by using the account to shift premium payments ... to other time periods during which the individual may have greater incentives or ability to earn higher income' (Fölster, 1996: 7).

The individual welfare account closely relates benefits (or withdrawals) to contributions (or deposits) made to the account. The contributions earn interest and mandatory contributions can be topped up by additional voluntary deposits. Benefits are payable, as in a standard social insurance scheme, on the occurrence of certain risks but when the account is exhausted, benefits continue to be payable (possibly on a means-tested or other conditional basis). This system provides incentives for persons not to claim benefits as the final amount in the account is available for pension payments. Thus the more paid in and the less withdrawn, the greater the final benefit to the individual. In addition, it is argued that individual welfare accounts would allow a greater degree of flexibility in meeting people's personal circumstances. The system could be operated either as a funded system or it could continue the current PAYG approach with a real reserve being slowly built up.

Individual welfare accounts have been implemented in only a very limited number of countries (for example, Malaysia, Brazil, Chile, Singapore and the United States of America), often in relation to only one aspect of the welfare system (such as unemployment in Chile). As the proponents of such plans have accepted, the transition costs to the new system would be high. Individual welfare accounts could be introduced for a younger age group only, leading to a gradual transition. An alternative approach might be the adoption of individual welfare accounts in specific areas of welfare policy, such as unemployment (Orszag and Snower, 2002). Under this system, employed people would make mandatory contributions to individual unemployment accounts and the balances in these accounts would be available to them in the case of unemployment (or perhaps for the purposes of life-long learning). While the system would largely smooth consumption over a person's employment life-cycle, government could also provide for redistribution by subsidising the contributions of low earners and paying benefits after the savings balance had been exhausted (as at present). However, in those accounts with a closing balance, this would be used to top up a person's pension, thus providing positive employment incentives.

REFUNDABLE TAX CREDITS

Refundable tax credits are basically cash payments made through the tax system. They may be offset against tax liabilities (thereby reducing the tax liability and/or leading to a cash payment to the individual depending on the outcome) or simply be paid directly to the individual with no reconciliation with the broader tax system. In the latter case, tax credits might better be described as 'notional tax credits' as they are simply using the tax system to make welfare payments and are not integrated into the general income tax system.

The scope of refundable tax credits can, in principle, vary enormously. Some, for example, have suggested that all tax credits should be made refundable, thereby effectively introducing a basic income system (see below). Under this approach, rather than an individual tax payer having their tax liability reduced by a personal tax credit, the credit would be paid directly to the individual and tax would be deducted in full on all additional income. However, no European country has introduced such a system. Actually existing refundable tax credits have tended to focus on two areas: child income support and in-work benefits.

Canada, for example, has introduced a national child tax benefit which is payable to all families up to a certain income and which then tapers down gradually until it is finally exhausted at a relatively high level of income. Although described as a tax credit it is, in fact, normally paid in cash and is not netted-off against a person's individual tax liability. In the United Kingdom, the Labour government has introduced a new child tax credit from April 2003 to provide a single, 'seamless' system of income-related support for families with children. The child tax credit brings together the support for children previously provided through the range of tax and welfare measures. This payment is payable in addition to the universal child benefit and provides support varying with the income of the family. The second area in which refundable tax credits have been introduced has been that of in-work benefits. The United States of America has been a pioneer in this area, introducing the earned income tax credit (EITC) in 1969. The United Kingdom has, more recently, led this approach in Europe, with the Labour government converting the existing in-work benefit (family credit) into a working family tax credit which has now been broadened into a general employment tax credit. The Netherlands has also recently introduced an in-work tax credit.

The advantages of refundable tax credits operate at two levels. The first is largely ideological. From a fiscal accounting perspective, tax credits – as opposed to welfare spending – *decrease* tax levels and *decrease* public spending. Thus for governments committed to reducing tax and controlling public spending they create a win–win situation. In reality, of course, this makes absolutely no difference from a macro (or micro) economic perspective. The same amount of money is still paid to the same people and, in so far as the tax credit reduces recorded levels of taxation, the same amount of taxation has to be raised elsewhere if the fiscal accounts are to be balanced. In fact, in so far as fiscal welfare is generally much less transparent and much less closely monitored than public expenditure, the transfer can be negative from a fiscal control and monitoring perspective[3]. Thus the 'benefits' of refundable tax credits at this level are entirely political.

The second level at which refundable tax credits are perceived to be advantageous is in relation to the practical administration of benefits. Here it is argued that payment of benefits through the tax system is more customer-friendly than through the means-tested

---

3 Although the lack of transparency and monitoring of fiscal welfare are not intrinsic parts of the system.

welfare system. Claimants are treated as part of the general tax system rather than part of a (potentially stigmatising) welfare system. It is argued that this is likely to lead to higher levels of take-up of benefits. It is difficult to gauge the extent to which this is true in practice. Almost all the advantages of payment through the tax system could also be achieved by way of payments though a reformed welfare system. In fact, as we have seen above, many refundable tax credits are not 'real' tax credits paid through the general tax system, but rather are welfare payments being described as tax credits and being paid by the tax authorities.

Overall, it would appear that the ideological reasons for adopting refundable tax credits are much more important for those countries which have chosen to adopt them extensively. It would be difficult for the UK and USA governments to argue for personal responsibility and to make the case that prolonged welfare dependency has pronounced negative effects while, at the same time, promoting wage subsidisation in a manner which leads to long-term receipt of welfare benefits. The adoption of employment tax credits allows a distinction to be maintained between 'bad' welfare and 'good' employment supports. This is obviously very important for the creation of a coherent governmental message on the objective of the welfare state.

BASIC INCOME

Proposals in relation to a basic income or analogous payments have a long history. These can be traced back at least as far as Thomas Paine's proposal to pay to every person reaching the age of 21 the sum of £15 'to enable him or her to begin the world' and to pay £10 per annum to every person at or over the age of 50 years 'to enable them to live in old age without wretchedness and to go decently out of the world' (1797/1992). In the 1930s proposals similar to basic income were advocated by Major Douglas as part of a social credit scheme. More recently, basic income has attracted serious consideration and, in some cases, support from mainstream political parties and trade unions. While the understanding of basic income varies somewhat from author to author, most would broadly agree with a definition of basic income as providing:

> ... an inalienable right for every citizen, regardless of age, sex, race, creed, labour market or marital status to a guaranteed, tax-free income, unconditionally. (Modified slightly from Parker, 1994: 6)

Some advocates of basic income, from what might loosely be described as a left-libertarian approach, see it as a means to provide a payment decoupled from labour market participation and to encourage the autonomy of the individual. Hinrichs et al. state that:

> ... the aim of a citizen's right to a basic income would not be to force people into employment; rather, it would aim to provide them with the adequate means of subsisting outside formal employment and hence of escaping the dictates of the labour market. In other words, it would seek not merely to prevent income poverty and 'poverty traps' but to create conditions under which voluntary non-participation in the labour market becomes a feasible and publicly recognised option, the exercise of which might even lead to the resurrection of communal forms of useful activity within civil society which would enable individuals to escape the dictates of both the private household and the labour market. (1988: 241)

Offe (1992: 70) argues that the right to a basic income would be based not on paid labour but on 'useful activities' including activities performed outside employment and the labour market and that the aim of the payment would be not (absolute) security but a sustainable level of risk and the maintenance of autonomous options concerning the citizen's responsible conduct of his or her life.

Most authors accept that the introduction of a full basic income is not realistically feasible in the short-term and there have been several proposals for partial basic income systems and suggestions as to how one might move towards a basic income system from existing welfare systems. Hinrichs et al. accept that 'a proposal to uncouple employment and income' could not be introduced immediately and suggest some first steps towards such a system such as:

> ... reducing the loss of retirement benefits incurred by employees when they deviate from standard working hours; subsidising time invested in social user activity outside the labour market (for example, participation in voluntary associations which provide social services); supporting parental leaves of absence through grants whose value is calculated according to the average income of all employees; or promoting gradual retirement by compensating individuals for their earning losses when their working hours are reduced after a certain age. (1988: 242)

While basic income (BI) has attracted a vast volume of literature – much of it supportive – it is probably fair to say that it does not represent a realistic policy option in many (if indeed any) European welfare states. Studies indicate that the introduction of basic income would require a significant increase in the tax rate in order to fund the basic income payments. In addition, studies of the dynamic impact of BI, that is, the impact it would have on issues such as economic growth, work incentives and labour market participation, are generally negative, although such economic projections must obviously be read with some caution, being highly dependent on the assumptions on which they are based. An Irish study found that BI would reduce work disincentives for those who are unemployed, but increase them for most employees and for women in the home (Callan et al., 2000). Overall, labour participation would be likely to fall somewhat, which could add to pressures of wage levels and potentially impact on inflation and competitiveness. In terms of the impact on economic growth, the study found evidence for potential positive effects to be rather limited and found the negative effects of higher taxes to be 'the most significant channel of influence' (2000). From a gender perspective, BI would be likely to reduce women's participation in employment which might also be seen as a negative effect, as giving women a greater incentive to undertake more unpaid caring work in the household. In addition, the introduction of basic income would require an increased role for the welfare system in delivering payments to all citizens. This, in turn, raises issues about the civil liberties implications of such a move and the potential for increased social control. From a gender perspective, it also raises issues about whether this would, in fact, benefit women or whether it might simply lead to a shift from private to public patriarchy.

KEY POLICY AREAS

This section will look at policy proposals which have been put forward in three important areas, namely working age policies, pension policy and gender and care.

It discusses approaches to addressing the policy challenges identified in Chapter 9 (drawing on the philosophies and technologies of welfare outlined in the previous sections).

WORKING AGE POLICIES

POLICY APPROACH

There is a widespread consensus amongst policymakers – in theory if not in practice – that policies should focus on increasing the employment rate with a particular emphasis on active labour market policies. Of course, the benefits of increasing the employment rate are dependent on employment leading to a decent income above the poverty line. Esping-Andersen et al. (2001) have made the point that in order to allow people to benefit fully from active labour market policies, there is a need for investment in children. They argue that active labour market policies are largely curative rather than preventative and that early investment in children is necessary in order to ensure that they have the maximum skill levels at an older age and can benefit from training and education policies. This is a very valid point, albeit one nor pursued here as the relevant policies fall largely outside the scope of this book.[4] However, active labour market policies, if properly designed and implemented, can have an important role to play both from a macro-economic and employment perspective. Studies in the United Kingdom suggest that active supply-side labour market policies can help the economy to grow more rapidly without leading to excessive wage inflation (Nickell et al., 2002).

EMPLOYABILITY

Unemployment policies no longer focus solely on financial support for those who are unemployed. Rather, the type of policy advocated by the EU and OECD (and followed to varying degrees in European countries) focuses on making people 'employable' by identifying the barriers to employment and by addressing those barriers. Employability, in this sense, is not a question of either/or (people who are job ready v. 'the unemployables'), but rather involves a continuum (Weinert et al., 2001). A range of factors are involved at the level of the individual (some alterable such as education, some unalterable such as age), the immediate context (for example, family, location, social networks) and in relation to labour demand (at both firm level and at a more macro-level). Issues identified as affecting employability include education, work experience, age, family circumstances, location, job seeking, psychological distress and literacy difficulties. Policy measures now respond to such issues by addressing motivational problems, providing information, providing education opportunities, shaping enterprising individuals, seeking to identify and refer people with literacy problems and so on. As Dean (1995) points out, unemployment support now 'not only acts upon the financial plight of the unemployed, and upon their job prospects, but also upon those attitudes, affects, conduct and dispositions that present a barrier to the unemployed returning to the labour market, and alienate them from social networks and obligations' (1995: 572). But these measures are no longer focused solely on 'the unemployed'. Rather, these active policies seek to promote employment for all, not just the groups traditionally considered to be relevant to the paid labour force, but also lone parents and people with disabilities. In the light

---

4 Esping-Andersen et al. (2001) also argue that welfare policies must address child poverty. However, the term 'child poverty' is potentially misleading. The data on child poverty refer, in fact, to families with children. In order to address 'child' poverty it is necessary to address poverty amongst (largely working age) parents. Thus the argument that in order to address working age poverty you must first address child poverty becomes somewhat circular, since in order to address child poverty you must address poverty amongst working age parents.

of these developments, Walters (1994) suggests that we can speak of the 'demise of unemployment' from a discursive and governmental perspective. He argues, first, that the growth of part-time, casual and self-employment is making it increasingly difficult to distinguish between employment and unemployment. And second, policies increasingly aim to 'activate' the entire working age population rather than just the traditional 'unemployed'.

TRANSITIONAL LABOUR MARKETS

Schmid (1998) has outlined a concept of 'transitional labour markets', focusing on five critical transitions during a person's life-cycle, that is, from education to the labour market, within employment, between unwaged and waged work, between employment and unemployment, and from employment to retirement. Rather than focusing on the traditional employment–unemployment nexus, he argues that policy must have regard to all these transitions (in both directions), with the traditional unemployment benefit (and related policies) being replaced by a series of policies to maintain and enhance income capacity (or employability) over the life-cycle, to guarantee income security during transitions within employment, and to provide income support during periods when income capacity is reduced. In particular, he envisages this re-orientation as implying a move from the concept of 'unemployment insurance centred on income maintenance for jobless people to a system of *employment insurance*' linked to other aspects of policy and aiming to increase the ability to adjust to labour market changes (1998). One of the factors which Schmid focuses on is the development of policies such as parental leave, family time off, childcare and related policies.

IMPLICATIONS FOR CARING

One effect of the emphasis on full employment for both men and women will be a fundamental change in the approach to payments to persons with family responsibilities and a refocusing of policy. In most European countries, there was not a particularly coherent approach to policy in this area in the past. As late as a decade ago, in many countries, lone parents were largely seen as long-term welfare recipients with no relationship to the labour market. But the ongoing changes in the labour market means that there is considerable pressure to make employment more family friendly (for example, the extension of maternity benefit, introduction of carer's benefit, pressures for paid parental leave) and to encourage or require lone parents to seek employment after a certain stage. Thus there is likely to be increased support for people with parenting or caring responsibilities (on a short-term basis) but increasingly conditional support for long-term parenting. This is discussed in more detail later in this section.

WORK INCENTIVES

One of the key issues in relation to the link between welfare and employment throughout the 1980s and 1990s was the question of work incentives (see, for example, OECD, 1994). If welfare rates are set at a level such that employment is financially unattractive, this will contribute to a disincentive to work. However, despite the numerous books and articles on this issue, there is a lack of consensus as to when exactly welfare rates (and related policy measures) became so high as to create a serious work disincentive and how much of an issue this really is in practice (Sjöberg, 2000b). Recent studies based on microsimulation of household incomes have, for example, argued that the presence of incomes of other household members is frequently a stronger contributor to 'high' replacement rates than the tax-benefit system (Immervoll and O'Donoghue, 2001).[5] There is a growing recognition that eligibility criteria, which make payment of benefits conditional upon job-search and related behaviour, 'can offset, or even reverse, the disincentive effects which arise when benefits are paid without such conditions' (OECD, 2000: Ch. 4). The OECD highlights the fact that the manner of implementation of eligibility criteria is probably more important than 'enacting strict legislation'. The main point to be taken from this study is that 'net replacement rates and durations of benefit payments alone are not decisive for the incentive impact of a benefit system, which can be properly assessed only by analysing them together with eligibility criteria' (2000).

ROLE OF NEW TECHNOLOGIES

Privatisation of benefits has a limited role to play in this area. Unlike the case of pensions, there appear to be few if any countries which have a purely private system of unemployment insurance covering any significant segment of the population. This is because unemployment is difficult to predict, open to moral hazard and adverse selection, and cyclical. In other words it will be quite difficult for an insurance company to predict the risk of unemployment in the case of an individual or group. Second, claims for unemployment could be affected by moral hazard on the part of employees, employers or both. Individuals might generally be better placed than insurers to predict their likelihood of losing employment and those at greater risk might be more likely to insure, leading to the problem of adverse selection. Finally, unemployment, rather than being randomly distributed, has peaks and valleys. However, a number of countries – the

---

5 In these studies replacement income is defined as total household income rather than that attributed solely to the individual.

Netherlands being a leader in Europe – have introduced elements of marketisation in their public employment services.

As we have seen, the United Kingdom has been a leader in the use of in-work benefits (through the medium of refundable tax credits). This has followed on the policy approach adopted in the United States of America where the Earned Income Tax Credit (EITC) has become an increasingly important policy measure. In general, evaluations have highlighted the positive role which such benefits play in increasing employment rates. However, there are a range of issues about the broader effects of in-work benefits (such as whether they simply trap people in low paid, low skilled work and subsidise low productivity enterprises) which are rarely addressed in policy studies. In addition, the potential of in-work benefits depends on the broader context of labour market policy (including the level of low paid employment and the minimum wage) and it may be that such policies will have limited transferability in a European context. Individual welfare accounts (IWA) would appear to have a potential role in this area, particularly if European states move more towards an employability insurance approach as proposed by Schmid (1998). IWAs would have the potential to facilitate such an approach with, for example, withdrawals being made to fund lifelong learning. However, such approaches are at a very early stage and the widespread enthusiasm for individual learning accounts has yet to be translated into large-scale practice. Finally, basic income is largely inconsistent with the current policy approach. As we have seen, econometric models suggest that such an approach would tend to decrease rather than increase the labour supply. In addition, the unconditionality of the BI approach fits uneasily with the more active labour market policy which tends towards greater (rather than less) conditionality.

PENSIONS POLICY

POLICY APPROACH

Unlike the area of employment supports where there is a broad political consensus about appropriate policy measures (if a wide divergence as to how they are implemented in practice), there is considerably more divergence about appropriate policy options in the area of pensions. Basically, the EU follows a parametric reform approach (European Commission, 2003a) while the World Bank (and to a lesser extent the OECD) argues for more systemic reform. The Third Way does not really provide any consistent approach in this area. And, as we have seen in Chapter 7, national governments adopt very different approaches in this area ranging from the neo-liberal focus of the United Kingdom to significant parametric reform in Sweden.

AREAS OF CONSENSUS

There is a broad consensus amongst all key policy philosophies on the need for a range of policy measures:

- *Increasing the employment rate*   This is a critical issue and can make a very important contribution to the affordability of the pension system. Detailed policy measures have already been outlined in the previous section.
- *Raising the effective retirement age*   At present in the EU15, the average effective retirement age (at which people actually withdraw form the labour force) varies from 58 to 65. One of the most critical policy measures will be to raise this age which has the double bonus that people remain in the labour force longer (contributing to pension financing and helping to achieve employment targets) and it reduces the period over which pensions must be paid.
- *Reducing early retirement*   A critical part of raising the retirement age will be to end and reverse existing policies which have lowered retirement age and facilitated labour shedding. As we have seen, while some countries have made steps towards this objective, others have, in the very recent past, continued to facilitate early retirement.
- *Reducing pension levels and relating these more closely to contributions*   There is a broad consensus amongst policy makers that there is a need to reduce high levels of pensions (where these exist) in order to use available resources in the most equitable manner. Of course, it is often difficult to reach agreement of any precise level at which pension levels can be said to be (too) high. In addition, there is a general trend to link pensions more closely to contributions in order to provide rewards for continued employment (or to avoid disincentives to employment). However, these type of policy measures can create difficulties for groups such as women who tend to have broken careers due to childbirth and rearing or people with disabilities. Linking benefits to contributions needs to be balanced with appropriate measures for people who do not work for 'socially' justified reasons, and there is inevitably a tension between these two policies.
- *Abolition of special privileges*   In principle most simply, there is agreement on the need to abolish special privileges for particular employment groups which are no longer (and may never have been) justified.

Although there is a broad policy consensus about such measures, they are not uncontroversial. In the case of pension levels, while there is nothing sacrosanct about a replacement rate of 75 per cent as opposed to 70 or 65 per cent, the impact of reductions depends critically on their size, incidence (by class and by gender) and the extent to which reductions in public benefits are made up for by increased private funding. Increasing retirement age in contrast – despite the strong objections it evokes in many countries – is arguably more equitable. Given longer life expectancy it is arguably more equitable to ask people to work for the same relative proportion of their lives rather than working for less and receiving a lower pension in return. But the strong opposition to increasing retirement age and the continued popularity of early retirement indicate that there are a range of broader labour market issues (such as job quality and flexible retirement) to be addressed if such policies are to be broadly acceptable to Europe's older workers.

THE CASE FOR A MULTI-PILLAR APPROACH?

The main area of policy controversy relates to the question of whether a systemic shift is required from a public PAYG pension to a multi-pillar approach as recommended by the World Bank. The Bank (1994) has long recommended a combination of a flat-rate, public tier focused on a poverty reduction, a mandatory private, funded, second tier, and a third voluntary savings tier. Few (if any) EU15 countries conform precisely to this approach although a number broadly follow this mix. The Bank has been very successful in encouraging the adoption of such an approach in the CEE countries in recent years with reforms adopted in Bulgaria, Croatia, Hungary, Kazakhstan, Lithuania and Poland. However, the Bank continues to argue that such a systemic shift is also required in the EU15 countries (Holzmann et al., 2003).

The arguments for such an approach (Holzmann et al., 2003: 9–10) are stated to include:

- improving work incentives – but this can also be achieved under a properly designed PAYG scheme;
- increasing saving and investment – but whether a funded scheme should or does increase savings is highly debated;
- accelerating the development of a country's capital markets and hence its economic growth – but again whether this will happen in practice is very dependent on a country's broader economic circumstances and not very relevant to countries which already have developed capital markets;
- providing a better return on investment – while the nominal returns on capital are currently higher than the implicit returns to a PAYG system (that is, wage growth), this is not a true comparison. Taking account of issues such as administration costs (which are higher in a private system), transition costs from a PAYG to

a funded system and, most importantly, taking account of the different levels of risk involved in 'investing' in private stock as opposed to overall wage growth, it is not clear that funded schemes do provide a better return (Geanakoplos et al., 1998); and
- diversifying risk – as returns to capital and labour differ over time, investing in both allows individuals (and the state) to diversify their risks. This argument is correct but the appropriate balance of investment then depends on an assessment of the relevant returns and risk and on the 'taste' for risk of the individual. It is not, in principle, an argument for a *minimal* public scheme.

In addition, private systems introduce a number of additional risks and costs. First, administration costs in private schemes tend to be significantly higher due to factors such as marketing costs. Second, private pensions tend to receive tax subsidies. As a recent OECD study has shown, on the assumption that such tax incentives lead essentially to savings diversion rather than creation, they lead to large net budgetary costs (Antolin et al., 2004). Third, as recent events have demonstrated – when share prices fell significantly – private pensions are by no means risk-free and pension fund values can fall as well as rise.

Modelling by the European Commission (2001a) suggests that a large-scale privatisation of public pensions is simply unfeasible due to the high transition costs involved in switching from one system to another. It did suggest that there might be a role for a partial privatisation of pensions. However, the study found that the main contributor to a balanced pension system was parametric reforms, such as raising the employment rate and increasing effective retirement age. A number of countries have introduced measures such as partial pre-funding of pension, for example, Ireland with the establishment of a National Pensions Reserve Fund into which 1 per cent of GNP per annum will be paid until 2025. The Fund is invested in international capital markets, thereby diversifying risk without introducing a private element into the public pension system.

ROLE OF NEW TECHNOLOGIES

We have already discussed the role of privatisation. The role of IWAs in this area is likely to be more limited given the significant transition costs and the difficulties of explaining the concept to a broad audience. However, IWAs in specific areas (such as unemployment) might have a role with the balance (if any) accruing in such accounts being used to provide an additional pension. In practice many countries have moved close to a partial basic income in the case of pensions, with most providing at least a flat rate pension at close to universal coverage. However, the flat rate and universal approach of BI sits uneasily with the move towards greater links between contributions and benefits and even for the 'first pillar' element of a pension system the additional cost of providing a fully universal as opposed to means-tested or insurance pension is far from negligible.

CONCLUSION

A number of countries – such as Sweden – have already taken measures which are likely to ensure adequate and sustainable pensions into the next decades. Others, such as the United Kingdom, have prioritised sustainability over adequacy, while others again such as the Czech Republic have not yet taken sufficient action to ensure that pensions will be sustainable. As the Swedish experience shows, correctly designed parametric reforms can be sufficient to achieve a balanced outcome without the higher risk involved in systemic reform. However, in other political, social and economic contexts, more systemic reforms have also been seen to be necessary. Given that there is no 'one right answer', the future direction of pension policy in Europe remains (and will remain) a matter of lively debate.

GENDER AND CARE

In this section we look at policy directions in relation to the gender structure of welfare systems and the development of supports for the 'new social risk' of caring for children and older people or people with disabilities. Unlike the two previous areas, gender and care have received much less detailed policy attention. In so far as gender is addressed, policy tends to focus on increasing labour market participation and actions which are perceived to be necessary to facilitate this (such as improved access to care). As we have seen in previous sections, both the current 'jobs, jobs, jobs' policy and the reform of pensions schemes have important gender impacts, but these have rarely been central to the debate. For example, increasing the employment rate of women has important implications for the development of caring supports (which are discussed below). However, such issues are, in general, seen as secondary to the main goal of raising the female employment rate. In the area of pensions, as we have seen, reforms such as tying benefits more closely to contributions or replacing public (redistributive) pensions with private (actuarial) pensions also have important implications for women, but again these are generally seen as secondary, calling for ameliorative measures to safeguard women's pensions rather than fundamental reconsideration of the policy approach.

GENDERED STRUCTURE OF WELFARE

There has been a significant shift in the gender structure of welfare systems since the 1980s. At that time, gender discrimination was common in many European welfare states. As a result both of the general increase in female participation and, more specifically, the EU directive on equal treatment for men and women (discussed in Chapter 4), direct discrimination on grounds of sex has been removed (at least in those areas covered by the directive). Family and survivors benefits remain outside the scope of the directive and here directly discriminatory provisions – such as payment of child benefits to the mother – remain in many welfare states. However, even here a number of member states have moved to introduce equality of treatment, for example in relation to widow's pensions. A number of aspects of pension systems – such as unequal pension ages – are also excluded from the scope of the directive, but again many European countries are moving slowly towards more equal treatment.

However, while indirect discrimination (that is, treatment which applies to both genders but disproportionately affects one and for which there is no objective justification) is also ruled out by the EU directive, the European Court of Justice has allowed member states a wide margin of discretion in deciding what is objectively justified. The result is that measures which disadvantage predominantly female groups such as part-time workers are still allowed under EU law – though again labour market pressures have tended to mitigate such measures in practice. But, of course, the EU directive itself is based around participation in the labour force (for example, persons leaving the labour force to care for children are not within the personal scope of the directive). So it only guarantees equality of treatment to women in so far as they behave like men in the labour force but does nothing to require men to assume more equal caring responsibilities. Policy measures such as those in relation to increasing labour force participation and reforming pensions tend to increase this pressure toward similar roles for men and women within the labour force. We turn now to the extent to which these policy pressures have led to reforms in the area of caring supports.

CARING FOR CHILDREN

Caring for children is not, of course, a 'new' risk facing parents. However, it has traditionally been seen as a private responsibility of the family and not one requiring a significant state role. This has now changed to a large extent with the very significant rise in mother's labour force participation. Policy reports tend to call for a fairly standard range of welfare measures to support female participation. Almost all studies also emphasise the need for flexible working arrangements such as part-time work, career breaks and flexible working. Esping-Andersen et al. (2001: 92) call for a combination of subsidies for childcare (meeting about two-thirds of the cost), extended maternity and parental leave and sickness absence covering children's sickness. The Kok Report calls for an increase in the 'availability, affordability and quality of childcare and eldercare' (Employment Taskforce, 2003: 39). But, in practice, support for childcare is both very diverse in form and quantity between member states. In the Scandinavian countries there are high levels of publicly provided or publicly subsidised crèches. In Ireland, in contrast, the formal provision of childcare is primarily through private (commercial) and community based crèches, with limited state support. But the largest source of childcare is in the informal sector, with childcare being provided by small-scale (largely unregistered) child minders or family members. The types of childcare policy which have been introduced in recent decades also vary significantly. In general, there has been a trend to increase support to services which will facilitate women (and men) in taking up employment. But as Morgan and Zippel (2003) point out, a number of European countries have introduced long-term, low parental care allowances which tend to encourage women to remain at home caring for children for the duration of the payment and, in so far as data is available, would appear to have the effect of reducing female participation (at least in the short-term).

At the Barcelona European Council in 2002, the EU set targets for childcare provision, which aim to provide childcare to at least 90 per cent of children between three and mandatory school age and at least 33 per cent of children under three. But as the Kok Report points out (Employment Taskforce, 2003: 40), very few member states, with the exception of the Nordic countries, come close to these targets. In fact, at present there is no reliable comparable measure of childcare support across EU countries. Very limited work has yet been carried out by the EU in terms of developing a comprehensive approach to the issues of childcare (such as that adopted in relation to, for example, pensions). The EU has adopted a directive on parental leave (agreed by the social partners) but this provides access only to unpaid leave and, while it required the introduction of such leave in the United Kingdom and Ireland where no such legal entitlement existed, its unpaid nature means that it has been of limited impact. Of course, the quality of childcare and early childhood education is of critical importance for the wellbeing of future generations. However, in these areas policy remains quite diverse and is primarily driven at a national level.

CARE FOR OLDER PEOPLE AND PEOPLE WITH DISABILITIES

Caring for disabled or old and infirm family members is also not a new risk. Indeed, given the high level of institutional care for old and disabled people in many European countries in the eighteenth and nineteenth centuries (both in poor law institutions, old folks homes and psychiatric hospitals), it is arguably not even a 'new social risk'. However, the extent to which the state is involved and the manner in which support is provided has changed significantly. While about 5 per cent of the population over the age of 65 are in institutional care in most European countries (except the South where the figure is much lower), there has been a general trend towards deinstitutionalistion and 'care in the community'. In addition, while the state did play an extensive role in the past, this was generally as a last resort when family care had broken down. There is, today, a greater acceptance that public support should be complementary to family support and should facilitate, in so far as possible, care in the community. However, as in the case of childcare, support is very diverse both in form and quantity across European countries. All countries provide both institutional and community care supports to varying degrees. Some provide cash payments either to the care provider (for example, the United Kingdom and Ireland) or to the person requiring care (Germany). Again, while policy reports tend to call for improved access to elder care, there is an absence of any attempt to co-ordinate policy in this area.

ROLE OF NEW TECHNOLOGIES

As we have seen, privatisation tends to be problematic from a gender perspective. Because women generally do less well in terms of market income, they tend to rely more on public redistribution. But moves towards privatisation tend to reduce the extent of redistribution. Therefore, any move towards privatisation requires very careful consideration of the gender impact of such an approach – something which has not always occurred in practice. In contrast, basic income is often portrayed as a gender-friendly approach. However, as we have seen, studies suggest that BI might tend to reduce female labour force participation so again any such approach would require careful consideration.

CONCLUSION

On the one hand, the development of supports for caring is indeed a dynamic area of European welfare policy which, as has been argued, goes against the images of widespread retrenchment or of frozen welfare states. On the other, in contrast to several previous stages of development of welfare policy, where policy developed in a number of European countries over a relatively short period, in broadly similar ways and with a high degree of diffusion, the development of care policies, to date, has been somewhat slow, very variable in form, and with a limited element of diffusion from one country to another. Despite its central importance, gender remains at the margins of both public policy and academic debates.

TOWARDS A EUROPEAN WELFARE STATE?

This book is about European welfare *states*. But in this concluding section we look at the current impact of EU policies on welfare states and the extent to which a European welfare state is developing (or is likely to develop).

THE ROLE OF THE EUROPEAN UNION

As we have seen in previous chapters, EU legislation in the area of welfare policy has been very limited. In the specific area of social security (which remains subject to unanimity) there has been only binding legislation in relation to free movement of workers, equal treatment for men and women in relation to public and occupational pensions, and most recently limited legislation on occupational pensions.[6] There have indeed been a range of recommendations – such as the 1992 Recommendations on minimum income and convergence of social protection policies – but these are not legally binding and have had a very limited effect (if any) on national welfare policy.

THE OPEN METHOD OF CO-ORDINATION

The indirect impact of measures such as the European Economic and Monetary Union (EMU), the growing importance of the Broad Economic Policy Guidelines (BEPGs) and the EU Treaty provisions on free movement of services have arguably had much more influence on welfare policy than has specific EU social policy instruments. Recognising the growing impact of economic and monetary policies in the social field (negative integration) and faced by a reluctance amongst many member states to adopt binding measures in this area (positive integration), the Commission, with the support of certain member states, developed the concept of the Open Method of Co-ordination (OMC).

As described by the European Council, the OMC involves:

> A means of spreading best practice and achieving greater convergence towards the main EU goals. This method, which is designed to help Member States progressively to develop their own policies, involves: fixing guidelines for the Union combined with

---

6 There has, of course, also been binding legislation in related areas including employment protection, health and safety at work, and anti-discrimination.

specific timetables for achieving the goals which they set in the short, medium and long terms; establishing, where appropriate, quantitative and qualitative indicators and benchmarks against the best in the world and tailored to the needs of different Member States and sectors as a means of comparing good practice; translating these European guidelines into national and regional policies by setting specific targets and adopting measures, taking into account national and regional differences; periodic monitoring, evaluation and peer review. (quoted in Schludi, 2003: 25)

While the European Employment Strategy can be seen as OMC *avant la lettre*, to date the OMC itself has been applied specifically in relation to social inclusion and pension policies (two of the four EU priority areas discussed at the beginning of this chapter). In each case this has involved member states producing national reports (based on an EU template) and involving varying degrees of consultation with national social partners and NGOs. These have then been compared and synthesised, leading to a Joint EU Council/ Commission Report. In the case of social inclusion policies, the process has included the adoption of a series of social inclusion indicators against which national progress can be measured. No EU *targets* have been adopted, although member states have been encouraged to set national targets and some have done so. In the case of pensions, the Joint Report agreed 'broad common objectives', but to date no indicators have been established.

Assessments of the OMC vary widely. Unfortunately, the dramatic growth in the quantity of literature on this topic has yet to be matched by a similar development in the quality or quantity of empirical research on its actual impact. Indeed, it is arguably too early in the process to come to any hard conclusions on its longer-term impact. However, recent academic reports commissioned by EU presidencies have seen the OMC as offering 'a promising wedge to break the institutional traps ... which relegate social protection policy inexorably within the preserve of national sovereignty' (Ferrera et al., 2000: 67) and as 'a powerful stimulus for policy learning and innovation' (Esping-Andersen et al., 2001: 258).

On the one hand, given the very limited nature of EU competence in the welfare area and the sclerotic pace of development, the OMC does mark an important new step in EU social policy which both gives the EU a (albeit limited) role in specific policy areas and which may give rise to greater intra-EU policy diffusion. On the other hand, it is important to be realistic about the likely impact of OMC in the short to medium term. Schludi (2003) has highlighted a number of limitations to the concept of benchmarking (even contextualised benchmarking as intended in the OMC).[7] He points out that learning from

7 In contrast, the World Bank advocacy of a one-size-fits-all multi-pillar approach is seen as decontextualised benchmarking.

abroad is only one possible factor for welfare state change; that learning *per se* may not lead to change as policy makers may refuse to or be unable to implement change; and that policy transfer may fail where it does not have sufficient regard to the context in which it operates, where it is incomplete or inappropriate. In addition, the practical impact of OMC to date is somewhat limited. In the case of the EES, which has been in place since 1997/8, it has been argued that 'there is no clear and at best mixed evidence that the EES has strongly promoted policy learning within member states or caused greater convergence among member states' employment policies' (Schludi, 2003: 42). And, as we have seen, employment policy is one area where there is the greatest degree of agreement as to appropriate policy approaches (albeit that this consensus is often internalised by member states to a limited extent). In the case of the pensions OMC, where there is a much greater level of policy divergence, while there has been much useful sharing of information and modeling of scenarios, the broad common objectives have been described as forming the lowest common denominator between EU social and economic policy makers on the one hand and between EU member states with their highly diverse pension arrangements on the other (Schludi, 2003: 31).

A EUROPEAN WELFARE STATE OR EUROPEAN SOCIAL MODEL?

So can we now see a European welfare state or is one developing? As we have seen, there remains a high level of diversity amongst European welfare states. But are European countries distinctive when compared with those outside Europe? The evidence suggests that there is something distinctive about European welfare states. First, in general they spend more than non-European countries, and spending is related to the level of economic development. In OECD Europe in 2001, spending varied from 16.5 to 29.2 per cent of GDP (GNP in the Irish case) compared to 6.1 to 18.5 per cent in the rest of the OECD. And, excluding Ireland, there is a much closer correlation between welfare expenditure and the level of economic development in Europe (see Figure 5.1) than there is outside Europe (correlation for OECD Europe of 0.65; for the rest of OECD this is 0.45 and the relationship between economic development and welfare spending for the *more developed* OECD countries outside Europe is strongly negative). Similarly, as we saw in Chapter 5, welfare outcomes in terms of income inequality and poverty are generally better in European countries and again are related to the level of economic development. Thus viewed from the outside, European (at least Central and Western European) welfare states do look distinctively different to those found in most other parts of the globe in terms of welfare spending and outcomes. But this was also the case 100 years ago and, as we have seen throughout this book, there remains a great diversity between European welfare systems. So, while we can see a distinctive *European social model*, we do not see a *single European welfare state* in any strong sense of the term. But can we say that national welfare systems are converging towards a more consistent model?

As we have seen in Chapter 5, there has been a degree of convergence in that all European welfare states, over time, adopted schemes in the main areas of welfare policy. And, as discussed in Chapter 3, depending to some extent on the countries one includes in the calculation, there has been a degree of convergence in terms of spending, with the Southern European countries converging towards the EU average and higher spending countries maintaining or moderating their spending levels. The role of the EU in all aspects of national life has also increased and we have moved from 'sovereign' welfare states to a system of semi-sovereignty with competence shared between the EU and national governments. However, as we have also seen, and as anyone working in European welfare systems will testify, there remains a very significant degree of divergence between different national systems not just in their detail but also in their objectives, their assumptions and the broader societal context in which they operate. And there is little indication that this diversity is lessening. The United Kingdom, for example, is on a policy trajectory which in many areas takes it further away from other European countries. The sovereignty argument also only goes so far. It would be simply a myth to suggest that national welfare states were ever fully sovereign and did not have to have regard to international financial pressures. And, while the impact of the EU has undoubtedly increased, in the area of welfare policy we should not lose sight of the fact that the preferred policy instrument has moved from the directly applicable regulation on free movement of 1958, to the binding (but requiring national implementing legislation) directive of 1979 to the non-binding OMC today.

However, one can argue that while we are not moving towards a European welfare state, there has been a Europeanisation of welfare policy making. As we saw in Chapter 1, the term 'Europeanisation' is used in two different ways. First, to describe the emergence and the development at the European level of distinct structures of governance. Second, to describe a set of processes through which the EU political, social and economic dynamics become part of a logic of domestic discourse, identities, political structures and public policies. There has been, albeit only in a weak sense, the emergence and the development at the European level of distinct structures of governance in the field of social protection. And both the EU legislation in the area and the OMC have at least begun a process through which EU dynamics become part of the domestic logic.

This process is, however, to date quite limited. An interesting case study is the introduction of welfare schemes to respond to the new social risk of care. If we were seeing a move towards a European welfare state one might expect to see a strong centralised European initiative in this area promoting convergence and a high degree of commonality between the quality and quantity of provision being introduced in member states. Neither of these is to be seen. There is little, if any, centralised policy initiative and the degree of diversity of policy (in both form and objective) is at least (if not more) divergent than has been the case in previous policy waves (such as the widespread introduction of family benefits in the 1930s and 1940s).

Summary

In this chapter we have:

- outlined a number of key philosophies of welfare including the approaches adopted by the World Bank, the EU Commission and the Third Way;
- looked at a number of new welfare technologies including privatisation, individual welfare accounts, refundable tax credits and basic income;
- examined key policy areas including working age policy, pensions and gender and care; and
- examined key EU developments and the extent to which a European welfare state is developing.

Discussion points

1 Compared to the post-War period, there is a much greater degree of consensus today about the role of the welfare state in Europe. Do you agree?
2 The future European welfare state should allow much more individual freedom and hence should be more privatised. Discuss.
3 The EU has played a very important 'demonstration role' in the development of welfare systems in new EU member states. Do you agree?

Supplementary reading

Materials on the philosophies and technologies of welfare and on three key policy areas are set out in the text. For an overview of key policy issues and a discussion of the role of the EU, see Ferrera et al. (2000) and Esping-Andersen et al. (2001). Other important recent books on the trajectory of welfare states include Castles (2004), Taylor-Gooby (2004) and Iversen (2005).

REFERENCES

Abrahamson, P. (1999) 'The Welfare modelling business', *Social Policy and Administration*, 33 (4): 394–415.

Abrahamson, P. (2003) 'The end of the Scandinavian model? Welfare reform in the Nordic countries', *Journal of Societal and Social Policy*, 2 (2): 19–36.

Adema, W. (2001) *Net Social Expenditure*. Labour Market and Social Policy Occasional Paper No. 52. Paris: OECD.

Adema, W. (2002) *Bosses and Babies*. Paris: OECD.

Adorno, T. and Horkheimer, M. (1972) *Dialectic of Enlightenment*. London: Verso.

Alber, J. (1981) 'Government responses to the challenge of unemployment: The development of unemployment insurance in Europe', in P. Flora and A.J. Heidenheimer (eds), *The Development of Welfare States in Europe and America*. New Brunswick: Transaction.

Alber, J. (1986) 'Germany', in P. Flora (ed.), *Growth to Limits*. Berlin: de Gruyter.

Allan, J. and Scruggs, L. (2004) 'Political partisanship and Welfare State reform in advanced industrial societies', *American Journal of Political Science*, 48 (3): 496–512.

Amenta, E. (1998) *Bold Relief: Institutional Politics and the Origins of Modern American Social Policy*. Princeton: Princeton University Press.

Andersen, K. (2001) 'The politics of retrenchment in a social democratic Welfare State', *Comparative Political Studies*, 34 (9): 1063–91.

Anderson, L.R.S. (2003) 'A global social policy?' PhD dissertation, University of North Carolina.

Antolín, P., de Serres, A. and de la Maisonneuve, C. (2004) *Long-term Budgetary Implications of Tax-favoured Retirement Savings Plans*. Economics Department Working Paper 393. Paris: OECD.

Arts, W. and Gelissen, J. (2001) 'Welfare States, solidarity and justice principles: Does the type really matter?', *Acta Sociologica*, 44 (4): 283–99.

Arts, W. and Gelissen, J. (2002) 'Three worlds of welfare capitalism or more? A state-of-the-art report', *Journal of European Social Policy*, 12 (2): 137–58.

Arts, W., Halman, L. and van Oorshot, W. (2003) 'The Welfare State: Villain or hero of the piece?', in W.A. Arts, L. Halman and J.A.P. Hagenaars (eds), *The Cultural Diversity of European Unity: Findings, Explanations and Reflections from the European Values Study*. Leiden: Brill.

Baldwin, P. (1990) *The Politics of Social Solidarity*. Cambridge: Cambridge University Press.

Baldwin, P. (1996) 'Can we define a European Welfare State model?', in B. Greve (ed.), *The Scandinavian Model in a Period of Change*. Basingstoke: Macmillan.

Baradasi, E., Lasaosa, A., Micklewright, J. and Nagy, G. (1999) *Measuring the Generosity of Unemployment Benefit Systems*. Working Paper 1999/8, Budapest: Hungarian Academy of Sciences.

Beneria, L. (2001) *Changing Employment Patterns and the Informalization of Jobs*. Geneva: ILO.

Beveridge, Sir William (1942) *The Beveridge Report*. Norwich: HMSO.

Blackburn, S. (1999) 'How useful are feminist theories of the Welfare State', *Womens' History Review*, 4 (3): 369–94.

Blair, T. and Schroeder, G. (1999) *Europe: The Third Way*.

Blekesaune, M. and Quadagno, J. (2003) 'Public altitudes towards Welfare State policies: a comparative analysis of 24 nations', *European Sociological Review*, 19 (5): 415–27.

Bock, G. and Thane, P. (1991) *Maternity and Gender Policies: Women and the Rise of the European Welfare States 1880s–1950s*. London: Routledge.

Boeri, T., Börsch-Supan, A. and Tabellini, G. (2001) 'Would you like to shrink the Welfare State?', *Economic Policy*, 9–50.

Boisard, P., Cartron, D., Valeyre, A. and Gollac, M. (2002a) *Time and Work: Duration of Work*. Luxembourg: Office for Official Publications of the EC.

Boisard, P., Cartron, D., Gollac, M., Valeyre, A. and Besançcon, J.-B. (2002b) *Time and Work: Work Intensity*. Luxembourg: Office for Official Publications of the EC.

Boix, C. and Stokes, S.C. (2003) 'Endogenous democratization', *World Politics*, 55 (4): 517–49.

Börzel, T.A. and Risse, T. (2000) *When Europe Hits Home: Europeanization and Domestic Change*. European Integration Online Paper 4 (15).

Bowles, S. and Gintis, H. (2000) 'Reciprocity, self–interest and the Welfare State', *Nordic Journal of Political Economy*, 26 (4): 33–53.

Boyer, R. (2002) *Is there a Welfare State Crisis? A Comparative Study of French Social Policy*. Geneva: ILO.

Bradley, D., Huber, E., Mahler, S., Nielsen, F. and Stephens, J.D. (2003) 'Distribution and redistribution in post-industrial democracies', *World Politics*, 55 (2): 193–228.

Bradshaw, J. and Finch, N. (2002) *A Comparison of Child Benefit Packages in 22 Countries*. Leeds: CDS.

Brewer, M., Goodman, A., Myck, M., Shaw, J. and Shepherd, A. (2004) *Poverty and Income Inequality in Britain: 2004*. London: Institute for Fiscal Studies.

Briggs, A. (1961) 'The Welfare State in historical perspective', *European Journal of Sociology*, 2: 221–58.

Bruce, M. (1961) *The Coming of the Welfare State*. London: Batsford.

Callan, T., Boyle, G., McCarthy, T., Nolan, B., Walsh, J., Nestor, R. and van de Gaer, D. (2000) *Dynamic Effects of a Basic Income: Phase 2 of a Study for the Working Group on Basic Income* (unpublished).

Cameron, D. (1978) 'The expansion of the public economy: A comparative analysis', *American Political Science Review*, 74 (4): 1243–61.

Carroll, E. (1999) *Emergence and Structuring of Social Insurance Institutions*. Stockholm: Swedish Institute for Social Research.

Carroll, E. (2003) 'The clear and present danger of the "globaloney" industry: Globalization concepts in welfare research and social opinion pieces since 1995', *Global Social Policy*, 3 (2): 195–211.

Castles, F.G. (ed.) (1993) *Families of Nations: Patterns of Public Policy in Western Democracies*. Aldershot: Dartmouth.

Castles, F.G. (1994) 'On religion and public policy: Does Catholicism make a difference?', *European Journal of Political Research*, 25 (1): 19–40.

Castles, F.G. (1998) *Comparative Public Policy: Patterns of Post-War Transformation*. Cheltenham: Edward Elgar.

Castles, F.G. (2004) *The Future of the Welfare State: Crisis Myths and Crisis Realities*. Oxford: Oxford University Press.

Castles, F.G. and Mitchell, D. (1993) 'Worlds of welfare and families of nations', in F.G. Castles (ed.), *Families of Nations: Patterns of Public Policy in Western Democracies*. Aldershot: Dartmouth.

Cigno, A., Casolaro, L. and Rosati, F.C. (2000) *The Role of Social Security in Household Decisions*. Working Paper 394. Munich: CESifo.

Cippola, C.M. (1976) *The Fontana Economic History of Europe,* Vol. 6 (2). Glasgow: Collins.

Clayton, R. and Pontussen, J. (1998) 'Welfare-State retrenchment revisited', *World Politics*, 51 (1): 67–98.

Collier, D. and Messick, R.E. (1975) 'Prerequisites versus diffusion: Testing alternative explanations of social security adoption', *American Political Science Review*, 69 (4): 1299–315.

Condorcet, J.-A.-N. (1795/1988) *Esquisse d'un tableau historique des progress de l'esprit humain*. Paris: Flammarion.

Conley, D. (2000) 'Home ownership, poverty and the Welfare State'. Paper, New York University.

Council of Europe (1998) *Gender Mainstreaming*. Strasbourg: Council of Europe.

Cousins, M. (1997) 'Ireland's place in the worlds of welfare capitalism', *Journal of European Social Policy*, 7 (3): 223–35.

Cousins, M. (2003) *The Birth of Social Welfare*. Dublin: Four Courts.

Daly, M. (1997) 'Welfare States under pressure: Cash benefits in European Welfare States over the last ten years', *Journal of European Social Policy*, 7 (2): 129–46.

Daly, M. (2000) *The Gender Division of Welfare*. Cambridge: Cambridge University Press.

Daly, M. (2001) 'Globalization and the Bismarckian Welfare States', in R. Sykes, B. Palier and P.M. Prior (eds), *Globalization and the European Welfare States: Challenges and Change*. London: Macmillan.

Dean, M. (1995) 'Governing the unemployed self in an active society', *Economy and Society*, 24 (4): 559–83.

Dion, M. (2005) 'The political origins of social security in Mexico during the Cárdenas and Ávila Comacho administrations', *Mexican Studies/Estudios Mexicanos,* 21 (1): 59–95.

Docherty, T. (1993) *Postmodernism: A Reader*. Hemel Hempstead: Harvester Wheatsheaf.

Duncan, S. (1995) 'Theorizing European gender systems', *Journal of European Social Policy*, 5 (4): 263–84.

Ebbinghaus, B. (2003) 'How the cases you choose limit the questions you ask', paper presented at the European Consortium for Political Research Conference, Marburg.

Ebbinghaus, B. and Manow, P. (2001) 'Introduction: Studying varieties of capitalism', in B. Ebbinghaus and P. Mannow (eds), *Comparing Welfare Capitalism*. London: Routledge.

Employment Taskforce (2003) *Jobs, Jobs, Jobs: Creating More Employment in Europe*. Luxembourg: Office for Official Publications of the EC.

Esping-Andersen, G. (1985) *Politics Against Markets*. Princeton: Princeton University Press.

Esping-Andersen, G. (1990) *The Three Worlds of Welfare Capitalism*. Cambridge: Polity.

Esping-Andersen, G. (1997) 'Hybrid or unique? The Japanese Welfare State between Europe and America', *Journal of European Social Policy*, 7 (3): 179–89.

Esping-Andersen, G. (1999) *Social Foundations of Postindustrial Economies*. Oxford: Oxford University Press.

Esping-Andersen, G., Gallie, D., Hemerijck, A. and Myles, J. (2001) *A New Welfare Architecture for Europe?* Report to the Belgian presidency of the EU.

European Commission (1994) *White Paper on Growth, Competitiveness and Employment*. Luxembourg: Office for Official Publications of the EC.

European Commission (1999) *A Concerted Strategy for Modernising Social Protection*. Luxembourg: Office for Official Publications of the EC.

European Commission (2001a) *Employment in Europe 2000*. Luxembourg: Office for Official Publications of the EC.

European Commission (2001b) 'Reforms of pension systems in the EU: An analysis of the policy options', *European Economy*, 171–222.

European Commission (2002) *Social Protection in Europe 2001*. Luxembourg: Office for Official Publications of the EC.

European Commission (2003a) *Adequate and Sustainable Pensions*. Luxembourg: Office for Official Publications of the EC.

European Commission (2003b) *Communication on Immigration, Integration and Employment*. Luxembourg: Office for Official Publications of the EC.

European Commission (2004a) *Making Work Pay*. Luxembourg: Office for Official Publications of the EC.

European Commission (2004b) *Development of a Methodology for the Collection of Harmonised Statistics on Childcare*. Brussels: European Commission.

Eurostat (2001) www.europa.eu.int/comm/eurostat/

Eurostat (2002) 'Women and men reconciling work and family life', *Statistics in Focus*, 9.

Eurostat (2003) 'How women and men spend their time', *Statistics in Focus*, 12.

Evans, M., Eyre, J., Millar, J. and Sarre, S. (2003) *New Deal for Lone Parents: Second Synthesis Report of the National Evaluation*. Leeds: CDS.

Fahey, T. (2002) 'The family economy in the development of welfare regimes: A case study', *European Sociological Review*, 18 (1): 51–64.

Ferge, Z. (2001) 'Welfare and "ill-fare" systems in central-eastern Europe', in R. Sykes, B. Palier and P.M. Prior (eds), *Globalization and European Welfare States*. Basingstoke: Palgrave.

Ferrera, M. (1993) *EC Citizens and Social Protection*. Brussels: EC Commission.

Ferrera, M. (1996) 'The "southern model" of welfare in social Europe', *Journal of European Social Policy*, 6 (1): 17–37.

Ferrera, M., Hemerijck, A. and Rhodes, M. (2000) 'The future of social Europe'. Report for the Portuguese presidency of the EU.

Flaquer, L. (2000) *Family Policy and Welfare State in Southern Europe*. Working Paper 185. Barcelona: ICPS.

Flora, P. (1986) 'Introduction', in P. Flora (ed.), *Growth to Limits*. Berlin: de Gruyter.

Flora, P. and Alber, J. (1981) 'Modernization, democratization, and the development of Welfare States in Western Europe', in P. Flora and A.J. Heidenheimer (eds), *The Development of Welfare States in Europe and America*. New Brunswick: Transaction.

Flora, P. and Heidenheimer, A.J. (eds) (1981) *The Development of Welfare States in Europe and America*. New Brunswick: Transaction.

Fölster, S. (1996) *Social Insurance Based on Personal Savings Accounts*. Working Paper 454. Stockholm: Industrial Institute for Economic and Social Research.

Fölster, S., Gidehag, R., Orszag, M. and Snower, D. (2002) *Assessing Welfare Accounts*. Discussion Paper 533. Bonn: IZA.

Förster, M.F. and d'Ercole, M. (2005) *Income Distribution and Poverty in OECD Countries in the Second Half of the 1990s*. Social, Employment and Migration Working Paper 22. Paris: OECD.

Frank, A.G. (1998) *ReOrient: Global Economy in the Asian Age*. Berkeley, CA: University of California Press.

Frye, T. (2003) 'State spending and globalization(s) in the post-Communist world',

Fultz, E., Ruck, M. and Steinhilber, S. (2003) *The Gender Dimensions of Social Security Reform in Central and Eastern Europe*. Budapest: ILO.

Gallie, D. and Paugam, S. (2002) *Social Precarity and Social Integration*. Brussels: EU Commission.

Garrett, G. (1998) *Partisan Politics in the Global Economy*. Cambridge: Cambridge University Press.

Garrett, G. and Mitchell, D. (1999) *Globalization and the Welfare State*. Working Paper 1999–04. Yale: Leitner Program.

Gauthier, A. (2001) 'The impact of public policies on families and demographic behaviour', paper presented at the ESF/EURESCO Conference, Bad Herrenalb.

Geanakoplos, J., Mitchell, O.S. and Zeldes, S.P. (1998) 'Would a privatized social security system really pay a higher rate of return?', in J. Arnold, S. Graetz and A. Munnell (eds), *Framing the Social Security Debate*. Washington, DC: Brooking Institution Press.

Gelissen, J. (2000) 'Popular support for institutional solidarity: A comparison between European Welfare States', *International Journal of Social Welfare*, 9: 285–300.

Genschel, P. (2002) 'Globalization, tax competition and the Welfare State', *Politics and Society*, 30 (2): 245–75.

Geurts, S., Kompier, M. and Gründemann, R. (2000) 'Curing the Dutch disease? Sickness absence and work disability in the Netherlands', *International Social Security Review*, 53 (4): 79–103.

Gilbert, B. (1966) *The Evolution of National Insurance in Great Britain*. London: Michael Joseph.

Gilbert, B. (1970) *British Social Policy 1914–1939*. London: Batsford.

Ginn, J., Street, D. and Arber, S. (eds) (2001) *Women, Work and Pensions*, Buckingham: Open University Press.

Girvetz, H. (1968) 'Welfare State', in D.L. Sill (ed.), *International Encyclopedia of the Social Sciences*. New York: Macmillan.

Goodin, R.E., Headey, B., Muffels, R. and Dirven, H.-J. (1999) *The Real Worlds of Welfare Capitalism*. Cambridge: Cambridge University Press.

Graham, C. (2002) *Public Attitudes Matter*. Washington, DC: World Bank.

Green-Pedersen, C. (2001) 'Welfare-State retrenchment in Denmark and the Netherlands, 1982–1998: The role of party competition and party consensus', *Comparative Political Studies*, 34 (9): 963–85.

Green-Pedersen, C. (2002a) *The Politics of Justification*. Amsterdam: Amsterdam University Press.

Green-Pedersen, C. (2002b) 'What to make of the Dutch and Danish "miracles"', in B. Södersten (ed.), *Globalization and the Welfare State*. London: Palgrave.

Green-Pedersen, C. (2004) 'The dependent variable problem within the study of Welfare-State retrenchment: Defining the problem and looking for solutions', *Journal of Comparative Policy Analysis*, 6 (1): 3–14.

Green-Pedersen, C. and Lindbom, A. (2002) 'Politics within paths: The trajectories of Danish and Swedish pension systems', paper presented at a conference.

Green-Pedersen, C., van Kersbergen, K. and Hemerijck, A. (2001) 'Neo-liberalism, the "Third Way" or what? Recent Social Democratic welfare policies in Denmark and the Netherlands', *Journal of European Public Policy*, 8 (2): 307–25.

Guillén, A.M. (1999) *Pension Reform in Spain (1975–1997): The Role of Organized Labour*. EUI Working Papers EUF 99/6. Florence: EUI.

Guillén, A.M. and Álvarez, S. (2002) 'Southern European Welfare States facing globalization: Is there social dumping?', in R. Sigg and C. Behrendt (eds), *Social Security in the Global Village*. New Brunswick: Transaction.

Guillén, A.M. and Álvarez, S. (2004) 'The EU's impact on the Spanish Welfare State', *Journal of European Social Policy*, 14 (3): 285–99.

Guillén A., Álvarez, S., and Adao e Silva, P. (2002) *Redesigning the Spanish and Portuguese Welfare States: The Impact of Accession into the European Union*. Working Paper 85. Harvard: Centre for European Studies.

Habermas, J. (1989) *Structural Transformation of the Public Sphere*. Cambridge: MIT.

Hacker, J. (2004) 'Privatizing risk without privatizing the Welfare State', *American Political Science Review*, 98 (2): 243–60.

Hall, P.A. (2003) 'Aligning ontology and methodology in comparative research', in J. Mahoney and D. Rueschemeyer (eds), *Comparative Historical Analysis in the Social Sciences*. Cambridge: Cambridge University Press.

Harris, J. (1977) *William Beveridge*. Oxford: Oxford University Press.

Haverland, M. (2001) 'Another Dutch Miracle? Explaining Dutch and German pension trajectories', *Journal of European Social Policy*, 11 (4): 308–23.

Hay, C., Watson, M. and Wincott, D. (1999) *Globalisation, European Integration and the Persistence of European Social Models*. Working Paper 3/99. Birmingham: University of Birmingham.

Heien, T. and Hofäcker, D. (1999) *How do Welfare Regimes Influence Attitudes?* Working Paper No. 9. Bielfield: University of Bielfield.

Herbertson, T.T. and Orszag, J.M. (2003) *The Early Retirement Burden*. Discussion Paper 816. Bonn: IZA.

Hicks, A. (1999) *Social Democracy and Welfare Capitalism*. Ithaca, NY: Cornell University Press.

Hicks, A. and Kenworthy, L. (1998) 'Cooperation and political economic performance in affluent democratic capitalism', *American Journal of Sociology*, 103 (6): 1631–72.

Hinrichs, K., Offe, C. and Wiesenthal, H. (1988) 'Time, money and Welfare-State capitalism', in J. Keane (ed.), *Civil Society and the State*. London: Verso.

Hirst, P. and Thompson, G. (1997) 'Globalization in question: International economic relations and forms of public governance', in J.R. Hollingsworth and R. Boyer (eds), *Contemporary Capitalism: The Embeddedness of Institutions*. Cambridge: Cambridge University Press.

Holzmann, R., MacKellar, L. and Rutkowski, M. (2003) 'Accelerating the European reform agenda' in R. Holzmann, M. Orenstein and M. Rutkowski (eds), *Pension Reform in Europe*. Washington, D.C.: World Bank.

Hong, Y.-S. (1998) *Welfare, Modernity, and the Weimar State, 1919–1933*. Princeton: Princeton University Press.

Huber, E. and Stephens, J.D. (2000) 'Partisan governance, women's employment, and the Social Democratic service state', *American Sociological Review*, 65 (3): 323–42.

Huber, E. and Stephens, J.D. (2001) *Development and Crisis of the Welfare State*. Chicago: University of Chicago Press.

Huberman, M. and Lewchuck, W. (2002) *European Economic Integration and the Labour Compact, 1850–1913*, Scientific Series 2002s-34. Montréal: Cirano.

ILO/Eurodata (2001) *Database on the Cost of Social Security (1949–1993)*. Geneva: Mannheim.

Immergut, E.M. (1992) *Health Politics: Interests and Institutions in Western Europe*. Cambridge: Cambridge University Press.

Immervoll, H. and O'Donoghue, C. (2001) *Welfare Benefits and Work Incentives*. Working Paper No. EM 4/01. Cambridge: EUROMOD.

Iversen, T. (1998) 'The choices for Scandinavian social democracy in comparative perspective', *Oxford Review of Economic Policy*, 14 (1): 59–75.

Iversen, T. (2001) 'The dynamics of Welfare State expansion: Trade openness, deindustrialization and partisan politics', in P. Pierson (ed.), *The New Politics of the Welfare State*. Oxford: Oxford University Press.

Iversen, T. (2005) *Capitalism, Democracy and Welfare*. Cambridge: Cambridge University Press.

Iversen, T. and Cusack, T. (2000) 'The causes of Welfare State expansion: deindustrialization or globalization?', *World Politics*, 52: 313–49.

Janoski, T. and Hicks, A.M. (eds) (1994) *The Comparative Political Economy of the Welfare State*. Cambridge: Cambridge University Press.

Jenson, J. (1997) 'Who cares? Gender and welfare regimes', *Social Politics*, 7 (4): 182–7.

Jütte, R. (1994) *Poverty and Deviance in Early Modern Europe*. Cambridge: Cambridge University Press.

Kangas, O. (1991) *The Politics of Social Rights*. Stockholm: Swedish Institute for Social Research.

Kautto, M. and Kvist, J. (2002) *Distinct or Extinct? Nordic Welfare States in the European Context*. Working Paper 7. Copenhagen: Danish National Institute of Social Research.

Kelstrup, M. (2001) *The European Union and Globalisation: Reflections on Strategies of Individual States*. Working Paper. Copenhagen: COPRI.

Kemeny, J. (1995) 'Theories of power in "The three worlds of welfare capitalism"', *Journal of European Social Policy*, 5 (2): 87–96.

Kemmerling, A. (2002) *The Employment Effects of Different Regimes of Welfare State Taxation*. Discussion Paper 02/8. Köln: MPIfG.

Kemmerling, A. (2003) *Report on the Social Dimension of Ezoneplus*. Working Paper 13. Berlin: Ezoneplus.

Kennedy, K.A., Giblin, T. and McHugh, D. (1988) *The Economic Development of Ireland*. London: Routledge.

Kerr, C., Dunlop, J.T., Harbison, F. and Myers, C.A. (1960) *Industrialism and Industrial Man*. New York: Oxford University Press.

Kim, H. (2000) *Do Welfare States Reduce Poverty?* Working Paper 233. Luxembourg: Luxembourg Income Study.

King, M.C. (2002) *Strong Families or Patriarchal Economies?* EUI Working Papers TRSC 2002/14. Florence: EUI.

Korpi, W. (1980) 'Social policy strategies and distributional conflict in capitalist democracies', *West European Politics*, 3 (3): 296–316.

Korpi, W. (1989) 'Power, politics, and state autonomy in the development of social citizenship: Social rights during sickness in eighteen OECD countries since 1930', *American Sociological Review*, 54: 309–28.

Korpi, W. (2000) 'Faces of inequality: gender, class and patterns of inequalities in different types of Welfare States', *Social Politics*, 7 (2): 127–91.

Korpi, W. and Palme, J. (1998) 'The paradox of redistribution and strategies of equality', *American Sociological Review*, 63 (5): 661–87.

Korpi, W. and Palme, J. (2003) 'New politics and class politics in Welfare State regress: A comparative analysis of retrenchment in 18 countries, 1975–1995', *American Political Science Review*, 97 (3): 425–46.

Koven, S. and Michel, S. (1990) 'Womanly duties: Maternalist politics and the origins of Welfare States in France, Germany, Great Britain, and the United States, 1880–1920', *American Historical Review*, 95: 1076–1108.

Koven, S. and Michel, S. (eds) (1993) *Mothers of a New World, Maternalist Politics and the Origins of Welfare States*. London: Routledge.

Král, J. (2004) 'The role of private pensions in the Czech pension reform', in *Reforming Public Pensions: Sharing the Experience of OECD and Transition Countries*. Paris: OECD.

Leisering, L. (2003) 'Nation state and Welfare State: An intellectual and political history', *Journal of European Social Policy*, 13 (2): 175–85.

Lewis, J. (1992) 'Gender and the development of welfare regimes', *Journal of European Social Policy*, 2 (3): 159–73.

Lewis, J. (1997) 'Gender and welfare regimes: Further thoughts', *Social Politics*, 7 (4): 160–77.

Lewis, J. (2002) 'Gender and Welfare State change', *European Societies*, 4 (4): 331–57.

Lindert, P.H. (1998) 'Poor relief before the Welfare State: Britain versus the Continent, 1780–1880', *European Review of Economic History*, 2: 101–140.

LIS (1980–2000) www.lisproject.org/keyfigures.htm

Lis, C. and Soly, H. (1979) *Poverty and Capitalism in Pre-industrial Europe*. Brighton: Harvester.

Lowe, R. (2004) *The welfare state in Britain Since 1945*. Basingstoke: Palgrave.

McIntosh, M. (1978) 'The state and the oppression of women', in A. Kuhn and A. Wolpe (eds), *Feminism and Materialism*. London: Routledge and Kegan Paul.

Mácha, M. (2002) 'The political economy of pension reform in the Czech Republic', in E. Fultz (ed.), *Pension Reform in Central and Eastern Europe*. Geneva: ILO.

Mackie, T. and Rose, R. (2000) *International Almanac of Electoral History*. London: Macmillan.

Maddison, A. (1991) *Dynamic Forces in Capitalist Development*. Oxford: Oxford University Press.

Maître, B., Whelan, C.T. and Nolan, B. (2002) *Household Income Packaging in the European Union: Welfare State Income and Welfare Regime*. EPAG Working Paper 35. Colchester: University of Essex.

Malthus, T.R. (1798/1992) *An Essay on the Principles of Population*. Cambridge: Cambridge University Press.

Mares, I. (2003) *The Politics of Social Risk*. Cambridge: Cambridge University Press.

Marshall, T. (1950/1992) *Citizenship and Social Class*. London: Pluto Press.

Mau, S. (2001) *Patterns of Popular Support for the Welfare State*. Discussion Paper FS III 01–405. Berlin: WZB.

Mishra, R. (1977) *Society and Social Policy: Theoretical Perspectives on Welfare*. London: Macmillan.

Mitchell, D. (1991) *Income Transfers in Ten Welfare States*. Aldershot: Avebury.

Mittelman, J.H. (2000) *The Globalization Syndrome*. Princeton, NJ: Princeton University Press.

Morel, N. (2003) 'Care policies and Welfare State transformation', paper presented at the RC19 Conference, Toronto.

Moreno, L. (2002) *Spain's National Background Report*. Madrid: WRAMSOC.

Moreno, L. and Arriba, A. (1999) *Welfare and Decentralization in Spain*. EUI Working Papers EUF 99/8. Florence: EUI.

Moreno, L. and Sarasa, S. (1992) *The Spanish 'Via Media' to the Development of the Welfare State*. Working Paper 92-13. Madrid: Instiuto de Estudios Sociales Avanzados.

Morgan, K. (2003) 'The politics of mothers' employment', *World Politics*, 55: 259–89.

Morgan, K. and Zippel, K. (2003) 'Paid to care: The origins and effects of care leave policies in Western Europe', *Social Politics*, 10 (1): 49–85.

Muffels, R. and Dirven, H.-J. (2001) 'Marketization of social security in the Netherlands', in J. Dixon and M. Hyde (eds), *The Marketization of Social Security: International Perspectives*. Westport, CT: Quorum.

Müller, K. (2002a) 'Between state and market: Czech and Slovene pension reform in comparison', in E. Fultz (ed.), *Pension Reform in Central and Eastern Europe*. Geneva: ILO.

Müller, K. (2002b) *The Political Economy of Pension Reform in Central and Eastern Europe*. Paris: OECD.

Mulligan, C.B., Gil, R. and Sala-I-Martin, X. (2002) *Social Security and Democracy*. Working Paper No. 8958. Cambridge: NBER.

Myles, J. and Pierson, P. (2001) 'The comparative political economy of pension reform', in P. Pierson (ed.), *The New Politics of the Welfare State*. Oxford: Oxford University Press.

Myles, J. and Quadagno, J. (2002) 'Political theories of the Welfare State', *Social Service Review*, 34–57.

Nickell, S., Nunziata, L., Ochel, W. and Quintini, G. (2002) *The Beveridge Curve: Unemployment and Wages in the OECD from the 1960s to the 1990s*. London: CEPR.

O'Connor, J. (1973) *The Fiscal Crisis of the State*. New York: St. Martin's Press.

O'Connor, J.S. (1993) 'Gender, class and citizenship in the comparative analysis of Welfare State regimes', *British Journal of Sociology*, 44 (3): 501–518.

O'Rourke, K.H. and Williamson, J.G. (2002) 'When did globalization begin?', *European Review of Economic History*, 6: 23–50.

OECD (1994) *Jobs Study*. Paris: OECD.

OECD (1997) *Employment Outlook*. Paris: OECD.

OECD (2000) *Employment Outlook*. Paris: OECD.

OECD (2003) *Main Economic Indicators*. Paris: OECD.

OECD (2004) *Social Expenditure Database 1980–2001*. Paris: OECD.

Offe, C. (1984) *Contradictions of the Welfare State*. Cambridge: MIT.

Offe, C. (1992) 'A non-productivist design for social policies', in P. van Parjis (ed.), *Arguing for Basic Income*. London: Verso.

Orenstein, M.A. and Haas, M.R. (2002) *Globalization and the Development of Welfare States in Post-Communist Europe*. Discussion Paper 2002–02. Cambridge: BCSIA.

Orloff, A.S. (1993a) 'Gender and the social rights of citizenship: The comparative analysis of gender relations and Welfare States', *American Sociological Review*, 58 (3): 303–28.

Orloff, A.S. (1993b) *The Politics of Pensions*. Madison, WI: University of Wisconsin.

Orloff, A.S. (1996) 'Gender and the Welfare State', *Annual Review of Sociology*, 22: 51–78.

Orszag, J.M. and Snower, D. (2002) *From Unemployment Benefit to Unemployment Accounts*. Discussion Paper 532. Bonn: IZA.

Paine, T. (1796/1992) 'Agrarian Justice', in *Rights of Man, Common Sense and Other Political Writings*. Oxford: Oxford University Press.

Palme, J. (1990) *Pension Rights in Welfare Capitalism*. Stockholm: Swedish Institute for Social Research.

Parker, H. (1994) 'Citizen's income', *Citizen's Income Bulletin*, 17: 4–8.

Pedersen, S. (1993) *Family, Dependence and the Origins of the Welfare State*. Cambridge: Cambridge University Press.

Peillon, M. (1995) 'Support for welfare in Ireland: Legitimacy and interest', *Administration*, 43 (3): 3–21.

Pensions Commission (2004) *First Report*. London: HMSO.

Pierson, C. (1998) *Beyond the Welfare State?* London: Blackwell.

Pierson, P. (1994) *Dismantling the Welfare State?* Cambridge: Cambridge University Press.

Pierson, P. (1996) 'The new politics of the Welfare State', *World Politics*, 48 (2): 143–79.

Pierson, P. (2000) 'Increasing returns, path dependence, and the study of politics', *American Political Science Review*, 94 (2): 251–67.

Pierson, P. (ed.) (2001) *The New Politics of the Welfare State*. Oxford: Oxford University Press.

Potůček, M. (1997) 'Splitting the Welfare State: The Czech and Slovak cases', *Social Research*, 64 (4): 1549–87.

Potůček, M. (2004) 'EU accession and Czech social policy', *Journal of European Social Policy*, 14 (3): 253–66.

Poulantzas, N. (1973) *Political Power and Social Class*. London: New Left Books.

Poulantzas, N. (1976) 'The Capitalist State: A reply to Miliband and Laclau', *New Left Review*, 95: 63–83.

Powell, M. (2004) 'In search of the dependent variable: Welfare change in Europe', Paper. University of Bath.

Przeworski, A., Alvarez, M., Cheibub, J.A. and Limongi, F. (1996) 'What makes democracies endure?', *Journal of Democracy*, 7 (1): 39–55.

Quadagno, J. (1988) *The Transformation of Old Age Security*. Chicago, IL: University of Chicago Press.

Radaelli, C. (2000) *Whither Europeanization? Concept Stretching and Substantive Change*. European Integration Online Paper 4 (8).

Ragin, C. (1994) 'Introduction to qualitative comparative analysis', in T. Janoski and A.M. Hicks (eds), *The Comparative Political Economy of the Welfare State*. Cambridge: Cambridge University Press.

Rake, K. and Daly, M. (2002) *Gender, Household and Individual Income in France, Germany, Italy, the Netherlands, Sweden, the USA and the UK*. Working Paper 332. Luxembourg: LIS.

Rayner, E., Shah, S., White, R., Dawes, L. and Tinmsley, K. (2000) *Evaluating Jobseeker's Allowance: A Summary of the Research Findings*. Leeds: CDS.

Rein, M. and Turner, J. (2001) 'Public–private interactions: Mandatory pensions in Australia, the Netherlands and Switzerland', *Review of Population and Social Policy*, 10: 107–153.

Rimlinger, G. (1971) *Welfare Policy and Industrialization in Europe, America and Russia*. New York: John Wiley.

Ringen, S. (1987) *The Possibility of Politics*. Oxford: Clarendon.

Rodrik, D. (1997) *Has Globalization Gone Too Far?* Washington, D.C.: Institute for International Economics.

Rose, N. (1996) 'The death of the social? Re-figuring the territory of government', *Economy and Society*, 25 (3): 327–56.

Ross, F. (1999) *'Beyond Left and Right: The New Partisan Politics of the Welfare State*. EUI Working Papers EUF 99/4. Florence: EUI.

Rothstein, B. (1992) 'Labor-market institutions and working-class strength', in S. Steinmo, K. Thelen and F. Longstreth (eds), *Structuring Politics: Historical Institutionalism in Comparative Analysis*. Cambridge: Cambridge University Press.

Said, E. (1993) *Culture and Imperialism*. London: Chatto and Windus.

Sainsbury, D. (1996) *Gender, Equality and Welfare States*. Cambridge: Cambridge University Press.

Sainsbury, D. (1999) *Gender and Welfare State Regimes*. Oxford: Oxford University Press.

Saxonberg, S. and Sirovátka, T. (2004) 'The role of social policy in seeking the balance between work and family after Communism', paper presented at the ISA Conference, Paris.

Scharpf, F.W. (2000) 'The viability of advanced Welfare States in the international economy: Vulnerabilities and options', *Journal of European Public Policy*, 7 (2): 190–228.

Schludi, M. (2003) *Chances and Limitations of 'Benchmarking' in the Reform of Welfare State Structures: The Case of Pension Policy*. Amsterdam: Amsterdam Institute for Advanced Labour Studies.

Schmid, G. (1998) *Transitional Labour Markets: A New European Employment Strategy*. Discussion Paper FS I 98–06. Berlin: WZB.

Schwartz, H. (n.d.) 'Down the wrong path: Path dependence, increasing returns and historical institutionalism', Paper. University of Virginia.

Scott, J.A. (1986) 'Gender: A useful category of historical analysis', *American Historical Review*, 91 (5): 1053–75.

Shalev, M. (2002) 'Limits of and alternatives to multiple regression in macro-comparative research', paper presented at a conference.

Siim, B. (1987) 'The Scandinavian Welfare State: Towards sexual equality or a new kind of male domination?', *Acta Sociologica*, 30 (3/4): 255-70.

Sirovátka, T. and Rabušic, L. (1998) *The Czech Welfare State and its Legitimacy*. Vienna: SOCCO.

Sirovátka, T., van Oorschot, W. and Rabušic, L. (1998) *Welfare State Solidarity and Support: The Czech Republic and the Netherlands*. Vienna: SOCCO.

Sjöberg, O. (2000a) *Duties in the Welfare State*. Stockholm: Swedish Institute for Social Research.

Sjöberg, O. (2000b) 'Unemployment and unemployment benefits in the OECD 1960-1990', *Work, Employment and Society*, 14 (1): 51-76.

Skocpol, T. (1985) 'Bringing the state back in: Strategies of analysis in current research', in P. Evans, D. Rueschemeyer and T. Skocpol (eds), *Bringing the State Back In*. Cambridge: Cambridge University Press.

Skocpol, T. (1992) *Protecting Soldiers and Mothers*. Cambridge: Belknap.

Skocpol, T. and Ritter, G. (1991) 'Gender and the origins of modern social policies in Britain and the United States', *Studies in American Political Development*, 5: 36-93.

Sleebos, J. (2003) *Low Fertility Rates in OECD Countries: Facts and Policy Responses*. Social, Employment and Migration Working Paper 15. Paris: OECD.

So, A.Y. (1990) *Social Change and Development: Modernization, Dependency and World-System Theories*. Newbury Park: Sage.

Sørensen, A. (2002) 'Gender equality in earnings at work and at home', in M. Kautto, T. Fritzell, B. Hvinden, J. Kvist and H. Uusitalo (eds), *Nordic Welfare States in the European Context*. London: Routledge.

Sörensen, K. and Bergqvist, C. (2002) *Gender and the Social Democratic Welfare Regime*. Stockholm: National Institute for Working Life.

Standing, G. (1999) 'Global feminization though flexible labor: A theme revisited', *World Development*, 27 (3): 583-602.

Steinmo, S. and Watts, J. (1995) 'It's the institutions stupid! Why comprehensive national health insurance fails in America', *Journal of Health Politics, Policy and Law*, 20 (2): 329-72.

Stephens, J. (1979) *The Transition from Capitalism to Socialism*. London: Macmillan.

Struyven, L. and Steurs, G. (2003) *The Competitive Market for Employment Services in the Netherlands*. Paris: OECD.

Suhrcke, M. (2001) *Preferences for Inequality: East vs. West*. Discussion Paper 150. Hamburg: HWWA.

Svalfors, S. (2004) 'Class, attitudes and the Welfare State', *Social Policy and Administration*, 38 (2): 119-38.

Swank, D. (2002a) *Global Capital, Political Institutions, and Policy Change in Developed Welfare States*. Cambridge: Cambridge University Press.

Swank, D. (2002b) 'European welfare states: Regionalization, globalization and social policy change', in T. Brewer, P.A. Brenton and G. Boyd (eds), *Globalizing Europe: Deepening Integration, Alliance Capitalism and Structural Statecraft*. Cheltenham: Edward Elgar.

Swank, D. (2003) 'Withering welfare? Globalization, political economic institutions and the foundations of contemporary Welfare States', in L. Weiss (ed.), *States in the Global Economy: Bringing Domestic Institutions Back In*. Cambridge: Cambridge University Press.

Swank, D. and Martin, C. (2001) 'Employers and the Welfare State', *Comparative Political Studies*, 34 (8): 889-923.

Swenson, P. (2002) *Capitalists against Markets: The Making of Labor Markets and Welfare States in the United States and Sweden*. New York: Oxford University Press.

Sykes, R. (1998) 'Studying European social policy – issues and perspectives', in R. Sykes and P. Alcock (eds), *Developments in European Social Policy*. Bristol: Policy Press.

Sykes, R., Palier, B. and Prior, P.M. (eds) (2001) *Globalization and European Welfare States: Challenges and Change*. Houndmills: Palgrave.

Taylor-Gooby, P. (1985) 'The politics of welfare: Public attitudes and behaviour', in R. Klein and M. O'Higgins (eds), *The Future of Welfare*. Oxford: Basil Blackwell.

Taylor-Gooby, P. (ed.) (2004) *New Risks, New Welfare*. Oxford: Oxford University Press.

Therborn, G. (1993) 'Beyond the lonely nation state', in F.G. Castles (ed.), *Families of Nations*. Aldershot: Dartmouth.

Therborn, G. (1995) *European Modernity and Beyond*. London: Sage.

Titmuss, R.M. (1974) *Social Policy*. London: Allen & Unwin.

Triplett, J.E. and Bosworth, B.P. (2003) 'Productivity measurement issues in service industries', *FRBNY Economic Policy Review*, September: 23–33.

United Nations (2000) *Replacement Migration: Is it a Solution to Declining and Ageing Population?* New York: UN.

United Nations Development Programme (1997) *Human Development Report*. New York: UNDP.

Usui, C. (1994) 'Welfare state development in a world system context: Event history analysis of first social insurance legislation among 60 countries, 1880–1960', in T. Janoski and A.M. Hicks (eds), *The Comparative Political Economy of the Welfare State*. Cambridge: Cambridge University Press.

Van der Veen, R., van der Trommel, W. and de Vroom, B. (2000) 'Institutional change of Welfare States', in H. Wagenaar (ed.), *Government Institutions: Effects, Changes and Normative Foundations*. The Hague: Kluwer.

Van Kersbergen, K. (1995) *Social Capitalism*. London: Routledge.

Van Oorschot, W. (1998) 'From solidarity to selectivity: The reconstruction of the Dutch social security system 1980–2000', *Social Policy Review*, 10: 183–202.

Van Riel, B., Hemerijck, A. and Visser, J. (2002) *Is There a Dutch Way to Pension Reform?* Working Paper WP 202. Oxford: Oxford Institute of Ageing.

Vodopivec, M., Wörgötter, A. and Raju, D. (2003) *Unemployment Benefit Systems in Central and Eastern Europe: A Review of the 1990s*. Washington, D.C.: World Bank.

Wallerstein, M. and Western, B. (2000) 'Unions in decline: What has changed and why', *Annual Review of Political Science*, 2: 355–77.

Walters, W. (1994) 'The discovery of "unemployment": New forms for the government of poverty', *Economy and Society*, 23: 265–90.

Weber, M. (1949) *The Methodology of the Social Sciences*. Glencoe: Free Press.

Weber, M. (1978) *Economy and Society*. Berkeley, CA: University of California.

Weinert, P., Baukens, M., Bollerot, P., Peschi-Gapenne, M. and Walwei, U. (2001) *Employability: From Theory to Practice*. Aldershot: Ashgate.

Weir, M. and Skocpol, T. (1985) 'State structures and possibilities for "Keynesian" responses to the Great Depression in Sweden, Britain, and the United States', in P. Evans, D. Rueschemeyer and T. Skocpol (eds), *Bringing the State Back In*. Cambridge: Cambridge University Press.

Welfare Commission (2002) *The Balance Sheet for the 1990s*. Stockholm: Ministry of Health and Social Affairs.

Wennemo, I. (1994) *Sharing the Costs of Children*. Stockholm: Swedish Institute for Social Research.

Wildeboor Schut, J.M., Vrooman, J.C. and de Beer, P.T. (2001) *On Worlds of Welfare*. The Hague: Social and Cultural Planning Office.

Wilensky, H.L. (1975) *The Welfare State and Equality*. Berkeley, CA: University of California Press.

World Bank (1994) *Averting the Old Age Crisis*. Washington, D.C.: World Bank.

World Bank (2000) *Balancing Protection and Opportunity: A Strategy for Social Protection in Transition Economies*. Washington, D.C.: World Bank.

World Bank (2003) *Social Protection Sector Strategy: From Safety Net to Springboard*. Washington, D.C.: World Bank.

INDEX